Y A N O M A M Ö

T H E   L A S T   D A Y S   O F   E D E N

Y A N O

A Harvest/HBJ Original

Napoleon A. Chagnon

MAMÖ

THE LAST DAYS OF EDEN

With a Foreword by Edward O. Wilson

Photographs by the author

Harcourt Brace Jovanovich, Publishers

San Diego   New York   London

Yanomamö: The Last Days of Eden is a substantially revised
adaptation of the Fourth College Edition of *Yąnomamö,*
published by Harcourt Brace Jovanovich College Publishers,
copyright © 1992, 1983, 1977, 1968 by Holt, Rinehart and Winston, Inc.

Library of Congress Cataloging-in-Publication Data
Chagnon, Napoleon A., 1938–
Yanomamö: the last days of Eden/Napoleon A. Chagnon;
with a foreword by E. O. Wilson.
p.   cm.
Originally published: New York: Holt, Rinehart and Winston, c 1983.
Includes bibliographical references and index.
ISBN 0-15-699682-0
1. Yanomamo Indians.   I. Title.
[F2520.1.Y3C5 1992]
306'.089982—dc20   92-1630

Designed by Camilla Filancia
Printed in the United States of America
First Harvest/HBJ edition 1992   A B C D E

For Carlene, Darius,

and Lisa with love

Contents

Foreword by Edward O. Wilson

The Yanomamö, arguably the most famous of preliterate peoples, weigh on our minds for their extraordinary traits: toughness, feistiness, courage, expansiveness, inventiveness, humor. Their chief chronicler, Napoleon Chagnon, strikes many of his friends and colleagues as basically similar in personality: tough, feisty, courageous. . . . He is, moreover—to their advantage and to ours—deeply devoted to the people he has chosen to study. The product of the conjunction of a culture and this particular anthropologist is the classic work *Yanomamö*.

The Yanomamö have special importance ethnographically as the last large unacculturated tribal aggregate on earth. They are the final tribes living strong and free in the style of the preliterate people first encountered by Europeans five centuries ago; all others with large populations and broad territory have been heavily modified or rendered physically extinct. I suspect that the Yanomamö way of life gives us the clearest view of the conditions under which the human mind evolved biologically during deep history.

A sense of urgency pervades this book, for Chagnon's account of the Yanomamö today portrays them on the edge of destruction. They are being corroded by the classic appurtenances of colonial invasion: religious conversion, assimilation into inferior roles within the "higher" culture, and depopulation by introduced diseases. None of these agents can be effectively resisted by the Yanomamö, whose original way of life will be irrevocably damaged within a decade if appropriate countermeasures are not taken. The fragility of Yanomamö culture alone makes the Chagnon report invaluable.

Chagnon has been pulled into the vortex. He wishes to involve the reader. His passion is not just for a culture but for Yanomamö as individual human beings—his friends and confidants of long standing, and *their* friends and allies and children. Early in the book we are given the indelible image of young Chagnon standing clad in loincloth and sneakers outside the hunting camp of a still-uncontacted Shamatari group, waiting to be invited in, his mouth too dry to give the traditional friendly whistle. The book ends with a middle-aged Chagnon crusading to spare the Yanomamö from further ruin.

The evolution of Chagnon's thought mirrors the more progressive trends of cultural anthropology during the past four decades. Chagnon was one of the earliest cultural anthropologists to incorporate the developing theory and methods of evolutionary biology. Consider how he links the rain-forest environment to Yanomamö biology and social structure. The environment, Chagnon finds, is highly productive for human populations at Yanomamö density. Whatever else befalls them, all members are relatively well fed by Western standards. Yet they are so fiercely combative and territorial that the level of their aggression within and between villages is legendary; they are indeed the "fierce people." What, then, is the essential resource, if any, for which they contend? By their own testimony and by Chagnon's observation, most serious fighting starts over women. At a deeper level, men and their kin are contesting the key limiting resource to their personal reproduction. In a protein-rich environment, reproduction by males is constrained primarily by control of access to women, whereas reproduction by women is ordinarily not limited by the number of males. The logic is simple: five women with a single husband can produce five times as many children as five males with a single wife. Thus do biologists, and increasingly, anthropologists, explain polygyny— the marriage of one man to several women. Whatever the use to which Chagnon's data and preliminary generalizations may eventually be put, their unique value cannot be doubted.

The exact demographic data assembled by Chagnon in this book (and elsewhere) is crucial. So is the detailed history of village fissioning and warfare he has traced across generations in Yanomamöland. While the history of the Yanomamö is different in scale from the history of England, Chagnon is their Macaulay. The intricate rules of kin classification, marital exchanges, and alliance, and in some cases the episodes of treachery and betrayal, fall together in a coherent network of cause and effect to create a true theory (as opposed to a mere skein of ad hoc explanations) subject to further testing. In the blending of biology and cultural analysis, nothing beats statistical data on the gritty details of life and death as put together by Chagnon. One peek, as the Chinese say, is worth a hundred finesses.

The cycles of Yanomamö life are easily broken, and the Yanomamö culture is easily destroyed by contact with the outside world, especially when acculturation is encouraged by well-meaning but cosmologically disoriented missionaries. The process is hastened by the continuing destruction of the rain forest to which Yanomamö culture has been so exquisitely adapted. The ethical dilemma presented by the light of these wonderful people is profound. Their culture is priceless to them and, because of the knowledge it provides, to the world at large. But they are highly intelligent human beings, rather than Paleolithic people frozen in time for our delectation, and they have free choice. The best we can hope to do for them, as Chagnon's master work makes clear, is to protect the Yanomamö and their environment until each group in turn can make a leisurely and decent accommodation between their world and ours.

Cambridge, Massachusetts
May 1992

Author's Preface

The Yanomamö are the last major primitive tribe left in the Amazon Basin, and the last such people *anywhere on earth*. They live in some 200 to 250 separate, fiercely independent villages and number approximately 20,000 people.

In this book, I describe their culture by focusing on the activities of a number of typical individuals. I talk about how they live, what they think and believe, what makes them happy and what makes them sad—and what makes them go to war with their Yanomamö neighbors.

Only a handful of Yanomamö were even vaguely aware that there were places called Brazil and Venezuela when I first began to live with and study them in the mid-1960s. That is still true today in the remote regions of southernmost Venezuela where my current field research takes me. The Latin American bureau chief of the *New York Times*, who recently accompanied me to a remote village, asked the village headman through me, "Where is Venezuela?" The headman scratched his head, shrugged, and pointed due south, toward Brazil. His answer would have been correct if he had pointed north, east, or west—any direction but south.

How long this remarkable situation can endure is an urgent question, and much of my recent effort has been devoted to keeping that possibility open for as long as possible. Increased contact with outsiders leads to epidemics and high mortality rates, and those Yanomamö who live in the few remaining inaccessible areas are actually better off than if they moved closer to the outposts of our kind of culture. But powerful forces in both Brazil and Venezuela are encouraging or compelling them to do so, in the name of progress, development, or Christianity.

It is unusual for an anthropologist to return repeatedly to the same people he has studied year after year for over a quarter of a century. He acquires some new factual information, scientific understanding, and a humanistic appreciation of the people and their culture, of course, but the return trips also evoke sadness and anger. Especially anger, because many things change for the worse and many people die of sicknesses they have never before suffered from in their history.

This book focuses on the people of one village, called Bisaasi-teri, the place where I began my work in 1964 as a graduate student at the University of Michigan. One of the main characters is the wise and unpretentious headman, Kaobawä. Another is a brash younger man, Rerebawä, not a native of Bisaasi-teri but married to a woman of the village. I discuss them and their families at length. While the narrative often depicts Yanomamö culture from the vantage point of these individuals, it also puts them and their activities into a larger context by contrasting them with many other people.

This village and its people are representative of the majority of the Yano-mamö. Approximately 25 percent of the estimated 20,000 Yanomamö live today in the area of my study, recently lived there, or have immediate ancestors who lived there sometime in the past fifty years. This area has historically been characterized by intense intervillage warfare, a phenomenon that very few anthropologists have been able to study firsthand. I therefore focused my research on how their warfare shaped their history and how they dealt with it during the time I lived with them.

A few of my colleagues object to my decision to view the Yanomamö culture in the context of warfare. But I did not arbitrarily choose this focus, the way many anthropologists seem to choose symbols, basket styles, myths, marriage rules, or some other aspect of tribal life. I chose it because I came to see that warfare was the Yanomamö's major preoccupation and affected almost everything they did. Ironically, I had started out to study something quite different—how much and what kinds of foods they ate. I had been trained to believe that what people ate determined a great deal about their lives.

Strange as it may seem, some cultural anthropologists do not believe that warfare ever played any significant role in our evolutionary past or that it might have been commonplace in contemporary tribal societies prior to their contact with the outside world. These anthropologists seem uncomfortable with the example of the Yanomamö. It is as if anthropology must prove that preindustrial man was like Rousseau's hypothetical noble savage. Some seem obliged to counter anthropological accounts of violence or warfare with special explanations. The most common of these is that if warfare is found, it must have been introduced by outsiders. Before then, the people lived tranquil, peaceful lives, addressing each other in altruistic kinship terms, selflessly helping each other, and unflinchingly sharing everything they owned with everyone else, especially their mates.

It is tempting to call this the "bad breath" theory of tribal warfare: Europeans landed in the Americas and breathed over the two continents, and all the previously peaceful natives began fighting each other. Something akin to this view was humorously captured in the film *The Gods Must Be Crazy*. A careless bush pilot discards an empty Coke bottle over the territory of the peaceful Bushmen of the Kalahari Desert. One of the Bushmen finds the bottle, and soon they are all fighting over it, and eventually mourning for the good old pre-Coke-bottle days when nobody fought over anything.

Other anthropologists admit that violence occurs in the tribal world but think that we should not talk about it. I recall a female colleague, early in my career, who seriously urged me to stop describing the warfare and violence I witnessed, saying, "Even if they are that way, we do not want others to know about it—it will give them the wrong impression." The wrong impression of what? On hearing of Darwin's theory that man was descended from the apes, the bishop's wife is reputed to have said, "Good Lord, let's hope that it isn't true. But if it is true, let's hope that others do not learn about it."

For better or worse, there is a definite bias in cultural anthropology favoring descriptions of tribal peoples that characterize them as hapless, hopeless, harmless, homeless, and helpless. For example, there was widespread excitement in my profession over the discovery of the "gentle Tasaday" of the Philippines, a timid cave-dwelling people. What occasioned the excitement was that they didn't even have a word for war. This was probably a good thing for the Tasaday—there were only twenty-six of them, and their only potential opponent was Ferdinand Marcos's army, with its tanks, automatic rifles, airplanes, and bombs. The Tasaday turned out to be a hoax.

The Yanomamö are definitely not that kind of a people, and it seemed reasonable to me to point that out, to try to capture the image of them that they themselves held. They frequently and sincerely told me, "*Yamakö waiteri no modahawä*" or "*Yanomamö täbä waiteri*" ("We are really fierce"; "Yanomamö are fierce people"). I never once heard any of them say, "We are truly cowards" or "We'd rather run than fight." And I cannot imagine a contemporary Apache, Cheyenne, or Crow Indian feeling comfortable with a description of his ancestors that denigrates them by suggesting that they were incapable of holding their own against their enemies or that they ran from them in fear.

Another criticism concerning my invoking the fierceness of the Yanomamö is that if a people does not act fiercely in everything they do, the descriptor is false. Thus I am wrong to call the Yanomamö the fierce people unless they sweat fiercely, drink fiercely, eat fiercely, dream fiercely, belch fiercely, and cook their food fiercely. This is an uncharitable criticism. In 1958, Elizabeth Marshall Thomas published a charming and influential book about the Bushmen of the Kalahari entitled *The Harmless People*. Many anthropologists were disappointed to learn, in the 1980s, that the homicide rate among the Bushmen was about the same as it was in Detroit. Bushmen didn't do everything harmlessly.

Many college students who have read earlier versions of this book have written to me expressing warm and sympathetic attitudes toward the Yanomamö and indicating concern for their future. I think this is because the Yanomamö, while being an exotic Amazonian tribe, are fundamentally like all the rest of us in universally human ways. The fact that warfare and violence occur in their culture is no more shocking to the normal reader than knowing how significant warfare and violence have been in our own culture and history. Yanomamö leaders and warriors, like our field commanders and soldiers, engage in warfare to protect and defend their people. They are the fathers, brothers, and sons of those back home on whose behalf they are acting, those who admire, encourage, and reward them and are grateful to them for having held their enemies at bay—often losing their lives to do so. To hold such a view toward one's warriors does not mean that a person revels in war and advocates killing, destruction, and mayhem. Almost everyone, including the Yanomamö, regards war as repugnant and would prefer that it did not exist. Like us, they are more than willing to quit—if the bad guys also quit. If we could all get rid of the bad guys, there wouldn't be any war.

In 1992, I invited Greg Gomez, a longtime friend and a man I regard as a brother, to accompany me on a field trip. Greg, an Apache, had read an earlier version of this book and was captivated by the quality, integrity, and texture of Yanomamö culture and by the valor of people like Kaobawä. He was reminded in many ways of how his own people had lived before the Mexicans and the Americans destroyed their society. He wanted to visit the Yanomamö so he could experience their kind of existence and get a feeling for what it was like to live among Native Americans who were still free and sovereign. During our brief stay he developed an intense spiritual feeling toward and bonds with the Washäwä-teri, the group we were visiting. The Washäwä-teri immediately recognized something different and special in him. He wasn't like the other foreigners they had seen; he even looked like a Yanomamö, although an unusually tall one. They asked me, privately, "Was Gregorio once a Yanomamö who decided to turn into a foreigner?" For his part, Greg saw them as Apaches who had not yet been forced to become foreigners in their own land. Perhaps they were like his Apache ancestors, but shorter and with no horses.

I think there is something of all of us in the Yanomamö, and something of them in all of us. Think of the vast expanse of time and space out of which we ourselves have come, and try to imagine in what ways it could have differed radically from what you are reading about here. As you do, assume that there exists just one group of bad guys, unidentified, but living nearby. No persons and no institutions constrain them. There is just you—and your kinsmen.

Note on the Spelling and Pronunciation of Yanomamö Words

The Yanomamö do not have a written language, and linguists and anthropologists have employed several means of representing specific sounds in their language.

The pronunciation of the word "Yanomamö" is nasalized through its entire length, and linguists usually add some sort of diacritical mark on one of the letters to indicate the nasalization. I have chosen not to do this. My justification is that any Yanomamö word containing an *n* or an *m* tends to be nasalized anyway. I have not indicated nasalization on any of the Yanomamö words I use in this book.

Their language has one sound that is not found in English, and I have flagged this by adding an umlaut (¨) over the letter *o* where the sound occurs. The vowel *ö* is pronounced like the umlaut *ö* in the German language or its *oe* equivalent, as in the poet Goethe's name.

I have also used the umlaut to distinguish between the phonemically distinct Yanomamö vowels *ahh* and *uhh*, the first being written *a* and the second *ä*. Both sounds exist in English, but we write them both as *a*. (The Yanomamö word *pata* has a totally different meaning than the word *pätä*; the first means "big," the second is a kind of insect.) Words with the vowel *ä* are pronounced with an *uh* sound, as in the word "duck." Thus, the name Kaobawä is pronounced *cow-ba-wuh*. It is entirely nasalized, but as I have said, I have not complicated the spelling by adding a diacritical to indicate this.

Some publishers prefer to eliminate all diacritical marks. This has led to various spellings of Yanomamö and to such mispronunciations as *Ya-no-ma-mo*. Some anthropologists and linguists have chosen to indicate the *oe* sound in Yanomamö by representing it as an *i* with a slash through it, leading to additional mispronunciations, like *Ya-no-ma-me* when the slash is dropped from the final *i*. To avoid some of these problems, I spelled the word as "Yanomama" in many of my earlier publications. In this book, however, the word is spelled with an umlaut over the final letter *o*.

YANOMAMÖ

THE LAST DAYS OF EDEN

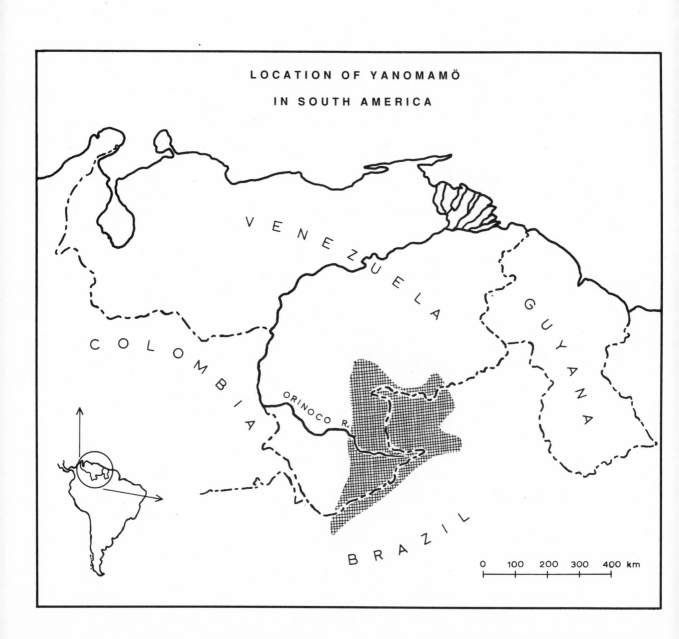

LOCATION OF YANOMAMÖ
IN SOUTH AMERICA

VENEZUELA

COLOMBIA

GUYANA

ORINOCO R.

BRAZIL

0   100   200   300   400 km

Introduction

A large tribe of tropical forest Indians inhabits the border region between Venezuela and Brazil. They are gardeners, and they have lived until very recent years in isolation from our kind of culture. Even the authorities in Venezuela and Brazil knew little about their existence until anthropologists began to go into the region. The most remarkable thing about the tribe, known as the Yanomamö, is how long they have managed, due to their isolation in their remote corner of Amazonia, to retain their native patterns of warfare and political integrity without interference from the outside world. They have remained sovereign and in complete control of their own destiny until only a few years ago. During most of my period of fieldwork the remotest of the uncontacted villages were still living under those conditions. Today, few villages remain that have not been directly contacted.

This book is a sort of case study about the Yanomamö and their sovereignty. It is based on my sixty months of residence in many of their villages, fieldwork that began in 1964—before the major vectors of change started to impinge on some of the villages. My initial fifteen months of field research, between 1964 and 1966, came at a time when little accurate information existed about Yanomamö culture, geographical distribution, tribal size, and cultural history. Even government maps of the area were grossly in error, showing, for example, the headwaters of the Mavaca River, where much of my work was focused, as the headwaters of the Siapa.

I will begin by describing an event that happened fifteen years before I went to live with the Yanomamö, an event that I was able to reconstruct from bits and pieces of information given to me by many Yanomamö informants, once I had learned their language. It was an event that had led to the development of many of the political relationships, alliances, and wars between villages that dominated Yanomamö social life while I was there, but about which I knew nothing for a long time.

The story contains a message about anthropological fieldwork, on the one hand, and about the nature of Yanomamö political organization, on the other. As to fieldwork, the lesson is that in some cases it is impossible to understand a whole society's social organization by studying only one village or community, for each community is bound up in and responds to its political ties with neighboring groups and to the obligations and pressures those ties impose. Regarding Yanomamö political organization, the lesson is that past events— history—must be understood before one can comprehend the current patterns one observes. As the Roman poet Lucretius said, "Nothing yet from nothing ever came."

The Killing of Ruwähiwä

The village of Bisaasi-teri was several days' walk from its southern neighbor, Konabuma-teri. Bisaasi-teri, about whose people much of this book centers, was a splinter village of a much larger village, Patanowä-teri. The Bisaasi-teri were at odds with the larger mother village, however, and were beginning to fission, or split away, from it to forge their own identity and make new allies. They saw an opportunity to strengthen their political image by cultivating a friendship with their southern neighbors in Konabuma-teri.

The recent history of both groups (the Patanowä-teri/Bisaasi-teri and the Konabuma-teri) had seen their gradual migration from northeast to southwest, as past wars and current alliances led the villages to relocate periodically in new areas of the virgin tropical forest. (The map in chapter 5, entitled "Historical Movements of Some Yanomamö Groups," shows these migrations.) The two groups spoke slightly different dialects of Yanomamö (but no different than, say, the dialects of North Carolina and upstate New York). Hunters from both groups began to encounter each other in the lands between their villages, and eventually, in the late 1940s, the groups began visiting and trading with each other. Apparently the trading visits became more frequent, and the members of the two groups got to know each other well.

In Yanomamö politics, members of allied villages often need each other's support, but often they cannot and do not trust each other very much— especially if the allies are not historically and therefore genealogically related, as was the case here.

The Yanomamö attribute to harmful magic almost all deaths other than those obviously caused by another human or by an animal, such as being shot with an arrow or attacked by a jaguar. Like all tribal populations, they suffer a high infant mortality rate—babies do not have a good chance of survival. A large number of babies die from a host of causes that we, with our scientific knowledge, could diagnose and prescribe for in precise, biomedical terms. But the Yanomamö do not have such knowledge. To them, babies die because someone has sent harmful spirits—*hekura*—to steal their souls, or someone has blown magical charms at them from far away, charms that have caused them to sicken and die. In every village, the shamans spend many hours attempting to cure sick children, as well as sick adults, by driving out the malevolent forces that have caused the illness and, in revenge, sending their own spirits and charms against the children of distant villages.

As the alliance with the people of Konabuma-teri was maturing, several children died in the village of Bisaasi-teri. The shamans of Bisaasi-teri began to suspect that the men of Konabuma-teri were secretly sending harmful charms and magic against their village and its children, and before long the Bisaasi-teri had convinced themselves that their new allies were truly their enemies.

Unaware of this development, one of the prominent men of Konabuma-teri arrived at Bisaasi-teri to visit and trade. His name was Ruwähiwä, and he came alone. He entered the village clearing in the traditional pose of the visitor, erect, proud, motionless, and showing no fear. The host men greeted him in the usual way, coming out with their weapons, cheering, hooting, and growling symbolic threats and intimidations as they inspected him. He was invited to take up a hammock until food could be prepared for him. When a gourd of plantain soup was ready, he was invited out to drink it before the house of the local headman. He squatted on his haunches, picked up the gourd, and drank, oblivious to his surroundings, happy to be welcomed in this customary way.

A man named Mamikininiwä approached silently from behind, a mature man of forty years whose decisions few dared to challenge. He carried the battered, worn remains of a steel ax hafted clumsily to a short, stout handle. Paying him no attention, Ruwähiwä continued to drink his soup. Then Mamikininiwä raised his ax high above his head and smashed it violently, sharp edge forward, into Ruwähiwä's skull. The visitor lurched forward, trying to stand, but he was mortally wounded. He fell to the ground and died in a pool of his own blood. Later that day, several old women carried his body off to his home village.

Thus began the war between the villages of Bisaasi-teri and Konabuma-teri, a war that was still going on fifteen years later, when I arrived, but that I was ignorant of then.

Ruwähiwä's group set about to avenge the killing. They enlisted the support of a third village, which was on friendly terms with the Bisaasi-teri, and persuaded that village to host a feast at which the Bisaasi-teri would be guests of honor. The men of a fourth village joined the Konabuma-teri in hiding outside the village.

The unsuspecting Bisaasi-teri came en masse for the occasion, men, women, and children. Shortly after the feast began, and while the Bisaasi-teri men were lying motionless and helpless in their hosts' hammocks, the signal was given, and the hosts suddenly set upon them with clubs, bowstaves, and arrows. A number of them died immediately, but some managed to escape from the village. Outside it, they ran into showers of arrows from the hidden archers. More died and more were wounded, some so badly that they did not live. Approximately a dozen men were killed that afternoon. A number of women and pubescent girls were taken captive and were never seen by their families again.

The survivors retreated deep into the jungle to the north and hid for many days, waiting for the wounded to recover enough to move on. Depressed and anguished, they finally sought refuge in a village to the north called Mahekodo-teri. This was early in the year 1951, a date recorded by James P. Barker, who a few months before had been the first missionary to make sustained contact with the Yanomamö. Barker was a witness to the Bisaasi-teri's arrival at Mahekodo-teri, which was the village he had chosen for his mission station.

The Bisaasi-teri left Mahekodo-teri about a year later and settled a little further down the Orinoco River. They were the people I lived with when I first went to work among the Yanomamö. But I knew nothing of this tragic event in their recent history when I joined them to begin my field research. The significance of it unraveled only slowly over the months as I learned their language better and sought to discover something of their history and recent settlement pattern. Not until then did much of what I had initially witnessed begin to make sense and their raids and political dealings with neighbors begin to become comprehensible.

Much of what follows in these pages is about Bisaasi-teri and the people who live there.

Chapter One

Chronicle of a Nabä's *Adventures in Yanomamöland*

Vignette

The Yanomamö, presently some 20,000 people, live in small villages thinly scattered over a vast and verdant tropical forest, the villages separated by many miles of unoccupied land. About 70 percent of them are in southern Venezuela, the remainder in adjacent areas of Brazil. They have no writing, but their language is rich and complex. Their clothing is more decorative than protective: well-dressed men sport nothing more than a few cotton strings around the wrists, ankles, and waist. They tie the foreskin of their penises to the waist string. Women dress about as scantily.

Much of their daily life revolves around gardening, hunting, collecting wild foods, collecting firewood, fetching water, visiting and gossiping with each other, and making the few material possessions they need—baskets, hammocks, bows and arrows, and the colorful pigments with which they paint their bodies. Their life is relatively easy in the sense that they can provide for themselves with about three hours' work per day. Most of what they eat they cultivate in their gardens, and most of that is plantains—a kind of cooking banana that is usually eaten green, either roasted on the coals or boiled in pots (photo 1). Their meat comes from a large variety of game animals, hunted daily by the men. It is usually roasted on coals or smoked and is always well done.

Their villages are round and open—and very public. One can hear, see, and smell almost everything that goes on anywhere in the village. Privacy is rare, although sexual discreetness is possible in the garden or at night while others sleep. The villages can be as small as 40 to 50 people or as large as 300, but in all of them there are many more children and babies than adults. This is true of most primitive populations and of our own demographic past. Life expectancy is short.

The Yanomamö fall into the category of tropical forest Indians called foot people. Avoiding large rivers, they prefer to live in the interfluvial plains of the major rivers. They have neighbors to the north, the Carib-speaking Ye'kwana, who are true river people and travel extensively along the major waterways in their large, elegant dugout canoes. For the Yanomamö, a large stream is an obstacle that can be crossed only in the dry season. They have traditionally stayed away from the larger rivers, and this is one reason for their lack of contact with outsiders, who usually come by water.

They enjoy traveling into the jungle in seasons when it abounds with ripe fruits and vegetables. Then the large village—the *shabono*—is abandoned for a few weeks, and everyone camps out a day or so away from the village and garden. On these trips, they erect temporary huts of poles, vines, and leaves, a separate hut for each family.

Two seasons dominate their annual cycle: the wet season, which inundates the low-lying jungle and makes travel difficult, and the dry season—the time of visiting other villages to feast, trade, and politick with allies. The dry season is also the time when raiders can travel and strike silently at their unsuspecting enemies. The Yanomamö with which I work still wage intervillage warfare, a phenomenon that affects all aspects of their social organization, settlement pattern, and daily routines. And it is not simply ritualistic war: in the area I work in, at least one-fourth of all adult males die violently. One particularly accomplished warrior I came to know had killed twenty-one people (I was almost the twenty-second), and several others, with fifteen or sixteen victims to their credit, approached that record. Over the nearly thirty-year span of my fieldwork, the warfare has diminished and, in some places, has nearly disappeared, but it is still common where I am currently working.

Social life is organized around the same principles utilized by all tribesmen: kinship relationships, descent from ancestors, marriage exchanges between kinship or descent groups, and the transient charisma of distinguished headmen who attempt to keep order within the village and whose responsibility it is to determine the village's relationships with other villages. Leadership positions are largely the result of kinship and marriage patterns—"big men," the leaders, come from the largest kinship groups within the village. They can, by their personal wit, wisdom, and charisma, become autocrats, but most of them are more nearly the greater among equals. They, too, must clear the gardens, plant crops, collect wild foods, and hunt. They are simultaneously peacemakers and valiant warriors. Peacemaking often requires the threat or actual use of force, and most headmen have acquired a reputation for being *waiteri*, or fierce.

The social dynamics within villages involve the giving and receiving of marriageable girls. Marriages are arranged by older kin, usually men—brothers,

1. *Bahimi, wife of the Bisaasi-teri headman, harvesting plantains, the cooking bananas that make up a large part of the Yanomamö diet.*

uncles, and the father. It is a political process in which girls are promised in marriage at an early age by men who are attempting to create alliances with other men via marriage exchanges. There is a shortage of women, due in part to a sex-ratio imbalance in the younger age categories but complicated by the fact that some men have multiple wives. Most fighting within the village stems from sexual affairs or the failure to deliver a promised woman—or from the out-and-out seizure of a married woman by another man. The fighting can sometimes lead to conflict of such an intensity that villages split up, or fission, each group becoming a new village and, often, enemies of each other.

But the conflicts are not blind, uncontrolled violence. There are graded forms of violence that range from chest pounding to club-fighting duels to shooting with deadly weapons. This gives the Yanomamö a good deal of flexibility in settling disputes without an immediate resort to lethal violence. In addition, they have developed patterns of alliance that serve to limit violence—trading and feasting with others in order to become friends (photos 2 and 3). These alliances can, and often do, result in intervillage exchanges of marriageable women, leading to additional amity between villages. However, no good thing lasts forever, and most alliances eventually crumble. Old friends become hostile and occasionally treacherous. The people of each village must remain keenly aware that their neighbors are fickle, and they must behave accordingly. The village leaders must traverse a thin line between friendship and animosity, employing political acumen and strategies that are both admirable and complex.

Each village, then, is a replica of all others in a broad sense. But each village is also part of a larger political, demographic, and ecological process, and it is difficult to understand a single village without knowing something of the larger forces that affect it and its historical relationships with all its neighbors.

Collecting Data in the Field

I have now spent over sixty months altogether with the Yanomamö, during which time I have learned their language and, to a point, have submerged myself in their culture and way of life. As my research has progressed, what has impressed me most is the importance that aggression has played in shaping their culture. I have had the opportunity to witness many incidents that expressed both individual vindictiveness and collective bellicosity. These ranged in seriousness from ordinary incidents of wife beating and chest pounding to

2. *Kaobawä, headman of Upper Bisaasi-teri, trading with his Shamatari allies for arrows, baskets, hammocks, and dogs.*

3. *Visitors dancing as a group around the* **shabono** *during a formal feast.*

dueling and organized raiding parties that set out to ambush and kill the men of an enemy village. One of the villages I discuss here was raided approximately twenty-five times during my first fifteen months of fieldwork—six times by the group among which I was living. And the history of every village I investigated, from 1964 to 1992, was intimately bound up in patterns of warfare with neighbors that shaped its politics and determined where it was located at any point in time and how it dealt with its current neighbors.

The fact that the Yanomamö have lived in a chronic state of warfare is reflected in their mythology, ceremonies, settlement pattern, political behavior, and marriage practices. Accordingly, I have made a special effort throughout this book to help the reader appreciate the effects of warfare on their culture in general and on their social organization and political relationships in particular.

The trying circumstances under which I have collected my data give a rough idea of what anthropologists mean when they speak of culture shock and fieldwork. Each field situation is in many respects unique, however, and the problems I encountered do not necessarily exhaust the range of possible problems anthropologists can have. But a few problems do seem to be nearly universal among anthropological fieldworkers, particularly those having to do with eating, bathing, sleeping, lack of privacy, loneliness, and the discovery that the people you are living with have a lower opinion of you than you have of them—or that you yourself are not as culturally or emotionally flexible as you had assumed.

The Yanomamö can be difficult people to live with, but I have also had colleagues acknowledge that they themselves have had difficulty in living with certain communities. The situation varies from society to society, and probably from one anthropologist to the next. I have done some limited fieldwork among the Yanomamö's northern neighbors, the Ye'kwana Indians, and, by contrast to many of my experiences among the Yanomamö, I found the Ye'kwana to be pleasant and charming, all of them eager to help and honor bound to show any visitor the numerous courtesies of their system of etiquette. In short, they approached the image of "primitive man" that I had conjured in my mind before I ever started doing fieldwork—a kind of Rousseau primitive—and it was sheer pleasure to work with them. Other anthropologists have noted similar sharp contrasts in the people they are studying. One of the most startling examples is in the work of Colin Turnbull, who first studied the Ituri Pygmies, and found them delightful to live with. He then studied the Ik, who lived on the desolate outcroppings of the Kenya-Uganda-Sudan border region, a people he had trouble coping with intellectually, emotionally, and physically. While it is possible for an anthropologist's reactions to a particular people to be personal and idiosyncratic, it nevertheless remains true there *are* enormous differences between whole peoples that affect the anthropologist in often dramatic ways.

Hence, what I say about some of my experiences is probably equally true of the experiences of many other fieldworkers. I describe them here for the benefit of any future anthropologists among my readers—because I myself could have profited by reading about the pitfalls and field problems of my own teachers. At the very least, I might have been able to avoid some of my more stupid errors.

The Longest Day: The First One

My very first day in the field showed me what my teachers meant when they spoke of culture shock. I had been traveling in a small aluminum rowboat propelled by a large outboard motor for two and a half days, going from the territorial capital of Puerto Ayacucho, then a small Venezuelan town on the Orinoco River, deep into Yanomamö country. On the morning of the third day, my party reached a small mission settlement, the field headquarters of the New Tribes Mission, a Protestant group comprised mostly of Americans that was working in two Yanomamö villages. The missionaries had come from these villages to hold their annual conference on the progress of their work, and the meetings were in session when I arrived. At the mission station we picked up a passenger, James P. Barker, the first non-Yanomamö to make sustained, permanent contact with the Yanomamö, in 1950. He had just returned from a year's furlough in the United States, where I had met him before I left for Venezuela. He had agreed to accompany me to Bisaasi-teri, the village I had selected for my base of operations, and introduce me to the Indians. This village was also his home base—he had been living with that particular group about five years—but he had not been there in over a year and did not plan to return permanently for another three months.

We arrived at Bisaasi-teri at about two in the afternoon and docked the boat along the muddy bank at the foot of the path the Yanomamö used to fetch their drinking water. It was hot and muggy, and my perspiration-soaked clothing clung uncomfortably to my body, as it did for the duration of my work. The small biting gnats called *bareto* were out in astronomical numbers, signaling the beginning of the dry season. My face and hands were swollen from the venom of their numerous stings. In just a few moments I was to meet my first Yanomamö, my first primitive man. What would he be like?

Greenhorn that I was, I had visions of entering the village and seeing 125 social facts running about altruistically, calling to each other in kinship terms and sharing food, each waiting anxiously for me to collect his genealogy. I would wear them out in turn. Would they like me? This was important to me; I wanted them to be so fond of me that they would soon adopt me into their kinship system and way of life. I had heard that successful anthropologists always got adopted by their people. I had learned, during my seven years of anthropological training at the University of Michigan, that kinship was equivalent to society in primitive tribes and that it was a moral way of life, "moral" being akin to "good" and "desirable." I was determined to work my way into their moral system of kinship and become a member of their society—to be accepted by them.

My heart pounded as we neared the village and could hear the buzz of activity within the circular compound. Barker commented that he was anxious to see if any changes had occurred while he was away and wondered how many had died during his absence. I nervously felt my back pocket to make sure my notebook was still there and was reassured when I touched it.

The entrance to the village was covered with brush and dry palm leaves, which we pushed aside to expose the low opening. The excitement of meeting my first Yanomamö was almost unbearable as I duck-waddled through the low passage into the village clearing.

I looked up and gasped to see a dozen burly, naked, sweaty, hideous men staring at us down the shafts of their drawn arrows. Immense wads of green tobacco were stuck between their lower teeth and lips, making them look even more hideous, and strands of dark-green slime dripped from their nostrils— strands so long that they reached down to their pectoral muscles or drizzled down their chins and stuck to their chests and bellies. We had arrived as the men were blowing *ebene*, a hallucinogenic drug, up each other's noses. As I soon learned, one side effect of the drug is a runny nose. The mucus becomes saturated with the drug's green powder, and the Yanomamö usually just let it dangle freely from their nostrils to plop off when the strands become too heavy (photo 4).

My next discovery was that there were a dozen or so vicious, underfed dogs snapping at my legs, circling as if I were to be their next meal, dodging in, grabbing my pants, ripping them, and darting back into the safety of the

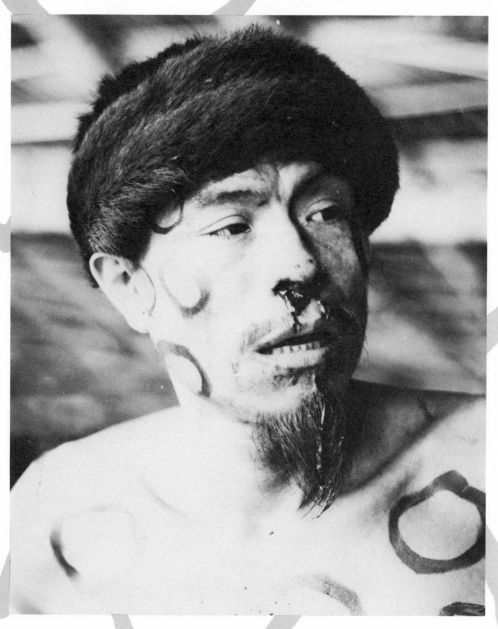

4. *Yanomamö man with monkey-tail headband and* ebene—*a hallucinogenic snuff powder*—*drizzling from his nostrils.*

pack to brace for another lunge. Helpless and pathetic, I could only stand there clutching my notebook. Then the stench of decaying vegetation and filth hit me, and I was almost sick to my stomach. I was horrified. What kind of welcome was this for someone who had come to live with these people and learn their way of life—to become friends with them? But when they recognized Barker, they put their weapons down and returned to their chanting, while keeping a nervous eye on the village entrances.

It seems that we had arrived right after a serious fight. Seven women had been abducted by a neighboring group the day before, and the local men and their guests had just that morning recovered five of them, in a brutal club fight that had nearly ended in a shooting war. The abductors, angry at losing five of their seven new captives, had vowed to raid Bisaasi-teri, and when Barker and I entered the village unexpectedly, the Yanomamö had feared that we were the raiders. On several occasions during the next two hours, the men of the village jumped to their feet, grabbed their weapons, nocked their arrows, and waited nervously for a noise outside the village to be identified. My enthusiasm for collecting ethnographic data diminished in proportion to the number of times such an alarm was raised. In fact, I was relieved when Barker suggested that we sleep on the other side of the river that night. "It will be safer over there," he commented casually. I was willing to take his word for that.

As we walked back down the path to the boat, I pondered the wisdom of having decided to spend a year and a half with these people before I even knew what they were like. I am not ashamed to admit that if there had been a diplomatic way out, I would have ended my fieldwork then and there. I did not look forward to the next day—and the months thereafter—when I would be alone with the Yanomamö. I did not speak a word of their language, and they were decidedly different from what I had imagined. Yes, they definitely were not what I had expected. Depressed, I wondered why I had ever switched my major from physics and engineering.

I had not eaten all day, I was soaking wet from perspiration, the *bareto* were still biting, and I was smeared with the red pigment with which the men painted their bodies, the result of a dozen or so rather complete examinations I had been given by as many pushy Yanomamö men. The examinations had capped an already grim day. The men would blow their noses into their hands, flick off as much mucus as would separate in a snap of the wrist, wipe the residue into their hair, and then carefully examine my face, arms, legs, hair, and the contents of my pockets. I asked Barker how to say, "Your hands are dirty." That comment got me this: the men spit a quantity of slimy tobacco juice into their hands, rubbed them together, grinned, and proceeded with the examination with what they considered clean hands.

Barker and I crossed the river and slung our hammocks. When he pulled his hammock out of a rubber bag, a heavy, disagreeable odor of mildewed cotton and stale wood smoke came with it, again almost making me sick. Even the missionaries are filthy, I thought. But within two weeks everything I owned smelled the same way, and I lived with that odor for the remainder of my fieldwork. My habits of personal cleanliness declined to such a level that I ceased to mind even the Yanomamö examinations, as I was not much cleaner than they were. After all, a man can't blow his nose gracefully when he is stark naked and, in evolutionary terms, the invention of handkerchiefs or Kleenex is millennia away. In fact, handkerchiefs may not be a very significant improvement, when you think of how thoughtlessly we carry around what we blow from our nostrils.

Life in the Jungle: Oatmeal, Peanut Butter, and Bugs

A fieldworker doesn't just plop down in the Amazon Basin for a year and get immediately into the anthropological swing of things. He will have heard a lot about horrible diseases, snakes, jaguars, electric eels, little spiny fish that can swim up his urine stream and get into his penis, quicksand, getting lost. Some of the dangers are real, although the imagination tends to make them more threatening than they really are. What my teachers had never bothered to tell me about, however, was the mundane and nonexciting side of life—like eating, defecating, sleeping, and keeping clean. These were the bane of my existence during the first several months of field research.

I set up my household in Barker's old mud hut, a few yards from the village of Bisaasi-teri, and immediately set to work building my own mud-and-thatch hut, with the help of the Yanomamö. Meanwhile, I had to eat and get started on my field research. I soon discovered how enormously time-consuming it was to maintain my body in the manner to which it had grown accustomed in the relatively antiseptic environment of the northern United States. Either I could eat adequately and be reasonably comfortable in fresh changes of clothes while doing little fieldwork, or I could do considerably more fieldwork and be less well fed and not as comfortable.

For instance, it was appallingly complicated to make oatmeal. First, it took two trips down to the river to haul the water. Next, I had to prime my kerosene stove with alcohol to get it burning—tricky when I was trying to mix powdered milk and fill a coffeepot at the same time. The alcohol prime almost always burned out before I could turn the kerosene on, and I would have to start all over. Or I would turn the kerosene on anyhow, hoping that the Coleman element was still hot enough, and start a small fire in my palm-thatched hut as the liquid kerosene squirted all over the makeshift table and the walls and *then* ignited. The amused Yanomamö onlookers quickly learned the English phrase "Oh, shit!" And later, when they discovered that the phrase offended the American missionaries, the Yanomamö delighted in using it in the missionaries' presence.

I usually had to try more than once with the alcohol. Then I had to boil the oatmeal and pick out the bugs. All my supplies, of course, were carefully stored in rat-proof, moisture-proof, and insect-proof containers, not one of which ever served its purpose adequately. Just taking things out of the multiplicity of containers and repacking them afterward was a minor project in itself. By the time I had hauled the water for cooking, unpacked my food, prepared the oatmeal, milk, and coffee, heated water and washed and dried the dishes, repacked the food in the containers, stored the containers in locked trunks, and cleaned up the rest of my mess, the ceremony of eating breakfast had brought me almost to lunchtime.

Having three meals a day was out of the question. My eventual solution was to eat one meal that could be prepared in a single container, or at most two, to wash dishes only when there were no clean ones left, to use cold river water, and to wear each change of clothing at least a week to cut down on the laundry problem—a courageous undertaking in the tropics. I reeked like a jockstrap that has been left to mildew in the bottom of a dark gym locker. I also became less concerned about sharing my provisions with rats, insects, the Yanomamö, and the elements, thereby eliminating the need for my complicated storage system.

I found I could get through most of the day on *café con leche*, heavily sugared espresso coffee diluted about five to one with hot milk. I would prepare this in the evening and store it in a large thermos. Frequently, my single meal was no more than a can of sardines and a package of soggy crackers. But at least two or three times a week I would do something more complicated, like making a batch of oatmeal or boiling rice to which I added a can of tuna fish or tomato paste.

I even devised a water system that obviated the trips to the river. I had the missionaries bring me a few sheets of tin roofing, out of which I made a rainwater trap; I caught the water on the tin surface, funneled it into an empty gasoline drum, and ran a plastic hose from the drum to my hut. When the drum ran empty in the dry season, I would get a few Yanomamö boys to fill it with buckets of water from the river, paying them in crackers—of which they grew all too fond all too soon.

I ate still less when I traveled with the Yanomamö to other villages. Mostly my travel diet consisted of roasted or boiled green plantains that I got from the Yanomamö, but I always carried along a few cans of sardines, in case I got lost or stayed away longer than I had planned. Peanut butter and crackers made a nourishing trail meal, and a simple one to prepare. It was nutritious and portable and required only one tool, a hunting knife, which was easy to clean by wiping the blade on a leaf or licking it clean.

More important, this food was one of the few the Yanomamö would let me eat in peace. It looked suspiciously like animal feces to them, an impression I encouraged by referring to the peanut butter as the feces of babies or cattle. They found that disgusting and repugnant. Although they did not know what cattle were, they were increasingly aware that I ate several canned products of such an animal. To them, the tin cans were containers made of "machete skins," but how the cattle parts got inside remained a mystery. I went out of my way to describe my foods in terms that sounded unpalatable to the Yanomamö, for it gave me some peace of mind while I ate. They wouldn't beg for a share of something they thought was horrible. Fieldworkers develop some strange defense mechanisms and strategies, and this was my particular form of adaptation. On one occasion, I was eating a can of frankfurters and growing very weary of the demands of one onlooker for a share. When he finally asked what I was eating, I replied, "Beef." Getting my attention by calling me by my Yanomamö name, he asked, "Shaki, what part of the animal are you eating?" I replied, "Guess." He muttered a contemptuous epithet but stopped asking for a share, although he was to get back at me later.

(The Yanomamö had trouble pronouncing "Chagnon," which sounded to them like their name for a pesky bee, *shaki*. And so that is what I became to them—the man called "Bee.")

Meals proved to be a problem in a way that had nothing to do with the inconvenience of preparing them. Food sharing is important to the Yanomamö in the context of displaying friendship and generosity or, in some cases, to demonstrate their ability to coerce others into giving them things. "I am hungry" is almost a form of greeting with them. I could not possibly have brought enough food to feed the entire village, yet in their begging they seemed to overlook this logistical fact. What became fixed in their minds was that I would not share my food with whoever was present—usually a small crowd—at each and every meal. They loved to watch me eat and to badger me as I did.

Nor could I easily enter into their system of reciprocity with respect to food. Every time one of them gave me something freely (or so I thought), he would dog me for months to pay him back, not necessarily in food but in knives, fishhooks, or axes. Thus, if I accepted a plantain from someone in a village I was visiting, he would most likely visit me later and demand a machete as payment for having fed me. I usually reacted to such demands by giving the person a banana, the customary reciprocation in that culture—food for food—but this could be a big disappointment for an individual who had nursed visions of that single plantain growing into a machete. Several years after the beginning of my fieldwork, I was approached by one prominent villager demanding a machete for a piece of meat he claimed he had given me five or six years earlier.

Although most of the Yanomamö knew I would not give in to their requests to share my food, some of them always showed up at my hut during mealtime. I gradually resigned myself to this and learned to ignore their persistent demands. Some of them would get angry, but most came to accept it as just a peculiarity of the subhuman foreigner who had come to live among them. If I did accede to a request for food, the hut quickly filled with Yanomamö, all demanding their share. The begging was not provoked by hunger, but by a desire to try something new or an attempt to establish a coercive relationship by getting me to accede to a demand. If one of them received something from me, all the others immediately had to test the system to see if they, too, could coerce me.

A few went to some lengths to make my meals downright unpleasant— to spite me for not sharing, especially if it was a food they had already tried and liked or a food that was part of their own cuisine. One day, for example, I was eating a cracker with peanut butter and honey. The Yanomamö will do almost anything to get honey, one of the most prized delicacies in their diet. One of my cynical onlookers—the fellow who had earlier watched me eating frankfurters—immediately spotted the honey and knew that I would not share the precious tiny bottle. It would be futile even to ask. Instead, he glared at me and said icily, "Shaki, what kind of animal semen are you pouring onto your food and eating?" The question had the desired effect, and my meal ended.

Finally, there is the problem of loneliness and separation from your own kind, especially your family. I tried to overcome the isolation by seeking personal friendships among the Yanomamö. But usually this only complicated my life, because all my so-called friends simply used my confidence to gain privileged access to my hut and my cache of steel tools and trade goods—and looted me when I wasn't looking. I would be bitterly disappointed that my erstwhile friends thought no more of me than to finesse our personal relationship with the sole intention of getting at my locked-up possessions, and my depression would hit a new low every time I discovered another instance of it. The loss of the possessions bothered me much less than the shocking awareness that to most of them I was nothing more than a source of desirable items. And that no holds were barred in relieving me of these, since I was a non-Yanomamö and therefore something subhuman.

The hardest thing I had to learn to live with was the incessant, impassioned, and often aggressive demands they made. The demands would become so unbearable at times that I would lock myself in my hut periodically to escape them. Privacy is one of our culture's most satisfying attributes, one we seldom think about unless suddenly we have none. But I did not want privacy for its own sake; I simply had to get away from the begging. Day and night, for almost the entire time I lived with the Yanomamö, I was plagued by demands like these: "Give me a knife, I am poor"; "If you don't take me with you on your next trip to Widokaiya-teri, I'll chop a hole in your canoe"; "Take us hunting up the Mavaca River with your shotgun, or we won't help you"; "Give me some matches so I can trade with the Reyaboböwei-teri, and be quick about it, or I'll hit you"; "Share your food with me, or I'll burn your hut"; "Give me a flashlight so I can hunt at night"; "Give me all your medicine—I itch all over"; "Give me an ax, or I'll break into your hut when you are away and steal all of them." I was bombarded by such demands day after day, month after month, until at times I could not bear to look at a Yanomamö.

It was not as difficult to become hardened to the incessant begging as it was to ignore the sense of urgency, the impassioned or whining tone of voice, and the intimidation and aggression with which many of the demands were made. It was likewise difficult for me to realize that the Yanomamö would not accept no for an answer unless my refusal also seethed with passion and intimidation—which it did after a few months. So persistent and characteristic is the begging that the early semiofficial maps made by the Venezuelan Malaria Control Service (*Malarialogía*) designated the site of the service's first permanent field station, next to the village of Bisaasi-teri, as *Yababuhii*—"Gimme." I would have to become more like the Yanomamö in order to get along with them: somewhat sly, aggressive, intimidating, and pushy.

I quickly saw that if I did not adjust in this fashion I could lose six months of supplies in a single day and would be spending most of my time ferrying people around in my canoe or taking them on long hunting trips. As it was, at first I did spend considerable time doing those things and did succumb often to the outrageous demands for axes or machetes—but things changed as I became more fluent in the language and learned how to defend myself socially as well as verbally. More important, had I failed to demonstrate that I could not be pushed beyond a certain point, I would have been the subject of even more ridicule, theft, and practical jokes than I actually was. In short, I had to acquire a certain proficiency in the Yanomamö's style of interpersonal politics and to learn how to imply subtly that unspecified but potentially undesirable consequences might follow if they did such and such. They act that way with each other constantly in order to establish the exact point at which an individual cannot be goaded or intimidated further without precipitating some kind of retaliation. As soon as I realized this and acquired the self-confidence to adopt their strategy, I could see how much of the intimidation was calculated to determine my flash point or my last-ditch position—and we got along better. Indeed, I even regained some lost ground.

It was a sort of political, interpersonal game that everyone played, a game in which all the players sooner or later have to give evidence that their bluffs and implied threats can be backed up with a sanction. I suspect that the frequency of wife beating is a component in this game, since it allows the men to display their *waiteri*, or ferocity, and demonstrate to others that they are capable of great violence. Beating a wife with a club is a way of displaying ferocity that does not expose the man to much danger—unless the wife has aggressive brothers in the village who will come to her aid. Apparently an important intention in wife beating is that the man has displayed his potential for violence, sending the message that other men ought to treat him with circumspection, caution, and even deference.

After six months, the level of demands from the Yanomamö in Bisaasi-teri became bearable. We had adjusted somewhat to each other and knew what to expect with regard to demands for food, trade goods, and favors. Had I elected to remain in this one village, the entire period of fieldwork would have been much more enjoyable. However, as I began to understand the social and political dynamics of this village, it became clear that I would have to augment my information by collecting data from many other villages. I therefore began making regular trips to at least a dozen neighboring Yanomamö villages. Since I had to establish my personal position in each new village I visited or revisited, the intensity of the begging remained relatively constant and high for the duration of my fieldwork.

For the most part, my own fierceness took the form of shouting back at the Yanomamö as loudly and passionately as they shouted at me, especially at first, when I did not know much of the language. They appeared to interpret my inability to understand their language as a hearing defect and would shout loudly at me whenever I didn't understand them. As I became more fluent and learned more about their political tactics, I became more sophisticated in the art of bluffing and brinksmanship.

An example is the time I paid one young man a machete (then worth about $2.50) to cut a palm tree and help me make boards from the wood, with which I fashioned a flooring in my dugout canoe to protect my possessions from the water that always sloshed around there. That afternoon, as I worked with one of my informants in the village, the long-awaited mission supply boat arrived and tied up across the river. Most of the Yanomamö ran down to see the supplies and try to beg items from the crew, but I continued to work in the village for another hour or so before going down to the river to visit with the men on the supply boat. When I got there, I noticed, with anger and frustration, that the Yanomamö had chopped up all my new floorboards into crude paddles to propel their own canoes, originally acquired from the missionaries, across the river to the supply boat. I knew that if I ignored the abuse I would be inviting the Yanomamö to take even greater liberties with my possessions in the future. So I got into my canoe, crossed the river, and docked among their flimsy, leaky craft, shouting loudly to attract their attention. They acted somewhat sheepish, but all had mischievous grins on their impish faces. A few of them came down to my canoe, and I launched into a spirited and angry lecture about their audacity and license. I talked about how just that morning I had paid one of them a machete for bringing me the palm wood, how hard I had worked to shape each board and place it in the canoe, how painstakingly I had tied each one with vines, how much I had perspired, how many *bareto* bites I had suffered and so on. Then, with exaggerated drama, I took out my hunting knife, cut every one of their canoes loose, and set them into the strong current of the Orinoco River, where they were immediately swept downstream. Their grins disappeared, and without looking back I huffed across the river again to resume my work.

The Yanomamö managed to borrow a canoe and, after some effort, recovered their dugouts. The headman of the village told me later, with an approving chuckle, that I had done the correct thing. Everyone in the village—except, of course, the culprits—supported my actions, and my status increased as a consequence.

Whenever I defended myself in such a way, I got along better with the Yanomamö afterward, and gradually I gained the respect of many. As I have said, a good part of their demeanor was designed to establish the point at which I would draw the line. Many of them, years later, would reminisce about those early days when I was timid, *mohode* ("stupid"), and a little intimidated, and when it was easy to bully me into giving my goods away for almost nothing. They laughed hysterically as they recited incident after incident in which they had duped me into giving them something and admitted how outrageous their demands had been.

Theft was the most persistent problem requiring defensive action. I could not keep everything I owned locked away in trunks, and yet the Yanomamö came and went in my hut at will. Eventually I developed this effective strategy for recovering most of the stolen items: I would ask a child who had taken the item, and then I would confiscate that person's hammock when he was not around, giving a spirited lecture to all within hearing on the antisociability of thievery as I stalked off in a faked rage with the thief's hammock slung over my shoulder. Nobody ever attempted to stop me, and almost all of them told me the technique was ingenious. By nightfall the thief would appear at my hut with the stolen item, or would send it with someone else, in exchange for his hammock. He would be heckled by the other villagers for having been caught and shamed into returning the item. The explanation usually was, "I just borrowed your ax. I wouldn't think of stealing it."

Prying into Yanomamö Secrets

Collecting Genealogies and Reproductive Histories

My purpose in living among the Yanomamö was to collect information on their genealogies, reproduction, marriage practices, kinship, settlement pattern, migrations, and politics. The most fundamental of the data was genealogical—who was the parent of whom, with such connections traced as far back as Yanomamö memory permitted. Like most primitive societies, the Yanomamö society is largely organized by kinship relationships, and figuring out this social organization essentially meant collecting extensive data on genealogies, marriage, and reproduction.

It turned out to be a staggering and frustrating problem. I could not have deliberately picked a more difficult people to work with in this regard, because of their very stringent taboos against mentioning the names of prominent living people or of deceased friends and relatives. They attempt to choose names for people so that when the person dies, and they can no longer use his or her name, the loss of the word from their language is not inconvenient. Hence, they name people for highly specific and minute parts of things, such as "toenail of sloth," "whisker of howler monkey," and so on, thereby being able to retain the words "toenail" and "whisker" but somewhat handicapped when they need to refer to these anatomical parts of sloths and monkeys. The name taboo even applies to the living, for one mark of a person's prestige is the courtesy others show by *not* using that person's name publicly. This is particularly true for the men, who are much more competitive for status than the women are, and it is fascinating to watch boys, as they grow into young men, demanding to be called in public either by a kinship term or by some such reference as "brother of Himotoma" or "nephew of Ushubiriwä." The more effective they are at getting others to avoid using their names, the greater is the public acknowledgment of their esteem and social standing. Helena Valero, a Brazilian woman who was captured as a child by a Yanomamö raiding party, was married for many years to a Yanomamö headman before she discovered what his name was. The sanctions behind the taboo are more complex than just fear: they involve a combination of fear, respect, admiration, political deference, and honor.

At first I tried to use kinship terms alone to collect my genealogies, but Yanomamö kinship terms, like those in all systems, tend to become ambiguous at the point where they include many possible relatives—as the terms "uncle" and "cousin" do in our own kinship system. In a community like Bisaasi-teri, where someone might have thirty cousins, you cannot get the right person simply by saying, "Call my cousin for me." Also, the system of kin classification merges many relatives that we normally separate by using different terms: the Yanomamö call both the actual father and the father's brother by a single term, whereas we call one "father" and the other "uncle." I was forced, therefore, to resort to personal names to collect unambiguous genealogies or pedigrees.

The villagers quickly grasped what I was up to, that I was determined to learn everyone's true name. This amounted to an invasion of their system of prestige and etiquette, if not a flagrant violation of it, and their reaction was brilliant but devastating. They invented *false names* for everybody in the village, systematically learned them, and freely revealed them to me. I smugly thought I had cracked the system and enthusiastically spent some five months constructing elaborate genealogies.

Since they enjoyed watching me work on the names and kinship relationships, I naively assumed that I was getting the most truthful information by working in public. This set the stage for converting my serious project into a hilarious game of the grandest proportions. Each informant would try to outdo his peers by inventing a name more preposterous or ridiculous than one I had been given earlier, the explanation for discrepancies being "Well, he has two names, and this is the other one." They even fabricated devilishly improbable genealogical relationships, such as someone being married to his grandmother or, worse yet, his mother-in-law—a grotesque and horrifying prospect to the Yanomamö. My practice was to have the informant whisper a person's name softly into my ear, noting that he or she was the parent of such and such or the child of such and such. The eager watchers would then insist that I repeat the name aloud, roaring in hysterical laughter as I clumsily pronounced it, sometimes laughing until tears streamed down their faces. The person named would usually react with annoyance and hiss some untranslatable epithet at me, which only served to reassure me that I indeed had the person's true name. Conscientiously checking and rechecking the names and relationships with multiple informants, I was pleased to see the inconsistencies disappear as my genealogy sheets filled with thousands of those desirable little triangles and circles.

My anthropological bubble burst when, some five months after I had begun collecting the genealogies, I visited a village about ten hours' walk to the southwest of Bisaasi-teri. In talking with the headman of this village, I casually dropped the name of the wife of the Bisaasi-teri headman, to show off a bit and demonstrate my growing command of the language and of who was who. A stunned silence followed, and then a villagewide roar of uncontrollable laughter, choking, gasping, and howling. It seems that I thought the Bisaasi-teri headman was married to a woman named "hairy cunt." It also came out that I was calling the headman "long dong," his brother "eagle shit," one of his sons "asshole," and a daughter "fart breath."

Blood welled in my temples as I realized that I had nothing but nonsense to show for my five months of dedicated genealogical effort and that I would have to throw out almost all the information I had collected on this, the most basic set of data I had come to get. Now I understood why the Bisaasi-teri had laughed so hard when they made me repeat the names they had given me, and why the person named had reacted with such anger and annoyance.

I would have to devise a new research strategy—an understatement to describe this serious setback to my work. The first change was to begin working in private with my informants, eliminating the horseplay and distractions that had attended the public sessions. The informants, who did not know what others were telling me, now began to agree with each other, and I managed to learn real names, starting with the children and gradually moving on to the adult women and then, cautiously, the adult men, a sequence that reflected the relative degree of intransigence at revealing the names. As I built up a core of accurate genealogies and relationships—which the various informants verified repetitiously—I could test any new informant by soliciting his or her knowledge about these core people whose names and relationships I was sure of. In this fashion, I was able to immediately weed out the mischievous informants who persisted in trying to deceive me. Still, I had great difficulty getting the names of dead kinsmen, the only accurate way to extend the genealogies back in time. Even my best informants continued to falsify the names of the deceased, especially if they were closely related. But the falsifications were not serious at this point and proved to be readily corrected as my interviewing methods improved. Most of the deceptions were of the sort where the informant would give me the name of a living man as the father of a child whose actual father was dead, enabling the informant to avoid using the name of a deceased kinsman or friend.

But the name taboo prevented me from making any substantial progress in tracing the present population back through several generations, without which data I could not, for example, document marriage patterns and inter-familial alliances over time. I had to rely on older informants for such information, and they were the most reluctant informants of all. Even as I became more proficient in the language and more skilled at detecting fabrications, my informants became better at deception. One old man, particularly cunning and persuasive, followed Mark Twain's theory that the most effective lie is a sincere lie. He made quite a ceremony out of giving me false names for dead ancestors. He would look around nervously to make sure nobody was listening outside my hut, would enjoin me never to mention the name again, and would act anxious and spooky as he grabbed me by the head and whispered a secret name into my ear. I was always elated after a session with him, because I would have added several generations of ancestors for particular members of the village, information others steadfastly refused to give me. To show my gratitude, I paid him quadruple the rate that I had been paying the others. When word got around that I had increased the pay for genealogical and demographic information, volunteers began pouring into my hut to work for me, assuring me they had changed their ways and had a keen desire to divest themselves of their version of the truth.

Enter Rerebawä: Inmarried Tough Guy

It was quite by accident that I discovered the old man had been lying. A club fight broke out in the village one day, the result of a dispute over the possession of a woman. The woman had been promised to a young man of the village, a particularly aggressive man named Rerebawä. He had inmarried— that is, he was from another village and had married into the village of Bisaasi-teri—and was doing his bride service, a period of several years during which he had to provide game and wild foods for his wife's father and mother and help them with certain gardening and other tasks. Rerebawä had already been given one of the daughters in marriage and had been promised her younger sister as his second wife. He became enraged when the younger sister, then about sixteen years old, openly began an affair with another young man of the village, Bäkotawä, and he challenged Bäkotawä to a club fight.

Rerebawä swaggered boisterously out to the duel carrying a ten-foot-long club, a roof pole he had impulsively cut from a house, as is the usual procedure. He hurled insult after insult at both Bäkotawä and his father, trying to goad them into a fight. They tolerated the bitter and nasty insults for a few moments, but Rerebawä's biting words soon provoked them to rage. They stormed angrily out of their hammocks and ripped off their own roof poles, returning the insults verbally, and rushed to the village clearing, where they took up positions some ten feet away from Rerebawä. He continued his insults, trying to goad them into striking him on the head with their equally long clubs. Had either of them struck his head—which he held forward prominently for them to swing at— he would have had the right to retaliate on their heads with his club. But his opponents, intimidated by his fury, backed down, refusing to strike him, and the argument ended. All three then retired pompously to their respective hammocks, exchanging nasty insults as they went. Rerebawä had won the showdown and thereafter swaggered around the village, insulting the two men behind their backs at every opportunity—so genuinely angry that he called the older man by the name of his long-deceased father.

As soon as I heard that name, which was not the same as the one I had recorded, I asked Rerebawä to repeat it, which he did willingly and contemp- tuously. Quickly seizing on the incident as an opportunity to correct my data, I confidentially asked Rerebawä to tell me more about his adversary's ancestors. He had been particularly brusque with me until now, but we soon became warm friends and staunch allies, partly because we were both outsiders in Bisaasi-teri. Like all inmarried Yanomamö sons-in-law, he had to put up with a considerable amount of pointed teasing and scorn from the locals (photo 5). With almost devilish glee he gave me the information I wanted about his adversary's deceased ancestors.

I asked about the dead ancestors of other people in the village and got equally prompt and unequivocal answers—he seemed to be angry at everyone in the village. When I compared his answers to those of the old man, it was obvious that one of them was lying. I challenged Rerebawä, and he explained, in a sort of "you damned fool, don't you know better?" tone, that everyone in the village knew that the old man was lying to me and that they were gloating over it when I was out of earshot. The names the old man had given me were those of the dead ancestors of people in a village so far away that he thought I would never be able to check them authoritatively. As it turned out, Rerebawä knew most of the people in that distant village and recognized the names— and also knew enough about recently deceased Bisaasi-teri to be sure that the old man had been lying.

I went over with Rerebawä all the Bisaasi-teri genealogies that I had presumed were close to their final form and had to revise them all because of the numerous lies and falsifications, many of them provided by the sly old man. Once again, after months of work, I had to recheck everything, but with Rerebawä's aid this time. Only the information about living members of nuclear

5. *Rerebawä, one of my closest friends and a constant companion
on long trips to remote villages.*

families turned out to be accurate; that about deceased ancestors was mostly fabrication.

Discouraging as it was to know I had to recheck everything yet again, it proved to be a major turning point in my fieldwork. From then on I took advantage of local arguments and animosities in selecting my informants and made more extensive use of informants who had married into the village in the recent past. I also began to travel more regularly to other villages to check on genealogies, seeking out villages whose members were on strained terms with the people about whom I wanted information. I would then return to my base in Bisaasi-teri and check the accuracy of the new information with local informants.

I learned to be scrupulous about selecting local informants so that I was not inquiring about *their* closely related kin. For each local informant, I had to keep a list of the deceased people that I dared not name in his or her presence. Even so, I would occasionally hit a new name that would send an informant into a rage or a sulk, such as that of a dead "brother" or "sister" (the Yanomamö classify many cousins as brothers and sisters) whose relationship I had not been aware of. That usually terminated the day's work with the informant; he or she would be too upset to continue, and I would be reluctant to risk the accidental discovery of another dead kinsman.

To inadvertently say the name of a dead person was always an unpleasant experience for me, and occasionally a dangerous one, depending on the temperament of the informant. On one occasion, I planned to visit a certain village to check my census list, but I knew that the village had been raided recently by its enemies and that a woman from the village had been killed by the raiders.

Killing women is considered bad form in Yanomamö warfare, and this was a particularly nasty case because the woman had been deliberately killed out of revenge. The incident started when raiders from her village, failing to bushwhack a man who had stepped out of his village at dawn to urinate, shot a volley of arrows into the village and beat a hasty retreat. Unfortunately, one of the arrows struck and accidentally killed a woman. On a retaliatory raid, the men of that village *deliberately* sought out and killed a woman—whose name I knew was on my census list, but I didn't know which one it was, because nobody dared say it.

My reason for going to the village was to update the census data on a name-by-name basis and estimate the ages of all the residents. I would be in very serious trouble if I got to the village and said the dead woman's name aloud. I would have to remove it from my list beforehand. But which name was it?

I called on one of my regular informants, who was usually cooperative, and asked him. He refused adamantly, explaining that she was a close relative—and he was angry that I had even raised the subject. I then asked if he would let me whisper the names of *all* the women of the village in his ear, and he could simply nod when I hit the right one. I thought we had become good enough friends to use such a procedure, and he agreed to it, but with an odd expression on his face. I began to whisper the names of the women, one by one. We were alone in my hut, so that nobody would know what we were doing or could hear us, and I read the names softly, continuing to the next each time his response was negative. But when I finally reached the dead woman's name, he flew out of his chair, enraged and trembling violently, his arm raised as if to strike me. "You rotten son-of-a-bitch!" he screamed. "If you say her name in my presence again, I'll kill you in an instant." I sat there, bewildered, shocked, and confused. And frightened, not only by his reaction but also by seeing what could happen to me if I tried to check a village's records without knowing that someone there had died or been killed since my last visit.

I reflected on the several articles I had read as a graduate student that explained the genealogical method, but I could not recall anything about its being potentially lethal. The furious informant left my hut and was never again invited back in that capacity. I was to have similar experiences in various villages, but fortunately the death had always occurred some time ago or the dead person was not too closely related to the individual into whose ear I whispered the forbidden name. Someone would usually caution me to desist from saying any more names lest I make people angry.

Not many days after that frightening incident, I took a group of men across the river in my canoe, promising to pick them up just before dark. On my return, as I sat quietly waiting in my canoe, I had the uneasy feeling that someone was watching, and I turned around to look up at the riverbank behind me. There was my informant, staring at me down the shaft of a drawn arrow that was aimed right at my chest. He held his position for what seemed like an eternity as we stared into each other's emotionless faces. Then he slowly relaxed the tension on his bowstring, turned, and disappeared into the jungle. I found myself trembling uncontrollably.

Kaobawä: The Bisaasi-teri Headman Volunteers to Help

I had been working on my genealogies for nearly a year when someone new came to my aid—Kaobawä, the headman of Upper Bisaasi-teri.

The village of Bisaasi-teri was split into two distinct groups, each with its own garden and circular house. They were in sight of each other but were on opposite sides of the Mavaca River at the point where it flowed into the Orinoco. Internal bickering and argumentation had become so intense and frequent that the villagers had decided to split into two groups, but they remained close to each other for protection against raids. I referred to the group that was slightly below the other on the Orinoco as the Lower Bisaasi-teri, and I called Kaobawä's group the Upper (upstream) Bisaasi-teri, a convenience the villagers themselves adopted. I spent most of my time with the members of Kaobawä's group, some 200 people when I first arrived. I did not have much contact with Kaobawä himself during the early months—he was somewhat retiring and quiet, and among the Yanomamö the rare quiet ones tend to go unnoticed when almost everyone is in the front row pushing and demanding attention.

Kaobawä showed up at my hut one day, after all the others had left, and volunteered to help me with the genealogies. He was "poor," he explained, and needed a machete. His only condition was that I promise not to ask him about his own parents and other close kinsmen who had died. He added that he would not lie to me, as many of the others had done (photo 6).

It was perhaps the single most important event of this first period of my field research, for out of this fortuitous circumstance evolved a very warm friendship, and among its many benefits was a wealth of accurate information on the political history of Kaobawä's village and related villages, highly detailed genealogical information, sincere and useful advice, and hundreds of valuable insights into the Yanomamö way of life. Kaobawä's familiarity with his group's history and his candidness were remarkable. His knowledge of details was almost encyclopedic, his memory nearly photographic. More than that, he was eager to see that I got a true picture, and he encouraged—indeed, he *demanded*— my going into details I might otherwise have ignored. If there were subtle nuances he could not express on the spot, he would have me wait while he checked with someone else in the village. He often did this checking clandestinely, giving me a report the next day and telling me who had revealed the new information and whether or not he thought that person was in a position to know.

With the information provided by Kaobawä and Rerebawä, I made enor-

6. *Kaobawä, the headman, alert for any telltale sign from the forest.*

mous gains in understanding the village interrelationships based on common ancestors and political histories, and I became lifelong friends with both men. And each of them was aware that I was learning about his recently deceased kin from the other. It was one of those quiet understandings that none of us would ever mention.

Once again I went over the genealogies, rechecking them with Kaobawä. It was a considerable task by this time, since they included about 2,000 names, representing several generations of individuals from four different villages. Rerebawä's information was very accurate, and Kaobawä's contributions enabled me to trace the genealogies even further back. After nearly a year of intensive effort, Yanomamö demographic patterns and social organization were beginning to make sense to me. Only now were the patterns through time starting to emerge from the data—the way kinship groups took form and exchanged women in marriage over several generations. And only at this point did I see that the fissioning of larger villages into smaller ones was a chronic and important feature of Yanomamö social, political, demographic, economic, and ecological adaptation. Now I could formulate more sophisticated questions, for I had a pattern to work from and to flesh out. Without the help of Rerebawä and Kaobawä, plus that of dozens of other informants, who knows how much longer it would have taken me to make sense of the plethora of details I had collected?

I spent a lot of time with those two men and their families, and got to know them much better than I did most Yanomamö. They frequently gave their information in a personal way that related themselves to the topic under discussion, and as time passed the formal informant-anthropologist relationship faded. We stopped keeping track of work and pay. Both spent hours talking with me without asking for anything, but if they ever did want something they just asked for it, no matter what the balance of reciprocity between us was. Both of them—and their respective families—appear frequently in the following chapters, to illustrate aspects of life in the Yanomamö culture. For many of the customary ways of another culture that anthropologists try to communicate, these two men and their families might be considered typical. In other ways they are exceptional. Either way, the reader will understand Yanomamö culture more intimately for having them as examples.

Individual Characteristics

Kaobawä was about forty years old when I first came to his village in 1964. I say about forty because the Yanomamö numeration system has only three numbers—one, two, and more-than-two—and it is hard to arrive at accurate ages or dates when an informant's language has no means of expressing them. Kaobawä is the headman of his village, meaning that he has certain responsibilities in the village's political dealings with other Yanomamö groups but little control over those within his group except when the village is engaged in conflict with an enemy. Political leadership and warfare are covered in a later chapter. It is enough to say here that headmen like Kaobawä are a lot like the North American Indian chief whose authority has been characterized this way: "One word from the chief, and each man does as he pleases." Leaders like Kaobawä do not usually give orders unless they are almost certain that the orders will be heeded. Most of the time they make suggestions or lead by setting an example. Before they give an order, they carefully assess the situation, privately consider what might happen, and, if convinced that the order will be followed, then they give it. It is especially touchy when there are several prominent men in the village, each not sure what will happen if he gives an order but keenly aware that his status will be diminished if he gives an order that is ignored. Visitors from other villages seem to play some role in defining who the real leader is when there are several contenders: the visitors seek out the particular leader they believe has the most prestige beyond his own village.

In addition, there are different styles of political leadership among the Yanomamö. Some leaders are mild, quiet, inconspicuous most of the time, but intensely competent. They act with restraint, but when they do act people listen and conform. Others are more tyrannical, despotic, pushy, flamboyant, and unpleasant to all those around. If confident that they are the true leaders, they shout orders frequently, are prone to beat their wives, and bully the weaker men. Some are very violent, and many conform to their wishes out of simple fear. I have met headmen who run the entire spectrum between these poles, in the seventy-five or so Yanomamö villages I have visited, and Kaobawä stands at the mild, quietly competent end of the spectrum.

He has had six wives thus far—and temporary affairs with as many more women, at least one affair resulting in a child that he has publicly acknowledged as his own. When I first met him he had just two wives, Bahimi and Koamashima. Bahimi had two living children then—others had died. She was the older and enduring wife, as much a friend to him as a mate. Their relationship was as close to what people in our culture think of as love as I have ever seen among the Yanomamö (photo 7). The second wife, Koamashima, was a girl of about twenty years with a new baby boy, her first child (photo 8). There was speculation

7. *Kaobawä and his oldest wife, Bahimi. She is his mother's brother's daughter and his favorite wife.*

8. *Koamashima and her first child. She is one of Kaobawä's younger wives, and because of her youth she enjoys his favors more regularly.*

that Kaobawä was planning to give Koamashima to Shararaiwä, one of his younger brothers, who had no wife; he occasionally allowed Shararaiwä to have sex with Koamashima, but only if he asked in advance. Kaobawä gave another wife to a different brother because she was *beshi* ("horny"); in fact, she had already been married to two other men, both of whom had discarded her because of her infidelity. Kaobawä had one daughter by her, who is being raised by Kaobawä's brother but is acknowledged to be Kaobawä's child.

Bahimi, the oldest wife, is about five years younger than Kaobawä and is his cross-cousin—his mother's brother's daughter. (It is customary in the Yanomamö culture for men to marry cross-cousins.) Bahimi was pregnant when I first met her, but she destroyed the infant, a boy, at birth, explaining tearfully that she had no other choice. The new baby would have competed for milk with Ariwari, her youngest child, who was still nursing, and rather than expose Ariwari to the dangers of an early weaning, she chose the other alternative. By Yanomamö standards, the marriage has been a warm and enduring one. Kaobawä claims that he beats Bahimi only "once in a while, and only modestly," and she, for her part, has never had affairs with other men.

Kaobawä is such a quiet, intense, wise, and unobtrusive man, staying on the sidelines while the others surrounded me and pressed their demands, that it came as something of a surprise when I learned that he was the headman of his village. He leads more by example than by coercion. He can afford to do so, at his age, for he established a reputation as a young man for being forthright and as fierce as the situation demanded, and the others respect him. Also, he has five mature brothers or half-brothers in the village whom he can count on for support, and several other mature "brothers" (parallel cousins, but called "brothers" in this kinship system) in the village who frequently come to his aid, though not as often as his real brothers. In addition, Kaobawä has given a number of his sisters to other men in the village and has promised his eight-year-old daughter in marriage to a young man who, as required in marriage alliances, is obliged to help Kaobawä, as are the other members of the young man's family. In short, Kaobawä's natural or kinship following is large, and partially because of this support he does not have to keep displaying his aggressiveness to maintain his position.

Rerebawä is a very different sort. He is much younger than Kaobawä, perhaps in his early twenties when I first met him (see photo 5). He has just one wife, but they have already had three children. He comes from a village called Karohi-teri, located about five hours' walk up the Orinoco and slightly inland, to the east of the river. Kaobawä's village enjoys amicable relations with Rerebawä's, and for this reason marriage alliances of the kind represented by Rerebawä's marriage into Kaobawä's village commonly occur between the two groups. Rerebawä told me that he came to Bisaasi-teri because there were no eligible women for him in his own village, a fact that I later confirmed through a census of the village and a preliminary analysis of its social organization.

Rerebawä is perhaps more typical of the Yanomamö than Kaobawä is, in the sense that he is chronically concerned about his personal reputation for aggressiveness and goes out of his way to make himself noticed, even if it means acting tough and brash. He gave me a particularly hard time during my early months of fieldwork by his intimidating behavior, teasing, and insults. He is, however, much braver than most others his age and is quite prepared to back up his threats with immediate action—as in the club-fight incident previously described. Moreover, he is fascinated by political relationships and knows the details of intervillage relationships over a wide area, as well as a great deal about the genealogies of his own and neighboring groups—knowledge that is important to leaders because it reflects politics and previous warfare, such as who killed who and who is likely to try to avenge someone's death. In this respect Rerebawä shows all the attributes for being a headman. But he has too many competent brothers in his home village to expect to move into the leadership position there.

He does not intend to stay in Kaobawä's group, however, and steadfastly refuses to make his own garden—an indication of a commitment to long-term residence. He feels that he has adequately discharged his obligations to his wife's parents by providing them with fresh game for several years. They should let him return with his wife to his own village, he says, but they refuse to do so, wanting him to remain permanently in Bisaasi-teri so he can continue to provide for them when they are old. To placate him, they even promised him their second daughter, their only other child, in marriage. Unfortunately, the girl was opposed and ultimately married another man—a rare instance of a Yanomamö woman having that much say in the choice of her husband.

Although Rerebawä has displayed his manhood and fearlessness in many ways, one incident in particular illustrates his character. Before leaving his own village to take his wife in Bisaasi-teri, he had had an affair with the wife of an older "brother" (probably a parallel cousin). When the affair was discovered, the brother attacked Rerebawä with a club. He responded furiously, grabbing a single-bit ax, soundly beating the brother with its blunt side, and driving him out of the village. The brother was so intimidated by the thrashing and the promise of more to come that he did not return to the village for several days. I visited this village with Kaobawä shortly after the fight, and Rerebawä was along to serve as my guide. He made it a point to introduce me to the man. He approached the brother's hammock, grabbed him by the wrist, and dragged him out on the ground, exclaiming, "This is the brother whose wife I screwed when he wasn't around." A deadly insult like that was usually enough to provoke a bloody club fight among the Yanomamö. This man only slunk sheepishly back into his hammock, shamed but relieved to have Rerebawä release his grip.

On another occasion, after I had been working among the Yanomamö for several years, Rerebawä accompanied me to a very remote village whose head-man, Möawä, had a well-deserved reputation for violence and killing—the man I have already mentioned, who had killed twenty-one people. Rerebawä and I had traveled alone to this village, as we often did during my fieldwork. I was collecting blood samples and had promised machetes to the families in exchange for their cooperation. Möawä especially despised several of the men of the village, and he angrily ordered me not to give them machetes—he wanted the machetes himself. I chose to ignore him, and after collecting my blood samples I started to give these men their machetes. At that, Möawä, an ax in his hand, rushed over to where I was sitting on a piece of firewood. He stood over me, raised the ax above his head, and, filled with rage, said he would kill me if I gave away one more machete. By then I had given out all but one, and I re-plied that I had saved it for him. He hissed contemptuously, but he put his ax down, snatched up the remaining machete, and stalked off in a rage. Then I looked over at Rerebawä. He had picked up my shotgun and had it aimed at Möawä—a brave gesture, considering that there were 300 people in that village.

Even though Rerebawä is fierce and capable of considerable nastiness, he has a charming and witty side as well. He has a biting sense of humor and can entertain a group for hours with jokes and clever manipulations of language. And he is one of the few Yanomamö that I feel I can trust. I will never forget my return to Bisaasi-teri for my second field trip after an absence of a year. When I reached the village, Rerebawä was in his own village visiting kinsmen, but as soon as he heard of my return he paddled downstream to see me. He greeted me with an immense bear hug and, tears welling in his eyes, exclaimed, "Shaki! Why did you stay away so long? Did you not know that my will was so cold while you were gone that I could not at times eat for want of seeing you again?" I felt the same about him—then and now.

Of all the Yanomamö I know, he is the most devoted to his culture's ways and values. I admire him for that, although I cannot say that I endorse all those values. By contrast, Kaobawä is older and wiser, a polished diplomat. He sees his culture in a slightly different light and even seems to question some aspects of it. While many of his peers enthusiastically accept all the explanations embodied in the culture's myths, he occasionally reflects on them, and even laughs at some of the more preposterous of them. Probably more of the Yanomamö are like Rerebawä than like Kaobawä, or at least they try to be.

Beyond the Bisaasi-teri and into a Remote Village

As my work with Kaobawä, Rerebawä, and all my other informants progressed, a significant anthropological problem emerged that I could solve only by visiting many distant Yanomamö villages to collect genealogies, demographic data, and local histories. This fieldwork was to lead me into some exciting and even dangerous adventures, for I would be contacting some Yanomamö who were totally unknown to the outside world, people who had never before seen foreigners.

First contact with a primitive society is a phenomenon that is less and less likely to occur in our shrinking world. Unknown tribes or villages are now very rare, and our generation is probably the last that will have the opportunity to experience that first contact. What follows is a description of one such situation, in the context of my scientific reasons for going into the unknown Yanomamö area.

The Scientific Problem

It was becoming increasingly clear to me that each present Yanomamö village was a relatively recent colony or splinter group of a larger village, and a fascinating set of patterns—and problems—arose from this. I could see that there were cause-and-effect relationships among a number of variables, including village size, genealogical composition, age and sex distributions, ecological and geographic variables, and marriage ties or alliances between families. Moreover, it was obvious that intervillage warfare had a powerful effect on village size and location—influencing how large a village got before it fissioned, or divided into two groups, and where the new groups moved to avoid old enemies, to get away from the group they had just separated from, or to seek new allies in a distant place. All this is discussed in detail later. It was the mere discovery that there was a pattern that had a marked influence on my fieldwork.

To fill out the pattern, I would have to travel to many villages in order to document the genealogical aspects of the pattern, take detailed censuses, and collect local versions of tribal history from all parties concerned. I also would have to map as best I could the locations of existing villages and of sites that the Yanomamö had abandoned in the recent past, sometimes to penetrate virgin, unknown forest as pioneers on the expanding frontier of their population. What was particularly exciting about this was the ecological parallels it suggested to the earliest development of agriculture—how our own ancestors in Eurasia and Africa spread agriculture into new lands, lands formerly inhabited by hunters and gatherers or lands that had never been inhabited by anyone.

Just getting to some of the new villages proved to be a staggering problem. First, Bisaasi-teri's old wars and current animosities hampered me in recruiting trustworthy guides who were politically able to visit some of the distant villages, or were willing to. Second, there were the political pressures the older men of the village put on many of my guides. These older men would have much preferred me to dispense all my trade goods in *their* village, and some of them went to great lengths to induce my guides to back out or to force me to turn back after I started. Third, some of the villages were a great distance away, their precise locations unknown even to my guides. They were uncontacted villages many days off, and often were mortal enemies of the Bisaasi-teri, with whom I had become somewhat identified.

My first year's research, which unraveled many details of previous wars, killings, and treachery, had showed me that the Bisaasi-teri had good reason for their hostility toward some of their distant neighbors, especially the members of a group of villages that they collectively referred to as the Shamatari.

The Shamatari were a congeries of many interrelated villages to the south, some of which had a long history of bitter warfare with the Bisaasi-teri. The Shamatari villages, all related to each other, had come into existence as larger villages fissioned into smaller ones, which grew, fissioned again, and spread into new lands, moving generally from northeast to southwest (see the map in chapter 2 entitled "Long-Term Movements of Seven Yanomamö Groups"). Two of the closest Shamatari villages lay immediately to the south of the Bisaasi-teri, and I visited both of them on foot during that first year—a ten-hour walk to the closest one, a two-day walk to the other. These two groups were on somewhat friendly terms with the Bisaasi-teri, and a number of intermarriages had recently taken place between them. They were becoming Kaobawä's allies, although mutual suspicion and occasional expressions of contempt still marked their relationship.

Far to the south and southeast of these two villages lay other Shamatari villages that were mortal enemies of the Bisaasi-teri. It became clear to me, as my data accumulated, that I needed to visit them. It would be quite an experience, because they were people who had never before seen outsiders. And the Bisaasi-teri—particularly Kaobawä and Rerebawä, who were genuinely concerned for my personal safety—chronically warned me about their treachery and viciousness.

The group of Shamatari I wanted to reach on my initial foray was known to the Bisaasi-teri as "Sibarariwä's village." Sibarariwä, the headman of the village, was hated by all the Bisaasi-teri for having engineered a treachery that had led to the deaths of many of them, including Kaobawä's father—the story is the one related in the introduction. Sibarariwä was *waiteri*—fierce—and had a widespread reputation for aggressiveness, even in villages whose people had never met him or anyone else from his village.

My first attempt to contact Sibarariwä's village was in 1966, near the end of my first field trip. It was unsuccessful, primarily because my three young guides, two from Bisaasi-teri and the third from the closest of the friendly Shamatari villages, Mömariböwei-teri, forced me to turn back. We set off up the Mavaca River, spending the first two days chopping our way through the large trees and tons of brush that clogged the river and made canoe passage difficult. No one had ascended the river that far in many years—perhaps seventy-five, to judge by clues in the historical sources. The last explorers ran into hostile Yanomamö and some died at their hands, according to Hamilton Rice, an explorer who traveled in the area in about 1920 and whose non-Yanomamö Indian guides urged him to avoid the upper Mavaca—which he did.

Apparently my young guides had assumed that the hardships would soon discourage me and I would turn back. Much to their consternation, I refused to, and on the third day we began to see signs that Shamatari hunters or travelers had recently crossed the Mavaca—we found flimsy footbridges made of poles and vines. The more of these signs we saw, the more worried my guides became. By nightfall they were adamantly against going any farther, and they even refused to sleep at the place where I had pulled in the canoe: it proved to be on a recently traveled trail that the guides concluded was used by raiders. Angered,

I had no choice but to go back downstream to a location more suitable to them, and we left for home the next morning.

There, the guides proceeded to press me for the payment I had promised them. I was reluctant to pay, because they had forced me to turn back. When I asked why they had agreed to go in the first place, I got this response: "For the machetes you promised us. We *never* thought we would get to the Shamatari."

It was too late that year to make another attempt, but on my next field trip to this area, in 1968, I tried again. This time I chose my guides more carefully—or at least I thought I did. I picked one older man, whose name translates into "piranha," who was from a village far to the north and had married into Kaobawä's village only recently. Thus, he had no personal reasons either to fear the Shamatari or to be despised by them, although he *was* from Kaobawä's village now, a possible source of hostility on the part of the Shamatari.

The other guide I picked was little more than a boy, whose name was Karina. I had met him briefly the year before, when he and his mother straggled into the Shamatari village of Mömaribówei-teri. They had both been abducted by Sibarariwä's group some ten years earlier, so that Karina had grown up in Sibarariwä's village and knew all the current residents. He had been terrified at the sight of me—his first glimpse of a non-Yanomamö—but subsequent visits to Kaobawä's village had exposed him to the missionaries there, and he had gradually lost his fear of foreigners (photo 9). Still, he was only about twelve or thirteen years old. Yet his age actually was an advantage in some re-spects—he was innocent enough to give me accurate names and simple genea-logies for all the people of Sibarariwä's village in advance of our trip, and he was flattered that someone like me would pay attention to him over others his age.

The first attempt in 1968 ended when I discovered that all my gasoline had been stolen and replaced with water—a common problem in the upper Orinoco, where gasoline is scarce, has to be hauled in by an eight-day river trip, and is vulnerable to filchers every step of the way, including the very people you have paid to bring it to you. We had gotten quite far up the Mavaca when I switched to one of the reserve gas tanks and the motor died—the tanks were full of water. We had to return to Bisaasi-teri, where my gasoline supplies were stored and where I could spend the night dismantling and cleaning the motor.

We set off again the next morning, and again we were far up the Mavaca when I switched to one of the reserve tanks. This time it wasn't water, but it wasn't gasoline, either—it was kerosene. Back down the Mavaca, clean the

9. *Karina, my young guide, when I first met him—a year before he led me into Shamatari country.*

engine the same night, and prepare to set off again. (I did the engine work at night to save time, and to let my dispirited guides see that we *were* making progress.) But by now—four or five days after the first start—the guides were growing impatient and weary. The older man failed to show up at all, and Karina said he was feeling ill and didn't want to go. I persuaded him that he would feel better in a day, and he finally agreed to try again.

He was the only guide I had at this point. Tired and depressed, I sat in my canoe wondering if I should even try to make the trip with just one twelve-year-old guide. It was a murky, dismal dawn, and I hadn't slept more than a few hours the last few nights. As I sat there, half ready to throw in the towel, a young man—Bäkotawä—appeared at the river to take an early bath. (He was the young man that Rerebawä had challenged to a club fight over Rerebawä's wife's younger sister.) He knew that my second guide had backed out and that I was down to just one. I asked him if he would be willing to go with me to Sibarariwä's village. He thought for a moment. "I'm a Bisaasi-teri, and they might kill me," he said. "But I could tell them that I'm really a Patanowä-teri, and they wouldn't know the difference." I turned to the ailing Karina, who lay whimpering in the canoe in the most comfortable spot I had been able to devise, using my pack and gasoline tanks as a couch. "Would you vouch for him if he said he was a Patanowä-teri?" I asked. Unenthusiastically, he grunted that he'd go along with the deception, remarking that it was better than being a Bisaasi-teri, which drew a glare from Bäkotawä. Thus, it was agreed that Bäkotawä would be my second guide. He rushed off to collect his hammock and a few items to trade, returning a few minutes later, ready for his great adventure into unknown lands where his older kin feared to tread. I had a second shotgun that I said he could use (he didn't even know which end to put the cartridges in), and this bolstered his confidence immensely.

And so we finally set off for the headwaters of the Mavaca in my large wooden dugout canoe, on top of which I carried a smaller, lighter aluminum boat for negotiating the upper waters that the big boat could not get through. My plan was to go as far as we could in the bigger boat, dropping off gasoline and other stores along the way for the trip back.

It was well along in the dry season, and the river was so low that we made it only about a day and a half upstream in the large canoe before we hit an insurmountable obstacle, two very large trees that had fallen across the river and were half submerged. (They had been there before, but the water had been high enough then for the canoe to get across.) The trees were too thick to chop through with our axes, and too far out of the water for us to drag the heavy dugout over. We had to leave the big canoe here, transfer everything to the smaller boat, and set off once more, badly overloaded, for the headwaters of the Mavaca.

Karina was feeling better and began to goad Bäkotawä, asking, "What would they do if they knew you were really a Bisaasi-teri? Maybe I might slip and tell them that you are Bisaasi-teri." Bäkotawä grew silent, then moody, then visibly nervous.

On the third day out, Karina rose to his knees, looked intently at the riverbanks on both sides, and exclaimed, "I know this place! We're getting close to Sibarariwä's village. Their trail to Iwähikoroba-teri is just a short way off the river, over there." He pointed to the east bank of the tangled, narrow river, a stream so small now that we could hardly have turned the boat around without lifting it most of the way. We proceeded a few hours farther upstream, slowly, because the river was not only shallow and narrow but was choked with deadfalls and branches through which we constantly had to chop our way.

About midday, we pulled over, unloaded the supplies, and dragged the boat up the bank. We would walk inland from here, for the river had become too narrow and shallow to proceed any farther. We were just entering a hilly region and could catch glimpses of high peaks covered with dense vegetation and punctuated with scraggy outcroppings of rock. We were in the headwaters of the Mavaca. Beyond the stark ridge ahead of us lay the almost legendary Shukumöna kä u, or "river of parakeets," and the homeland of the Shamatari—the lair of the dreaded Sibarariwä.

At that time the Shukumöna kä u (the Siapa River) was not even correctly shown on official maps of Venezuela. Its true location and course were not established until 1972, when aerial radar maps of the region were commissioned. Most earlier maps incorrectly showed the headwaters of the Mavaca River as the Siapa. We were truly in unexplored country.

I divided the supplies into those we would take inland with us and those we would leave behind for the return trip, and was somewhat alarmed over the relatively small amount of food we had. In my concern over the gasoline and the sputtering motor, I had neglected to restock the food after each of the aborted trips. There was enough for several days, but if we failed to contact the Shamatari we would have to ration ourselves carefully.

Karina said the village was to the southeast, indicating the distance in the Yanomamö manner of pointing to where the sun was now and where it would be when we reached the village. It was about a four- or five-hour walk by his description, and that meant we would reach the village just before dark—not the best time to arrive on a first contact. The Yanomamö like to have as much daylight as possible when they come into a strange village, so that they have time to make friends and assess the situation. But we set off with our backpacks at about two o'clock, and soon we were running into fresh signs of human activity—footprints made the day before, husks of palm fruits, discarded items of no value, broken twigs where someone had cleared a trail, and so on. My heart began to pound, for clearly we were close to Sibarariwä's village.

A ferocious rain, the onset of the rainy season, hit us after about an hour, and we had to stop and huddle together under a small nylon tarp I always carried. That cost us an hour, and we decided it would be better to camp for the night—we would reach the village too late in the day to make friends. We ate some boiled rice and strung our hammocks in an abandoned temporary hut a Shamatari hunter had put up months earlier. As dusk settled, Karina resumed his teasing of Bäkotawä about the nastiness of Sibarariwä's group, again reminding him mischievously that he was really a Bisaasi-teri, not a Patanowä-teri. Bäkotawä lay sullenly and unhappily in his hammock, and I scolded Karina for his ill-natured humor. At dawn, as we were packing to leave, Bäkotawä quietly and forcefully told me that he was going no farther, that he intended to return to the boat. He frankly admitted, "*Ya kirii* [I am frightened]."

I was not going to turn back now. I gave him a share of the food and a quick lesson in how to load and fire the shotgun, along with a box of twenty-five cartridges. I told him we would be gone about three days (indicating the duration by three fingers) before we would rejoin him at the boat. He assured me that, though he was frightened here, he would be safe and secure at the boat and would camp there to wait for us. Karina and I set off to the southeast. Bäkotawä disappeared silently into the shadowy forest, heading north, toward the boat.

Karina and I walked for several hours, continuing to run into fresh signs of Yanomamö travelers. We found footprints that had been made just that morning, last night's rainwater still oozing into the depressions. A banana peel here, a discarded bunch of palm fruits there. We were getting very close.

Karina grabbed my arm and whispered excitedly, "The village is just beyond the top of this hill." We crept to the ridge and looked down into the valley below, where we saw a gigantic, well-kept banana plantation surrounding an extremely large, circular *shabono*, the largest I had ever seen until now. We were there! Karina peered intently and then urged me to follow. In a few minutes we were in the garden, and soon we could see the back of the *shabono* roof. But something was wrong: there was no noise. No babies crying, no men chanting to the *hekura* spirits, no smoke, no dogs barking, no buzzing of voices. The shabono was *broke*—empty. Karina looked at me and said, "Shit! *A da kuu* [Go ahead, say shit, like you always do]."

Deserted, but only recently. Karina went to investigate the garden and came back a few minutes later with a pile of ripe plantains and the news that someone had been in the garden that morning to harvest plantains. He guessed that Sibarariwä's group was camped out, but camped close enough that they could easily harvest food from the garden. They might be farther upstream, he thought, at a place where they often camped at this time of year, when certain wild fruits were in season. We decided to leave our packs in the abandoned village and strike off to find them. The sun was high. We had all afternoon to look.

By now I was down to my sneakers, my shotgun, and a red loincloth I had borrowed from one of the Bisaasi-teri men (I had given away all my new loincloths). My intention was to avoid looking strange when I contacted these people, and wearing a loincloth in their favorite color of red, instead of my regular clothing, would help. Karina had only his bow, several arrows, and a large wad of now-aging tobacco tucked behind his lower lip—and his own loincloth. As we walked, we saw fresher and more abundant signs of Sibarariwä's group, and I knew that we would soon come upon them. Dusk had begun to settle when we smelled smoke and, a few minutes later, saw a lazy cloud of bluish smoke drifting through the gray forest and rising slowly to the treetops. Then we heard babies crying and the chatter of many voices. We had found the camp at last.

We approached quietly and cautiously, stopping at a small stream just short of the campsite to wash. Scolding, Karina urged me to clean up—my legs were all muddy and my loincloth dangled haphazardly down to my scratched knees. We were now in *his* country, and *he* was taking charge of the expedition. I made myself as presentable as I could, washing off the mud and perspiration, straightening my loincloth, and tying my sneakers, but we had no feathers or red *nara* paint to add the final touches. Karina handed me his bow and arrows and took my shotgun, commenting, as he headed for the camp: "They might be frightened of your shotgun, so I'll take it. You carry my bow and arrows, and wait for me to tell you to come in. They'll really be scared to see a *nabä* [non-Yanomamö]." He disappeared into the jungle and whistled a signal to alert the people that a visitor was coming in. A chorus of cheers, whistles, and welcoming hoots rebounded through the darkening jungle, punctuated by an accompaniment of barking dogs.

The absurdity of my situation and the magnitude of what I was doing suddenly hit me. Here I was in the middle of an unexplored and unmapped jungle, a few hundred feet from an uncontacted group of Yanomamö who had a reputation for enormous ferocity and treachery, led to them by a twelve-year-old boy. It was getting dark. I was wearing nothing but a borrowed red loincloth and torn, muddy sneakers, and I was clutching a bow and three skinny arrows as if I knew what I was doing.

An ominous hush fell over the forest. Karina had obviously told the group that I was waiting, and they were pondering what to do. Disquieting recollections flashed through my head of Kaobawä's tales about the Shamatari. I thought about his intense warnings of the hazards in trying to find them. They would pretend to be friendly, he had said, but when my guard was down they would fall on me with bowstaves and clubs and kill me, as they had his people. Perhaps they would do it on the spot. Or they might wait until I had taken up a hammock, as a visitor is expected to do, and lay there defenseless. Perhaps they would do it at night, while I slept, or just before dawn. Silence. Anxiety. My temples pounded. I wanted to run. I could hear the hushed buzzing of voices and the sound of people moving around in the jungle, spreading out. Some of them were leaving the camp. I knew they were surrounding me. Could I really trust Karina? Was someone even now staring at me down the long shaft of a war arrow?

Karina suddenly appeared on the trail and motioned for me to come— to present myself. He urged me to hurry. I tried to give the customary visitor's announcement, a whistle, but my dry lips wouldn't pucker, and only a pathetic hiss of air came forth. I walked past Karina and noticed his curious look. Was it the same look he had had when he told Bäkotawä he would vouch that he was a Patanowä-teri? But it was too late now to consider any such weighty implications, and far too late to do anything about them.

Then a host of growling, screaming men, naked and undecorated, swarmed around me, prancing nervously. Their long, bamboo-tipped war arrows, nocked in the strings of their powerful bows, were pointed menacingly at my face. I stood my ground, motionless and as poised as I could manage, trying desperately to keep my legs from wobbling, hoping I looked dignified, defiant, and fearless.

After what seemed like an eternity, one of them gruffly told me to follow him to one of the temporary huts. As we went toward it, I could see young men scrambling to clear off the ground and straighten a *nara*-stained cotton hammock—intended for my use. They worked quickly and nervously, scattering as I approached. Karina placed my shotgun at the back post, and I reclined in the hammock, striking the visitor's pose—one hand over my mouth, staring at the space above me, and swaying gently. I felt as if I was on display in Macy's window, with a noontime crowd peering in.

Eventually a few of the bolder men came closer, hissing commands to the others to "Get some food prepared, quickly." They whispered excitedly to each other, describing the smallest and most private of my visible body parts. "Look at how hairy his legs are. Look at all that ugly hair on his chest. Look how pale he is. Isn't his hair an unbelievable color—*frarefrare*, like a ripe banana. Isn't he strange looking, and did you see how 'long' he was when he was standing there? I wonder if he has a regular penis. What are those skins he has tied to his feet?" Overwhelmed by curiosity, the bolder and older of the men came closer yet, duck-waddling right up to me. Then a hand came forward and cautiously and ever so delicately touched my leg. The hand retracted quickly, accompanied by a hiss of amazement from its owner—"Aaahhh!" A chorus of admiring tongue clicks followed from the less bold, and then more touches and hisses. Soon many hands were touching me all over and pulling at all my body hairs. Repeatedly they smelled my spoor on their red-stained cupped hands, clicking their tongues and marveling that someone so different could be so similar. Just a bit "longer," hairier, and lighter than they were. Then I spoke, and again they marveled. I spoke a "crooked" version of Yanomamö, like the Bisaasi-teri do, but they understood me: "*Whaaa! A akahayuwo no modahawä* [He is capable of language]."

Soon we were jabbering away like long-lost friends. They scolded me for not having come sooner. It seems they had known about me for some time and had wanted to meet me. The Reyaboböwei-teri had told them, passing on what they knew from having met me personally and what they had heard from the Mömariböwei-teri and the Bisaasi-teri. (The Yanomamö language is very precise about what is known firsthand and what has come from secondhand, or hearsay, sources.) I was flabbergasted at the detail and accuracy of what they had heard. They knew I had a wife and two children, and the sexes and approximate ages of my children. They repeated with incredible accuracy conversations I had had with Yanomamö in many different villages. One of them wanted to see the scar on my left elbow. When I asked what he meant, he described in minute detail a bad fall I had taken several years earlier, while on a trip to the Reyaboböwei-teri—I had slipped on a wet rock and landed on my elbow, which bled profusely. He even repeated quite accurately the string of Yanomamö vulgarities I had uttered, and my angry complaint to my guides about their goddamned trails that stupidly went straight up and down steep hills when they could more efficiently go around them. For people who had never seen a non-Yanomamö before, they certainly knew a great deal about at least one of them!

I stayed several days and was able to make my first census of the group. However, Karina had let it out that I had a small treasure of trade goods at my boat, and they were eager to hike to the river to examine the goods—and to see what a boat was. They were also disappointed that Bäkotawä had not come along—they "wouldn't have harmed him, but would have befriended him." After I finished a systematic check of the genealogical data that Karina had given me about the current families and had long visits with the families, I reluctantly agreed to take some of the men to the boat and its cache of gifts.

It had taken Karina and me at least six hours of walking to get to the camp from the boat, but the men were in a hurry to see the boat and the trade goods, and they made fast work of guiding us back to the river—we ran most of the way. They carried only their weapons. No food and no hammocks. We left for the boat about midday, but I couldn't see what they planned to do for sleeping or eating that night. I must have assumed that they would spend the night in their abandoned *shabono*, which they could probably reach by dark after spending an hour at the boat.

We came to the spot where we had separated from Bäkotawä. Soon after, we came on two expended shotgun shells, then two more, and another two, and so on. It appeared that Bäkotawä had fired the gun every few minutes on his retreat to the boat, and it was obvious that he would have been out of ammunition by the time he reached it.

When we crossed the last rise before reaching the spot where I had left the boat, I saw, to my horror, that boat, motor, gasoline, food, tarps, and trade goods all were gone. Bäkotawä had panicked and taken off, leaving me stranded among people he was sure were going to kill us all.

It was a decidedly unenviable position for me to be in. Nobody except a few Yanomamö even knew where I was. I couldn't walk out, for that would have taken at least two weeks in the best of circumstances. And it had been raining regularly since I arrived. The river was rising fast, meaning that the land between me and Bisaasi-teri was beginning to flood. I spent a miserably wet night huddled under my small tarp wondering what to do. I concluded that the only feasible way to get out was to go by river.

My first idea was to build a raft, similar to the log palisades the Yanomamö erect around their villages. The men who had accompanied me from the village stayed to help, and with the one machete I had we set about cutting numerous trees and vines for the raft. At the end of the day we assembled it in the river, and when I stepped onto the raft it promptly sank. You already know what Karina told me to say.

The next day we went to Plan II: building a "trough" of the sort that the Yanomamö use at ceremonial feasts. It is a bark trough, which they fill with plantain soup, but the same trough, when reinforced with a few branch ribs, is occasionally used as a temporary canoe suitable only for floating downstream (photo 10). It is a kind of "throwaway" canoe that might do for the circumstances I was in. We scrapped that plan when the villagers said there were no suitable trees nearby to make the trough. We sat around some more and talked about options, and again concluded that the only logical way out was by river.

The villagers suggested that since foreigners know how to make canoes, why couldn't I, a foreigner, just make one? I tried to explain that it wasn't quite that simple, that canoe making is a complex enterprise, and that I was from one of those foreign villages where we had to "trade" with others for our canoes—we had "forgotten" how to make them, as others had "forgotten" how to make clay pots and had to trade for them. They insisted that it was easy to remember lost arts. I said that it took axes to make canoes. They said they had axes at the village and sent young men running off to fetch them. The young men returned in record time, after dark, with two of the most miserable axes I have ever seen. They were worn down by years—perhaps decades—of heavy use and were about a third the size they had been when new. But the men's confidence inspired me, and we set about hunting for the largest, pithiest tree we could find—one that could be easily hollowed out and would suffice for a single voyage. We found one, cut it, and began hollowing it out. It took all day. It looked like a long, fat cigar with a square notch cut in it. We dragged it to the river to test it.

I knew that it would roll over as soon as any weight was put into it, so I had devised an outrigger system, which served also as a pair of seats where the poles were lashed to the gunwales. For the outrigger, I lashed a pithy long pole parallel to the axis of the canoe (photo 11). To our great surprise and my

10. Woman in a bark canoe. These canoes are occasionally made by the Yanomamö for a single trip downstream or for fording rivers. After a few days they sag, leak, and deteriorate beyond use.

11. The canoe I made to descend the Mavaca River with Karina, who clutches one of our hand-hewn paddles.

personal delight, the canoe floated when Karina and I got into it . . . but just barely. We spent much of another day whittling canoe paddles—one for Karina, one for me, and one for a spare.

The villagers had given me a large number of bows and arrows in exchange for the small knives that I had carried in my pack as welcoming gifts. When we loaded these into the outrigger and then climbed in ourselves, very gently, we sank. We unloaded the bows and arrows, and every nonessential item we could find in my pack. I kept only my notes, hammock, food, camera, medical kit, and a small transistor radio for monitoring broadcasts from the mission. With our burden thus reduced, we climbed in again. This time, the water rose to only about half an inch from the gunwales. We could float, and could stay afloat, as long as we kept in perfect balance.

I said earlier that the Yanomamö are "foot" Indians rather than "river" Indians, and Karina is perhaps the classic example of what that means. If the Yanomamö had decided to be river Indians, they might now be extinct. For all my passionate injunctions to Karina that it was hazardous to lean too far to the right or the left, we probably swamped and sank thirty or forty times in the first two days. He ignored everything I said, and whenever he leaned too far one way or the other, he froze as he watched the water pour in—a posture he stoically maintained while we went under. Each time, we had to dog-paddle the canoe to the bank and bail it out before we could go on.

It still amazes me that we made it all the way back to where we had left the large canoe. And it amazes me even more that Bäkotawä had left the large canoe there when he passed. He had stopped everywhere else and collected all my stores of gasoline, and he would have been much more comfortable if he had also taken the big canoe.

Eventually we made it back to Bisaasi-teri in the big canoe, to the genuine relief of Kaobawä and Rerebawä, who had assumed the worst—that Sibarariwä's group had killed me. And Bäkotawä's return several days before had provoked much anxiety in the village.

I knew it would be unprofessional of me to hunt Bäkotawä down, when my mind was so full of vindictive plans for his future. In antiseptic anthropological terms, I wasn't in a very cultural relativistic mood. The inevitable confrontation came later; its details are discussed in my *Studying the Yanomamö*. He is alive and well today, and we greet each other pleasantly, but he doesn't go on any trips with me.

So that is what it can sometimes be like to meet an uncontacted tribe of

South American Indians. I have had other experiences that were far more dangerous. On one occasion, my hosts came close to killing me as I slept (see chapter V in *Studying the Yanomamö*). More recently, in 1990 and 1991, I contacted other Yanomamö villages that had never been visited, but these experiences were much less dramatic, although they were scientifically very productive. The results of these trips, discussed in several of the following chapters, have led to significant new insights into Yanomamö culture and political history.

Finally, if any of you readers ever visit the Yanomamö, I advise you to take your own red loincloth and under no circumstances be so foolish as to borrow one from them. My crotch began to itch even before Karina and I started our descent in our makeshift canoe. When we camped after our first hectic day of many capsizings, I examined my skin by flashlight. I was scarlet from knee to navel with an odious rash I had contracted from the borrowed loincloth. You can't imagine how silly I looked and felt, lying naked on my back, legs spread apart, shaking Desenex foot powder all over my crotch, while a twelve-year-old warrior kept saying disdainfully, "I told you not to give yours all away. You never listen to me."

Chapter Two

The World Around the Yanomamö

Tribesmen everywhere must come to terms with the physical environment in which they live in order to survive and to produce offspring who will carry on their traditions. The physical environment, however, contains not only lands, forests, resources, and foods but many other things as well. One of the most compelling features of the environment is the *other people* who inhabit it. In the tribal world, security ends at the edge of the village. Those who live elsewhere are often strangers and potentially are enemies; at the very least, their actions cannot be directly controlled by orders or laws from the people of the village. Each community is like a small sovereign nation trying, like all sovereign nations, to maintain and defend its independence.

From the vantage point of the members of a particular community—a village, for example—the world beyond has both a physical and a sociopolitical dimension, and the community must come to grips with both. Anthropologists usually refer to this process as cultural adaptation: the social, technical, and ideological means by which people adjust to the world that impinges on them. Much of that world is ontologically real, in the sense that an outsider from a different culture can see and document it in a fashion that other observers can verify. But much of it lies hidden in the minds of the observed natives, whose cultural traditions, interpretations, and assumptions infuse it with spirits, project into it meanings, and view it in a way that the outsider can discover only by learning the language and, through the language, the intellectual dimensions of the culture.

To me, one of the more intriguing aspects of the Yanomamö adaptations to their natural environment is the relationship of ecology and culture to the dispersion of their villages over the landscape as settlements fissioned and relocated in new areas.

A similar process clearly was of enormous significance in our own culture's early history, when agriculture was developing and leading to the rapid growth of populations, the event that we call the "agricultural revolution." What we can learn from studying the Yanomamö settlement patterns may shed light on many aspects of our own history, a history we know now only through archaeology.

Jungles, Rivers, and Mountains

Kaobawä's village is located at the confluence of the Orinoco River and the Mavaca, one of its larger tributaries at that latitude. The village lies at an elevation of about 450 feet above sea level on a generally flat jungle-covered plain that is interrupted occasionally by low hills. None of the hills qualifies as a mountain, but in nearby areas the terrain is quite rugged and hilly and difficult to traverse on foot—the kind of terrain into which beleaguered people can flee to escape their more powerful neighbors, as we shall see.

Most of the rivers and streams arise in the hills as tiny trickles that are dry at some times of the year but become dangerous torrents at other times. A sudden heavy rain can dramatically alter even the larger streams, and the Yanomamö therefore avoid large streams when selecting their garden and village sites. In the more remote villages, I got great pleasure from bathing and drinking in those pure, cool streams that drain the tropical forest and eventually tie into the mighty Amazon and Orinoco far downstream.

While not mountains, the hills do reach heights of 3,500 feet in some places. Almost all of them are covered with jungle, but far to the east of Kaobawä's village, in the Parima mountains, relatively large natural savannas occur at higher elevations, and one finds some Yanomamö villages there. But much of the lowland area is inundated during the wet season, making it impossible to travel in the lowlands and unwise to locate a village and garden there.

The jungle is dense and contains a large variety of palm and hardwood trees. Their canopy keeps sunlight from reaching the ground, and on overcast days the jungle is usually dark and gloomy—from the inside looking out, it is not green but appears to be shades of gray. Scrub brush and vines grow almost everywhere, making travel by foot difficult. Along the rivers and streams, where sunlight can penetrate, luxuriant vegetation grows, a haven for many kinds of birds and animals.

Trails and Travel

The Yanomamö villages are thinly scattered over this vast tropical land-scape. Distances between villages can be as short as a few hours' walk or as long as a week or ten days of walking, depending on the political relationships between groups. Warfare between villages is what generally keeps them widely separated, and alliances of various sorts and descent from common ancestors are factors that tend to reduce the distance.

All the villages have trails leading out into the jungle and to various villages beyond. Many trails simply go to the gardens that surround the village and terminate there. The jungle trails tend to take a direct path through brush, swamps, rivers, and hills—annoyingly direct at times, when they go straight up a steep hill to the peak and then straight down the other side instead of following the easier terrain an anthropologist might have chosen.

A Yanomamö trail is not easy to see, let alone follow, particularly one that is used only sporadically, and it takes experience to recognize the trails. The most certain clues are numerous broken twigs at about knee height, for the Yanomamö constantly snap off twigs with their fingers as they walk. Another frequent sign is a foot-worn log across a stream or ravine, usually so slippery that at first I had to shimmy across them on hands and knees while my companions roared with laughter. Most of the trails cross streams and rivers and often run in the stream for several hundred feet. It is easy to get lost on these trails, for it is never obvious when the trail leaves the stream and continues across land. When I first began my field work, the Yanomamö would say, "*Kahä wa baröwo* [You take the lead on the trail, we'll follow]." Within minutes, they would be laughing hysterically as I wandered off the trail and ended up in an impenetrable thicket.

Friendly neighbors visit regularly, and the most used trail from Kaobawä's village went south, to the two friendly Shamatari villages of Reyaboböwei-teri and Mömariböwei-teri. Hardly a week of the dry season went by without someone, usually a small group of young men, coming to Bisaasi-teri from one of the Shamatari villages, or vice versa. Young men can make the trip easily in a day, for they travel swiftly and carry nothing but their bows and arrows. A family might also make it in one day if it kept moving, but it would be a dawn-to-dusk trip for women carrying their babies or trade items. Should the whole village decide to go, it might be a two- or three-day trip.

On one occasion, Kaobawä invited me to accompany his entire village on a trip to Mömariböwei-teri. I had already been there several times and knew that it was a hard eight-hour walk for a young man, so I packed my supplies accordingly, and we set off. We walked about twenty minutes inland, to the south, and then stopped to let the women and children rest. Much to my dismay, that was where we made our first night's camp. We were barely outside their garden! It would have taken at least a week to reach our destination at that pace. I went on alone, with a young man to guide me, spent a day and a night visiting, and was back home before the Bisaasi-teri even reached the village.

The more frequently used trails have numerous temporary camping places along the way, collections of quickly assembled pole huts—*yanos*—in various stages of repair, where earlier travelers have spent a night or two.

Walking entails certain risks for the Yanomamö. For one thing, they have no shoes or clothing, so thorns are always a problem. A party of ten men can rarely go more than an hour without someone stopping suddenly, saying the Yanomamö equivalent of "Ouch!," and sitting down to dig a thorn out of his foot with the tip of his arrow point. While their feet are hardened and thickly callused, walking in streams and through muddy terrain softens the calluses, and then the thorns can penetrate deeply.

Snakebite is another hazard. While it is something of an honor to go first on the trail, it also more dangerous, because of poisonous snakes, which tend to bite the first person who disturbs them. A surprisingly large number of Yanomamö die of snakebite, and almost all of them, if they live long enough, eventually get bitten. Most of the bites are not fatal, although all are painful. I have treated several nonfatal bites with antivenin, but none of these cases was serious. The cure—several largish ampules of injectable antivenin—was usually more painful than the bite itself. In my more recent fieldwork, I have used an electrical stun gun, a hand-held, battery-operated self-defense instrument whose low-amperage, high-voltage charge can disable a person for several minutes. I had an electrical engineer reduce the voltage from 40,000 to about 15,000 and used the device to "shock" the area of the snakebite. In cases reported in other parts of the world, this technique has been known to dramatically reduce the severity of the snakebite and seems to neutralize the venom. A few snakebites can be severe enough to cause the loss of a limb or the loss of its use. One of my Yanomamö friends had lost a leg some fifteen years prior to my arrival; the leg had rotted away and fallen off. He got around well enough by hopping on his remaining leg. Snakebites are almost as frequent in the garden or near the village as they are on remote trails, and one must always be careful around the firewood pile and in the garden. With this in mind, the Yanomamö try to keep their gardens and paths weeded. Abandoned gardens attract snakes because they also attract rodents.

In Kaobawä's area, most of the travel between villages occurs from September through March, the dry season. During the wet season, long stretches of the trails are under water, and small lakes replace the swampy lowlands. Communication between villages nearly ceases at the peak of the rainy season, and most villages are cut off from outside contact. Streams that were mere trickles in March become raging torrents in May and June. If a group must travel in the wet season, it can make simple pole-and-vine bridges to cross the smaller streams but has to take wide detours around large streams. The bridges are essentially a series of **X** frames linked together by long poles (where the legs of the **X** cross) and vine railings, with a gap of ten to fifteen feet separating each **X** all the way across. These bridges usually wash out within a few weeks, but occasionally a few of the poles last into the dry season.

Technology

Much of Yanomamö technology is like the pole-and-vine bridge—crude, easily fashioned from immediately available materials, effective enough to solve the current problem, but not destined to last forever. Perhaps the one artifact that an archaeologist would be likely to find in any quantity in ancient abandoned sites is the crude, poorly fired clay pot traditionally used by the Yanomamö (photo 12). It is nearly an inch thick at the bottom and tapers to almost nothing at the rim. It is undecorated, very fragile, and pointed at the bottom. Women, considered clumsy by the men, are rarely allowed to use the pots. They are often used to prepare food for a feast, and the men do all that work. The pot is shaped by the coil technique of winding strips of clay in a spiral, and the firing is done by simply stacking brush and wood around it. When it breaks— usually fairly soon—the men use the pieces as the grinding surface for preparing their hallucinogenic snuff powder. The pieces are also used as griddles on which to cook a kind of bread made from the grated pulp of the cassava plant. Clay pots were relatively common when I began my field research, but they had almost completely disappeared by the late 1970s. As we shall see later, only the members of a few villages made the pots and traded them to their neighbors.

Yanomamö technology is very straightforward. No tool or technique is so complex that it requires specialized knowledge or raw materials, and each village can produce every item it needs from the resources immediately available in the jungle. Nevertheless, some specialization in manufacturing does occur, although political alliances have more to do with it than the distribution of resources: the people deliberately create shortages in order to have occasion to trade with distant neighbors. Yanomamö technology could almost be classified with that characteristic of hunters and gatherers, except that the Yanomamö are horticulturalists.

Their bowstaves, some five to six feet long, are made of palm wood. One species of palm grows wild, and the other, the preferred kind, is cultivated for its fruit. The wood of both is very dense, brittle, and hard; one cannot even drive a nail into it. Bowstrings are made from the fibers of the inner bark of a tree. The bark is stripped off in long, narrow pieces and twisted into thick cords by rolling the fibers vigorously between the thigh muscle and the palm of the hand. The finished cords are so strong that the Yanomamö also use them as hammock ropes. The bowstave is painstakingly shaped by shaving the stock with the incisors of a wild pig; this pig's lower projecting teeth become razor sharp from eating, and the entire mandible serves as a wood plane for making bows. The completed bow is oval or round in cross section and is very powerful—comparable in strength to our own hunting bows. With age and use, the bows become brittle and may shatter when drawn too hard. That's why one often sees bystanders put their hands in front of their faces when someone picks up a bow and draws it back to test it.

A pencil-shaped splinter of palm wood is also used for one type of arrow point, the curare-poisoned *husu namo* point. The foot-long splinter is weakened about every two inches along its length by a cut going partially through the wood; this causes the splinter to break off inside the target and send the curare into the bloodstream. This arrow point is primarily used for hunting monkeys, although it is also used in warfare. A monkey can pull out an ordinary arrow, but it cannot pull out a point that has broken off deep in its body. The curare gradually relaxes the monkey, so that it falls to the ground instead of clinging to a branch and dying high in the tree. The Yanomamö must carry a supply of extra curare points in their bamboo quivers, for the points break when they strike anything and usually must be replaced after every shot. The points are manufactured in large bundles—thirty or forty—in several villages near Kaobawä's, and they are prized trade items (photo 13).

The poison comes from a vine that is leached in hot water, to which other vegetable ingredients are added to make the substance adhere to the wood

12. Clay pots like these were common when I began my fieldwork, but they have been almost completely replaced by aluminum ware that is traded from village to village.

13. Man painting curare poison on palm-wood arrow points. The poison is leached with hot water and painted on in many coats over glowing embers. The water evaporates, leaving a sticky poison coating.

splinter. The men often wrap a leaf around the poisoned point to keep the rain from dissolving the poison as they travel. In some areas, other vegetable poisons are used, one of which is a hallucinogen. In a pinch, the men can scrape the poison off and get high by snuffing it deeply into their nostrils.

The arrow-point quivers—*tora*—that all the men wear dangling down the middle of their backs are made from a section of bamboo, usually about three inches in diameter and fifteen to eighteen inches long. A natural joint in the bamboo forms the bottom of the quiver, and the open top is covered with the skin of an animal, usually a snake, a monkey, or a jaguar. The bamboo grows wild in large stands, and some villages specialize in the trading of bamboo quivers. The quiver generally contains several arrow points, fibers, resin, and strings for repairing arrows, and sometimes a magical charm or two, for luck. A piece of old bowstring ties the quiver around the neck. A pair of *tomö nakö*, or agouti-tooth, knives, which are needed to trim arrow points made of bamboo—*rahaka*—are attached to the outside of the quiver, and occasionally so is a fire drill.

The drill, made from the wood of the cocoa tree, is in two pieces. One piece is about ten inches long and lanceolate—in the shape of a lance head. Along its edges are several holes worn by the friction of a longer, round piece of wood that is rapidly spun between the palms of the hands. The lower piece is held down by the foot, and the other is spun into it until the friction produces a glowing dust, which is quickly fed with tinder until a fire ignites. Working in pairs, the men take turns with the drill; as one, spinning downward with his palms, gets to the bottom of the stick, the other starts at the top, and so on. The drill is wrapped in leaves to keep it dry. Today, matches are in ample supply as trade goods in villages that have contact with outsiders, and the matches are traded far inland. Like the clay pot, the fire drill is rapidly disappearing, even in the most remote villages.

Arrows are made from six-foot-long shafts of cultivated cane, and are often taken for spears by people seeing them for the first time. Two long black feathers from the wing of the *paruri*, a bird like a wild turkey, are attached as fletching, in such a way as to cause the arrow to spin when shot. A thin fiber from a cultivated plant was traditionally used to attach the fletching, but white cotton thread received in trade from the missionaries is now common. A nock is carved from a piece of hardwood, using the small agouti-tooth knife. The nock looks something like a golf tee, except that it has a notch in it for the bowstring. It is stuck into the shaft behind the fletching, held in place by pitch and fine fibers wrapped tightly around the arrow shaft.

Three kinds of arrow points are used interchangeably, with spare points carried in the quiver. The most effective for the killing of large game, such as tapir, is a lanceolate point, about eight to twelve inches long, made from a section of bamboo. These are often painted with red, black, or purple pigments, and some of them acquire a reputation and a history, if they have taken many animals. The histories are recited in great detail when the point is traded to another owner, and much raising of eyebrows, clicking of tongues, and expression of amazement accompanies the transaction as the new owner praises his trading partner's generosity in giving up so valuable and lucky a property. The bamboo points are fastened to the arrow shaft simply by pushing one of the sharp ends into the pith of the arrow cane as far as it will go, usually about one-eighth the length of the point itself. To prevent the arrow shaft from splitting, about two inches of the tip is bound with fine but strong cord. The next most effective arrow point is the curare-smeared, pencil-like palm-wood point. The third kind is a barbed point that is used primarily for hunting birds. The barb is made from a sliver of bone, often a monkey bone. It prevents the arrow from coming out after it hits a bird, and the weight of the arrow shaft, plus its unwieldiness, keeps the bird from flying away. A fourth kind of arrow point, made out of a twig with many branching stems, is usually fashioned on the spot in a few seconds and is discarded after one or two uses. Small birds, often sought for their decorative feathers, are shot with such points—the archery equivalent of a shotgun shell.

The Yanomamö diet does not rely heavily on fish, but at certain times of the year fish are abundant and are easily taken. One method is just to wait for the end of the rainy season, when areas of the jungle that have been flooded by the overflowing rivers begin to dry out, leaving pools of fish stranded. It is a simple matter to wade into the pools and catch dozens of fish by hand. Another way of catching fish is by poisoning small streams. A poison made of wild lianas is put into the water upstream of a small dam constructed of sticks and mud. Stunned by the poison, the fish float or swim clumsily down to the dam and come to the surface, where the women and girls scoop them up by hand or in large circular baskets, biting the larger ones behind the head to kill them (photo 14). Sometimes the women are shocked by eels while fishing, and the eel must be found and killed before the work can continue.

I cannot leave the subject of technology without describing some of the Yanomamö's barbering implements and practices. One implement is a splinter from a certain reed—*sunama*—with which they shave the top of their heads bald, making a tonsure, and trim their pudding-bowl-shaped bangs. The sliver of reed is wrapped around the finger and scraped over the scalp, neatly cutting the hair off with no more discomfort than if they were shaving with a dull razor blade. Men with deep scars on their heads acquired in club fights look particularly grotesque to an outsider, especially when they rub on red pigment to enhance the scars. The size of the tonsure varies markedly from area to area. The Shamatari, for example, sport relatively small tonsures, about three inches in diameter. The Yanomamö to the north and east of Kaobawä's village shave so much of their heads that they look as if they have only a narrow fringe of hair, like a black strap wrapped around the head just above the temples. Women wear the same hairstyle as the men do.

If head lice become extremely bothersome, the people shave their heads completely, since it takes a great deal of time to groom (delouse) someone, and reinfestation is rapid. While such grooming is an expression of affection or friendship, it can also become tedious. Children are often shaved when their lice become too bad for their parents to handle (photo 15). Old people, no longer concerned about their looks, also frequently shave off all their hair. I was amused to learn that the Yanomamö get revenge on the lice by eating them or by biting them to kill them. But having head lice is not as primitive as many of us assume. I recall that once when I was in elementary school the county nurse had to come in to delouse all of us, whether we needed it or not.

Hallucinogenic Drugs

The jungle supplies several highly prized plant products that the Yanomamö use in the manufacture of hallucinogenic snuff powders. The most widely distributed of these plants is the *yakowana* tree, whose soft and moist inner bark is dried and ground into a powder. To this are added snowy white ashes made from the bark of another tree. The mixture is moistened with saliva and kneaded by hand into a somewhat gummy substance, which is then placed on a piece of heated potsherd (or now, in some villages, the top of a gasoline drum) and ground into a fine green powder.

But a more desirable hallucinogen comes from the *hisiomö* tree, whose tiny, lentil-sized seeds are painstakingly peeled, packed into ten- or fifteen-inch-long wads shaped like cylinders, and traded over a wide area. The tree has a spotty

14. Women collecting
stunned fish with baskets
in a small stream that has
been dammed with brush
and mud. The men put
barbasco poison in the
water upstream to stun
the fish, and the women
catch them.

15. Children delousing
each other during a break
from playing. Sometimes
head lice become so
numerous that it is easier to
shave a child's head bald.

distribution, and villages located near natural groves tend to specialize in the *hisiomö* trade. It is not only a more desirable drug than *yakowana* but is more powerful. Like *yakowana*, the seeds are kneaded with ashes and saliva and then pulverized into a green powder on a piece of heated potsherd. A smooth stone, often a stone ax (which the Yanomamö find on the surface when they clear and burn new gardens), is used to grind the substance into a powder. Several other plants are also used as hallucinogens. The Yanomamö cultivate a variety of small bushes of the genus *Justicia* and snuff these, but they are less potent and less desirable than the first two. All the drugs in their powdered form are known by the generic name of *ebene*.

The men—women do not take the drugs—usually make a new batch of *ebene* every day, and sometimes several groups of men in a village all make their own batches. It takes much kneading and grinding to produce half a cupful, enough for several men, depending on their appetites and whether it is *hisiomö* or *yakowana*. The men then paint themselves elaborately with red pigment, put on their fine feathers, and gather around the front of the host's house. A long hollow tube, or *mokohiro*, is used to blow the powder into the nostrils. With one finger, a small amount, about a teaspoonful, is pushed into one end of the tube. The other end, which has a large hollowed-out palm seed as a nostril piece, is put into a companion's nose. The green powder is then blown into the nasal cavity in a powerful, long burst of breath that starts slowly and terminates in a vigorous blast (photo 16).

The recipient grimaces, chokes, groans, coughs, gasps, and often rubs his head excitedly with both hands, or he holds the sides of his head as he duck-waddles over to a convenient post, which he leans against while waiting for the drug to take effect. He usually takes a blast of *ebene* in each nostril, sometimes two in each, and freshens the effect with more blasts later. The recipient's eyes immediately get watery and his nose runs profusely—long strands of green mucus begin to drip from each nostril. Dry heaves are common, as is out-and-out vomiting. Within a few minutes, he is having difficulty focusing and starts to see spots and blips of light. His knees get rubbery, and he walks as if he has had too many cocktails. Profuse sweating is also common, and the recipient's pupils get large. Soon the *hekura* spirits can be seen dancing out of the sky and down from the mountaintops, rhythmically prancing along their trails to enter the chest of their human beckoner, who by now is singing melodically to lure them into his body, where he can control them—send them off to harm his enemies or cure his sick kinsmen.

16. *Blowing* ebene *powder into another man's nostrils. The initial pain is severe, but the effects are eventually pleasant.*

The trade in *hisiomö* seeds was unexpectedly interrupted by changes in the warfare patterns while I was living in Kaobawä's village, and the response by some individuals served as a fascinating illustration of the kind of ingenuity that must lie behind the whole process of plant domestication. Rerebawä, who had grown quite fond of the drug, took it upon himself to make sure that his supply could never again be cut off by wars. He made several trips to an area far to the northeast, where the tree abounded, and brought back many seedlings. Some of them he transplanted in his native village, and others he transplanted in Kaobawä's village. Still others he traded inland, to men in the Shamatari villages. While many of the seedlings did not survive, some did—and later produced significant quantities of seeds.

The Yanomamö quickly disperse through trade the novel or more desirable varieties of their cultigens—domesticated plants whose wild ancestors may or may not be known—and when they discover such plants in distant villages, they bring home seedlings, cuttings, or seeds for their own gardens. For a while, a new variety or plant is remembered as having come from a particular village, but over time the people forget and tend to think that they have always had it. It should be recalled that the Yanomamö are highly dependent on cultivated plantains, a domesticated plant that was introduced to the Americas after Columbus—yet they believe that they have always cultivated it, and they have origin myths about it.

Shelter

All the Yanomamö's house construction materials come from the jungle —poles, vines, leaves. But they make a sharp distinction, as do most people, between domestic and natural, that is, between Culture and Nature, and the focal point of the distinction is the village and its surrounding garden. The things found here are *yahi tä rimö*, "of the village," or Culture. Everything else is *urihi tä rimö*, "of the forest," or Nature.

The village may be constructed of natural things, but it becomes cultural through the intervention of human effort and its transformation of the natural materials. The permanent house and its central plaza, collectively, is called the *shabono*, and it is probably one of the most labor-intensive products in the Yanomamö culture. A high degree of planning and cooperation is necessary to build a village, not to mention the many days of work.

Unfortunately, a *shabono* lasts only two years or so before the leaves of the roof begin to leak or the roofing becomes so infested with roaches, crickets, and other insects that the structure must be burned to the ground to get rid of them. Roaches can become so numerous that they create a constant buzzing noise, which increases in intensity when someone's head passes close to the roofing and alarms the bugs, or when some such item as a bow and arrow is placed in the roof thatch. Kaobawä's village was once so infested that every time someone moved, dozens of roaches fell from the roof and scurried away. The roaches can be as large as small birds or so tiny that they can crawl in between the elements in a camera lens. For some reason, they loved my Sony shortwave radio. After 1985, I began using a portable computer, and it, too, became a favorite nesting and foraging place for the roaches. Concerned about possible damage to the computer, I improvised a homemade "roach trap": a large piece of duct tape, sticky side up, with a fragrant dab of peanut butter in the middle, which I left on top of the computer for a few nights. None of them made it more than one step onto the duct tape—where they remained fixed until dawn, their antennas twitching impatiently.

The *shabono* looks like one large round communal house at first glance, but in fact it is a coordinated series of individual houses (photo 17). Each family builds its own section of the common roof. The men usually do the heavy work of fetching the poles for the frame, placing them into the ground or overhead, and weaving the thousands of leaves that go into the thatch. The women and older children help in the thatching and in gathering the leaves and vines, the major materials in the structure. If the *shabono* is to have a palisade, the men do this heavy building.

If the *shabono* is to replace an old one that has been burned down, it might be located on that same spot or a few yards away—as long as it is not in a depression and likely to be flooded in the rainy season. If it is a new location altogether, the primary consideration is how close the village's enemies and allies are, and, secondarily, the suitability of the land for gardens. The Yanomamö prefer to build their *shabonos* on a slight rise, so that when it rains no pools are left standing in the central clearing. Families whose houses are in the path of draining rainwater dig small ditches all around them, to divert the runoff from coming into their sleeping quarters or quenching their fires.

The four main posts of each house are sunk into the ground in holes dug with a stick or machete, the dirt being scooped out by hand. Two short poles about five feet high are set at the back of the house and two longer ones, about ten feet high, at the front. Each two poles are about eight to ten feet apart, to accommodate hammocks, and this also determines the distance between the

17. *A small Yanomamö village as seen from the air. The village is at the edge of its plantain garden and close to the Toototobi River.*

front and back posts. Cross poles are lashed to these, horizontal to the ground and near the tops of the upright posts. Long slender saplings—*hanto nahi*—are now placed diagonal to the cross poles, about a foot to eighteen inches apart, and lashed to them with vines. The saplings, twenty to thirty feet long, run from near ground level at the rear of the house, arch up over it and bend under their own weight into a gentle arc, and end about twenty to twenty-five feet off the ground. Vines are strung between the saplings, perpendicular to them, about every fifteen inches. These hold the long-stemmed leaves most often used in roofing, *bisaasi kä hena*, from which comes the name of the village of Bisaasi-teri—"roofing-leaf people."

The thatching begins from the bottom. A long-stemmed leaf is slid under the second vine up and bent down over until it rests on the first vine (photo 18). Another leaf is placed a few inches to the side of the first, and so on, until the row runs the entire length of the individual house. Then the second and higher rows are added, with a scaffolding of poles and vines erected as the roof progresses. The weight of the leaves bends the saplings further, and when the roofing is nearly completed support poles must be added to hold up the overhang. These poles are often embedded in the ground and tied to the *hanto nahi* tips to keep the roof from blowing off in a strong wind. In club fights, the support poles are often ripped out and used as weapons—and the roof may sag or break as a result.

When each of the houses is finished, there will be a circle of them separated from each other by a few feet of open space. These open spaces are thatched over, and now the village looks like one continuous, communal, circular roof surrounding an open plaza. Occasionally one sees an unroofed gap a few feet wide, and sometimes a section of village that is not connected to neighboring houses at either end. Such a village appears to be composed of discrete sections, as it is, but in the region around Bisaasi-teri there usually are no sections separated by open space. Elsewhere, to the north and east, Yanomamö villages are seldom unified structures of the kind just described. There, individual sections of a village might even be double-gabled, that is, have houses with double-pitched roofs. This is a feature that could well have been introduced from the outside, since the Yanomamö on the north and northeast periphery of the tribe have had regular contact with the Ye'kwana, Carib-speaking Indians who have a long history of contact with Europeans, and with the missionaries who work among the Ye'kwana and Yanomamö.

The physical size of a village is determined by two important variables, at

18. *Thatching the* shabono *roof with leaves from the* bisaasi kä hena *plant.*

least in the area around Bisaasi-teri. The first and most obvious is how many people there are in the group. Because warfare is common in this area, the villages tend to grow fairly large before they fission. A village must have at least eighty to a hundred people before it can fission, but here many of them grow much larger. (We will go into this further in chapter 4.)

The second determinant of the physical size of a village is its politics— the extent to which the members of the village have entered into alliances and exchange regular visits with neighboring groups as a part of their political strategy, a necessary strategy in Kaobawä's area. Alliance obligations require visits by all the members of an ally's village, and the host village has to be large enough to accommodate them, along with its permanent residents. The physical dimensions may be such that a hundred or so visitors can be accommodated at one time. In a word, where alliances between villages are an inherent part of the political strategies, a Yanomamö village that numbers eighty people is physically larger than a village of eighty in an area where alliances of this sort are less important.

Elevation and temperature also affect the style of construction. When I visited some Yanomamö villages in the Parima highlands, which are at an elevation of about 2,500 to 3,000 feet, I was puzzled to see that their *shabonos* had large masses of banana leaves hanging from the high point of the roof almost to the ground. I discovered the reason on the first night I slept in one of these villages. The air temperature dropped to about 60 degrees Fahrenheit, and the high humidity made it feel as if it was 40 degrees. The banana leaves kept the heat from the hearths from escaping too rapidly. Unfortunately, they also prevented the smoke from escaping. I felt like a smoked monkey each morning—but people who have no clothing or blankets apparently can tolerate a good deal of smoke if it means keeping warm.

A new *shabono* is a pleasant place to be. It is clean, smells of fresh-cut leaves, and has a cozy, tidy appearance. It is something like living inside an enormous new wicker hamper.

The wind, however, can be destructive. It blows off the leaves and, when very gusty, can get under the roof, rip it off, and blow it away into the jungle. The Yanomamö sometimes throw heavy branches and poles on the roof to hold the leaves down, and I have already described the support poles they install. But the most common defense against wind is magical. The shamans rush forth and chant incantations at *Wadoriwä*, the spirit of the wind, pleading with him to stop the blowing. He seldom does. Often the shaman of an enemy village is accused of causing the spirits to make the violent winds, and the local shamans retaliate by urging *Wadoriwä* to blow their roofs off, too.

When the Yanomamö travel to another village or go on an extended food-collecting trip in the jungle, they make a simpler house, the *yano*. It is roughly triangular in shape, with two back poles and one front pole. One of these huts can be erected in a few minutes, and a whole group—all the members of a village—can create a homey camp of them in about half an hour. The roofing material is usually the long, broad leaves of the wild banana, the *kediba*, a few of which suffice for a waterproof roof that will last several days. Later travelers who come across such huts simply string up their hammocks for the night, hoping that the roof will not leak. But the roof always leaks, and a traveler may spend most of the night futilely adjusting and readjusting the decayed leaves to keep the rain out. The dripping-roof problem is almost as prevalent in the permanent villages, as the leaves get old and dry. Nothing is less pleasurable than to wake up in the night because you have the sensation that you are wet—and to discover that you *are* wet, because the roof right above you is leaking and water is pouring into your hammock. You and your hosts then spend the rest of the night poking at the roof with sticks, trying to readjust the leaves to stop the leak or move somewhere else where the rain will not bother you.

A permanent *shabono* will be surrounded by a ten-foot-high palisade if the residents are afraid of enemy attacks. The palisade is made of stout poles, or logs, and stands a few feet from the lower part of the *shabono* roof. The logs are sunk a foot or so into the ground and lashed together with vines. The palisade is kept in good repair only if the threat of raids is high; otherwise, the people pilfer the wood for their cooking fires. Village entrances, whether the entrance is through the palisade or directly into the village, are covered with dry brush at night, so that the slightest movement will wake the dogs and alert the residents. Villages without palisades are more vulnerable, but the people have a way of stacking their firewood under the low end of the roof to prevent a nocturnal assassin from getting an easy shot. In the darkness, everyone looks alike, and the Yanomamö even had me stack my pack and other containers, like camera cases, against the back of my roof to add some protection against would-be raiders.

The Food Quest

Wild Foods

The jungle provides the Yanomamö with countless varieties of plant and animal food. Some is seasonal and some is available most of the year, although access to it may be restricted by rainfall. It would be possible for a Yanomamö group to live entirely on the wild foods in its environment, if the group was small and remained migratory. Indeed, most of the villages in Kaobawä's area regularly go on *waiyumö*—go camping—for long periods, usually breaking up into groups of about thirty or forty. They subsist heavily on wild foods, especially palm fruits and game, and they time the camping trips to coincide with the ripening of wild fruits. They lead a relatively sedentary life at the temporary camps, but they usually hedge their subsistence bets by bringing along a supply of plantains from their gardens. The camping trips are a time of fun and relaxation, affording a respite from gardening and allowing the Yanomamö to vary their diet with the many kinds of seasonal wild produce. In many regards, the trips are similar to our vacations.

The most commonly taken game animals in Kaobawä's area are two varieties of large game birds that resemble our pheasant and turkey (*marashi* and *paruri*), two species of wild pig, several varieties of monkeys, tapir, armadillos, anteaters, alligators (caiman), deer, rodents, and a host of small birds. Many varieties of insects, fish, larvae, tadpoles, and freshwater crabs are eaten with gusto. In some areas, large snakes are also eaten, but they are not considered especially desirable—anacondas and boa constrictors in particular. Large toads and frogs are eaten in some regions. Certain species of caterpillars are a prized food, as are the fat white grubs of the insect that lays its eggs in the pith of palm trees and the grubs that live in the seeds of many palm fruits. In the Parima area, some groups eat the flesh of jaguars, a habit that Kaobawä and his people regard as peculiar. On the other hand, Kaobawä's people rarely eat the flesh of the capybara, the world's largest rodent, which abounds in the lowlands and reaches 100 or 150 pounds (it looks like a giant beaver, but with no tail). Fish are taken in considerable abundance in certain seasons, and as fishhooks and fishing line have been introduced and become more common, fish are of increasing importance in the diet of those Yanomamö who have access to fishing tackle.

In short, the Yanomamö are able to exploit a wide variety of animal protein resources, and they enjoy a high standard of living by world health standards—as my medical-research colleagues found during their intensive studies in the 1960s and 1970s. With more foreigners coming into the area and taking up permanent residence, the situation will change rapidly—and it already has along the major river ways where permanent missions have been established. Their personnel hunt with guns, flashlights, and canoes, both day and night, and seine fish from the rivers with nets. The meat is often stored in kerosene freezers and dispensed generously to the many tourists who are beginning to flock to the missions to see the "wild Indians."

Vegetable Foods

The vegetable foods most commonly exploited by the Yanomamö are the fruits of several species of palm and hardwoods, brazil nuts, tubers, the seedpods of a native wild banana, and a host of lesser items, including some delicious mushrooms. One can gorge endlessly on palm hearts without getting full, and I have joined the Yanomamö in orgies of palm-heart eating in which the consumption of forty or fifty pounds among some dozen people was not unusual. Westerners buy hearts of palm in small, expensive tins or bottles and regard them as a delicacy, but if they are all one has to eat for several days, even they can quickly get tedious.

The two commonest palm fruits are called *kareshi* and *yei*. The latter is about the size of a hen's egg, the former about half as large. Both fruits have a leathery skin and a large, hard seed inside. Between the skin and the seed is a thin layer of slimy, sticky, stringy flesh, somewhat sweet to the taste, that is sucked or chewed off the seed. The overall flavor of both, however, reminded me of a grade of inexpensive soap, and eating them often made my throat burn. The seeds of both are roasted, smashed open with a stone, and the white flesh inside eaten. A third palm fruit, *ediweshi*, abounds in swampy areas. It is a tangerine color, about the size of a large hen's egg, and is covered with hundreds of small scales, not unlike fish scales. *Ediweshi* fruits look like tiny red hand grenades. When the dry fruit falls from the tree, it is leathery and difficult to peel. The Yanomamö throw the fruits into a pond (where most of them have fallen anyhow) and wait for them to soften. Then the scaly skin can be scraped off with the fingernails. Underneath is a thin layer of yellowish, soft, sometimes slimy flesh that has a pleasant cheesy taste. It was great fun to go collecting *ediweshi* fruits with the Yanomamö. We would probe around in knee-deep muddy water to find them, and when we had accumulated a half bushel or so, we would gather around the pile to eat and gossip. My personal reaction to all the palm fruits I have described is that it takes a tremendous number of them, acquired at great effort, to fill your belly.

Wild honey is one of the Yanomamö's most prized foods, and they will go to great extremes to get it. If someone spots a bee's nest, all other plans for the day are dropped and honey becomes the top priority. And when a person returns to the village later than expected, it is safe to assume that he or she has run across a cache of honey on the way.

Most of the honey—there are many kinds—is harvested by smoking out the bees, ripping the combs from the nest (which is often a hollow tree), and soaking wads of leaves in the liquid that remains in the nest. The honey-soaked leaves are then rinsed in water. If nobody has a container for the water, a shallow pit is dug in the ground, lined with broad leaves, and filled with water. The Yanomamö dip the combs into this watery pit and eat them, larvae and all. The watery liquid is likely to have many larvae, a few smoke-stunned bees, and a lot of other debris floating around in it. The Yanomamö dip the liquid out in cups fashioned from leaves, or, if they have a cooking pot, they pass the pot around and drink from it, blowing the debris aside first. If the nest is unusually large, they squeeze out their honey-soaked leaves onto a pile of broad leaves and wrap this up to take home. They also use leaf-lined pits filled with water to make beverages from a variety of palm fruits. The fruits are skinned and kneaded by hand in the water until it is sweet enough, and the beverage is consumed by dipping cupfuls out of the pit.

Collecting Grubs and Other Gathering Techniques

One of the most ingenious gathering techniques is the process of collecting the large, fat palm-pith grubs. First, the Yanomamö fell a large palm and eat the heart. Many days later, they return to the decaying tree and chop it apart to get at the soft, spongy pith inside. In the meantime, a species of insect will have laid its eggs in the pith, and the eggs will have developed into large grubs—some the size of mice. The grub looks like a very large housefly maggot. As the Yanomamö dig out the pith with sticks, they encounter the fat grubs, perhaps fifty or sixty of them in a good-sized tree. The squirming grub is bitten behind the head and held tightly in the teeth. A strong pull leaves the head and entrails dangling between the teeth. These are spit out, and the remainder of the grub is tossed, still squirming, into a leaf bundle. Grubs damaged by the digging sticks are eaten raw on the spot. The leaf bundles containing the grubs are tossed onto the coals of a fire and roasted, rendering them down into liquid fat and a shriveled white corpse. The corpse is eaten in a single gulp, the fat enthusiastically licked from the leaves and fingers. I ate a number of different kinds of insects while with the Yanomamö, some of them quite tasty, but I could never bring myself to eat the palm-pith grubs. A missionary who had tried them said they tasted like very fat bacon, but I suppose anything fat that is cooked over a smoky fire will taste like bacon. What fascinated me about the palm-grub collecting is that it comes close to being an incipient form of animal domestication. The Yanomamö fell the tree with the clear intention of providing fodder for the insect eggs, which will turn into grubs for the Yano-mamö to harvest.

Anthropologists are always running into strange or exotic customs, which they generally take in stride because someone is always topping them. Well, I think I have discovered one of the strangest among the Yanomamö, involving maggots. There is a certain wildflower in which a particular insect lays its eggs. They hatch into small white maggots that crawl like an inchworm. I was watching a man carefully extract these maggots from the flower one day, and after he had two or three he had a friend stick them into his ear. Dumbfounded, I asked him what he was doing, and he said, "I've got a lot of wax in my ear, and it itches. The maggots will eat the wax and clean out my ear." Sure enough, the maggots live on a waxy substance inside the flower, and apparently they will eat any kind of wax. By and by, the maggots crawled out of the man's ear, full of wax. He said it tickled a bit, but that was better than the itching.

Another interesting Yanomamö hunting technique is their way of taking armadillos. Armadillos live several feet underground in burrows that can run for many yards and have several entries. When the Yanomamö find an active burrow, as determined by the presence around the entry of a cloud of insects found nowhere else, they set about smoking out the armadillo. The best fuel for this purpose is a crusty material from old termite nests, which burns slowly and produces an intense heat and much heavy smoke. A pile of this material is ignited at the entry of the burrow, and the smoke is fanned inside. The other entries are soon detected by the smoke rising from them, and they are sealed with dirt. The men then spread out on hands and knees, holding their ears to the ground to listen for armadillo movement in the burrow. When they hear something, they dig there until they hit the burrow and, with luck, the animal. They might have to try several times, and it is hard work—they have to dig down two feet or more. On one occasion, after the hunters had dug several holes, all unsuccessful—they even missed the burrow—one of them ripped down a large vine, tied a knot in the end of it, and put the knotted end into the entrance. Twirling the vine between his hands, he slowly pushed it into the hole as far as it would go. As his companions put their ears to the ground, he twirled the vine, causing the knot to make a noise, and the spot was marked. He broke off the vine at the burrow entrance, pulled out the piece in the hole, and laid it on the ground along the axis of the burrow. The others dug down at the place where they had heard the knot and found the armadillo on their first attempt, asphyxiated from the smoke.

Gardening

Although the Yanomamö spend at least as much time hunting as they do gardening, in most areas the bulk of their food comes from cultivated plants. Early visitors to the region consistently described the people as hunters and gatherers, but that was a characterization based on misinformation or on the romantic assumption that a tribe so unknown and remote had to be living in the most primitive conditions imaginable and therefore had to be hunters and gatherers. Upwards of 80 percent to 90 percent of the Yanomamö's food is from their own gardens in most areas, a factor that profoundly influences all their political, economic, and military activities. Of the domesticated foods, plantains are far and away the most important item. To be sure, this horticultural emphasis is certainly a post-Columbian phenomenon, but it is reasonable to assume that before they had plantains they relied heavily on manioc, maize, and several indigenous varieties of cultivated tubers.

The Yanomamö are constantly alert to the potential of the regions in which they hunt as future sites for villages and gardens, for their warfare patterns dictate that they must eventually move their villages to new areas. When I hunted with them, evening conversations around the campfire frequently revolved around the merits of that particular spot as a possible garden site. It is the hunters who usually find the site for a new village when a long move is required. The best land will not be heavily covered with low, thorny brush, which is difficult to clear and burn, and will have relatively few large trees, which require much labor to fell. Ideally, a new site will have a light tree cover, will be well drained, and, most important, will not be inundated in the wet season. It will also be near a reliable water source. One of their conceptions about potential new garden sites is implied in their definition of the word for savanna, or *börösö*. Savanna to them is not a stretch of treeless land, but a jungle

with widely spaced trees that can readily be cleared for gardening. They occasionally refer to a potentially useful tract of jungle by the same term they
use for a cleared garden—*hikari täka*, a "hole" in the jungle where there is a
garden.

The first step in making a new garden is to cut the smaller trees and low
brush. The larger trees, *kayaba hii*, are left standing until the undergrowth has
been cleared. The large trees usually have very strong vines weaving through
them high up in their canopies. The Yanomamö often will chop almost through
the trunks of a clump of large trees and finish off the biggest one. When it
topples, the vines drag the others down with it. The larger trees are felled
with steel axes and left lying on the ground for several weeks while the
branches and leaves dry out. Especially large trees are felled by chopping them
from scaffolds ten feet or more above the ground, where the trunk is not
so thick.

My older informants said that they did not have steel axes when they
were young and had to kill large trees by cutting a ring of bark off the base
of the trunk with a crude stone or by burning brush and deadfall wood piled
around the base of the tree. The dead tree would drop its leaves, allowing
enough light to reach the ground for crops to grow, but the trunk would be
left standing. These informants also maintained that making a garden was a lot
more work in those days because they had to scour a large area to accumulate
enough wood and brush for the fires. Today steel axes are common; even
uncontacted villages often have almost-new ax heads that have been traded
along from villages that have links with the mission posts, where most of the
trade in steel tools originates. Still, I have contacted remote villages where steel
axes not only were rare, but the few they had were so badly worn from previous
use that at least half the blade was gone.

The rate at which steel tools and other Western items are now entering
the region is nothing short of incredible. One Catholic missionary I knew well,
Padre Luis Cocco, gave the members of his village—some 130 people—over
3,000 steel machetes in a fourteen-year period, plus hundreds of axes, aluminum
cooking pots, knives, and several hundred thousand meters of nylon fishing line
and an equivalent number of steel fishhooks. The items were quickly dispersed,
through trade, not only to the villages immediately adjacent to his but far inland,
to the most remote villages. Other mission posts that have established permanent
contact with the Yanomamö likewise provide large quantities of these items to
villages on both the Venezuelan and the Brazilian side of the border. Before the

arrival of the missionaries, the Yanomamö appear to have obtained steel tools from the Ye'kwana Indians to their north, who have had contact with Westerners for 200 years. The Ye'kwana, a people who have carried the art of dugout-canoe making to a high level of sophistication, would travel as far as Georgetown, in present-day Guyana, to trade with the English colonials there, long before Westerners had penetrated into their area to establish permanent contacts. Whole villages of Yanomamö would go to the Ye'kwana villages and work there for several months to earn steel tools and other items. The tools would eventually be traded farther and farther inland, to remote Yanomamö villages whose members had never seen a Ye'kwana. The northern Yanomamö villages and the Ye'kwana still maintain a relationship, which has occasionally and erroneously been described as slavery.

I draw attention to the trade in items from outside the culture for several reasons. First, it should be made clear that the Yanomamö have had access to some steel tools for as long as a hundred years, and perhaps longer in the areas near the Ye'kwana. This might be of importance in explaining the rapid population growth over the past 125 years that I have documented among several large clusters of Yanomamö villages—a "population explosion" that might be related both to the introduction of an efficient and productive cultigen, the plantain, and to the use of steel tools, which make gardening more efficient and productive. Second, I want to emphasize that the word "uncontacted" as applied to some villages is a relative term: the residents of such villages may never have seen outsiders, but they or their ancestors could have benefited from items introduced into the New World by Europeans—such as steel tools and certain cultivated plants.

Useful items often spread rapidly between cultures, a process that does not require direct contact, and such items often set off changes in a recipient culture that transforms it into a new and different culture. Classic examples abound in the anthropological literature. For example, the nomadic equestrian buffalo-hunting cultures of the Great Plains came into existence only *after* the introduction of firearms, via the French and English traders in Canada, and the introduction of horses, via the Spaniards in Mexico. Prior to these introductions, the cultures of the Great Plains that we know either from anthropology textbooks or from Hollywood films simply did not exist in those forms. Again, many of the dramatic cultural processes and situations that we encounter in the highlands of New Guinea and in much of Micronesia and Polynesia owe their present form to economies based on the cultivation of the sweet potato, a plant that was brought to these areas from the New World after the discovery of the Americas in the sixteenth century. Similarly, many traditions and technoeconomic factors affecting Western European culture took form because of plant crops borrowed from the Americas. Karl Marx once mused that the industrial revolution could not have succeeded without the white potato, a cheap and efficient food to sustain a large labor force; the potato came to Europe from the Andes. What would pizza be without tomato sauce—the tomato being yet another New World plant introduced to Europe after Columbus? And let us not forget to add quinine, tobacco, and cocaine to our list.

Thus, the Yanomamö clear their trees with steel tools today, often not knowing the provenance of the tools or caring much, other than that "We got this ax from the Monou-teri" or "The machete came from the Abruwä-teri." And they plant their sites primarily with a crop, plantains, that was introduced to the New World after Columbus.

Larger trees are usually felled toward the end of the wet season, although I have seen the Yanomamö do this kind of work at other times of the year, especially when military relationships dictated a different schedule. In general, jungle clearing tends to be a wet-season activity and the burning of brush and small branches a dry-season one. But felled timber can be burned even during the rainy season if it has had two or three days of sunshine in a row to dry out. Only the smaller branches are burned, along with the brush and scrubby vegetation, and it is not necessary to wait for the large trunks to dry. They are left lying helter-skelter on the ground and serve as firewood or makeshift boundaries between patches of food crops belonging to different families.

Other Garden Products

Many kinds of foods and nonfood cultigens can be found in most Yanomamö gardens. Among the more important foods not yet mentioned are several root crops. Manioc, a starchy root staple widely found throughout the Amazon Basin, is cultivated in small quantities by most Yanomamö. They usually grow the "sweet" variety, a variety that contains little or no cyanic acid, a lethal poison that must be leached from the manioc pulp before the pulp can be eaten. When the pulp of the poisonous manioc is exposed to the air, as it is when the plant is uprooted and peeled, the toxin oxydizes into hydrocyanic acid (related to the substance used in gas chambers for executions). The Yanomamö in the north are beginning to grow more of the "bitter," or poisonous, manioc, however; the neighboring Ye'kwana have diffused both the plant and the proper refining techniques into the Yanomamö area. In Kaobawä's area, the sweet manioc variety is dominant. It is refined into a pulp by grating the roots on rough rocks. This moist white pulp is shaped into thick patties (cassava bread) about ten inches in diameter and cooked on both sides on a hot piece of broken pottery (photo 19). Ye'kwana cakes are much larger—up to three feet across. In general, the Yanomamö prefer foods that require little processing—a kind of "take it from the vine and throw it on the fire" attitude that applies to vegetable and animal food alike.

Three other root crops are widely cultivated and provide substantial amounts of calories in the Yanomamö diet. One is called *ohina*, a South American variety of taro (of the genus *Xanthosoma*). Sweet potatoes (*hukomo*) are also cultivated, as is a potatolike root known in Spanish as *mapuey* and in Yanomamö as *kabiromö* or, in a slightly different variety, *ahä akö*. All these usually are roasted in the hot coals of the hearth, peeled with the fingers, and eaten without condiments. However, the Yanomamö occasionally make a salty-tasting liquid from the ashes of a certain tree and dip their food in it. (The salt is probably calcium chloride rather than sodium chloride.) When the Yanomamö first taste salt, they detest it, claiming that it "itches" their teeth and gums, but they gradually become addicted to it and beg for it frequently.

Perhaps another dozen food items of lesser importance are grown, but not all of them in every garden. Avocados, papayas, and hot peppers are among the more common of these.

Several important nonedible cultigens are also found in nearly all Yanomamö gardens. Arrow cane is grown for its long, straight shafts, which are dried in the sun and made into arrows. The arrows are exceptionally long by our standards—six feet—are light and springy, and can penetrate completely through the body of an animal or a man.

Without a doubt, the most significant nonfood cultigen in the Yanomamö garden is tobacco, to which the men, women, and children as young as ten are all addicted. Their word for "being poor," *hori*, means literally "to be without tobacco." They chew rather than smoke the tobacco, although the chewing is perhaps better described as sucking. Each family cultivates its own tobacco patch and jealously guards it from theft—a common problem, since neighbors are always likely to run out by giving too much away in trade or having a crop fail. Tobacco is the only crop that is sometimes fenced off, to remind avaricious neighbors that the owner is serious about protecting his crop. The fence, a flimsy corral of thin sticks stuck into the ground and laced together with vines,

19. *Kaobawä's younger brothers preparing packs of cassava bread and smoked meat
at the end of a feast. The food will be given to the guests to eat on their way home.
Yanomamö's cassava bread is smaller and moister
than that made by their Carib neighbors.*

would never prevent theft; it is merely a proclamation that the owner intends to defend his tobacco plants vigorously. I have even seen some Yanomamö bury booby traps in their tobacco patches—sharp, long splinters of bone that can remain buried in a poacher's foot for a long time.

The method of preparing tobacco is somewhat complex. It is harvested by selecting individual leaves at the peak of maturity. The leaves are then tied together by their stems, fifteen or twenty at a time, and hung over the hearth to cure in the heat and smoke of the fire. The dry leaves are stored in large balls, which are wrapped in other leaves to keep out insects and moisture. As needed, several leaves of the cured tobacco are removed from the ball, dipped in a calabash of water to moisten them, and kneaded in the ashes of the campfire until the entire leaf is coated with a muddy-looking layer of ash. (The ashes of certain woods are preferred over others.) The ashy leaf is then rolled into a short, fat, cigarlike wad, which is often bound with fine fibers to hold it in shape. With conspicuous pleasure, the large wad is placed between the lower lip and the teeth, and the user reclines in his or her hammock with a blissful sigh to suck on the gritty, greenish, and very large wad. The Yanomamö are quite sociable with their tobacco. When someone removes a wad and lays it down for a second, another might snatch it up and suck on it until the owner wants it back. The borrower may be a child, a buddy, a wife, a stranger, or, if willing, an anthropologist. It should be obvious that this kind of tobacco usage contributes significantly to the rapid spread of viruses and infectious diseases, at both the village and the regional level.

Cotton is also an important cultigen. Cotton yarn is used in hammocks as well as in "clothing"—a word one must interpret loosely, since Yanomamö clothing is largely symbolic or decorative. Indeed, a well-dressed man often sports nothing more than a string around his waist to which is tied the stretched-out foreskin of his penis. As a young boy matures, he starts to act masculine by tying his penis to his waist string, and the Yanomamö use this developmental phase to specify a boy's age: "My son is now tying up his penis." A certain amount of teasing takes place at that age, since an inexperienced youth will have trouble controlling his penis. It takes a while for the foreskin to stretch to the length required to keep it tied securely, and until then it is likely to slip out of the string, much to the embarrassment of its owner and the mirth of older boys and men. Sometimes an older boy or an adult man will accidentally come untied, to his great embarrassment—for to him it is like being completely naked. So circumspect are the men that even in the heat of a serious fight or duel they will cease hostilities for a moment if one of the contestants comes untied. I once saw a duel in which two men were pounding each other violently on the chest when the penis string of one of them came untied. Both, without a word, stopped until the man got himself tied up again, and then they resumed slugging it out.

The women, too, are careful and modest, despite being clothed no more fully than the men. A girl or woman is always careful, when rising from a sitting position, to cross her legs to conceal as best she can her naked pubes.

Take my word for it, a penis string is not comfortable. Wherever clothing is available, as at mission posts, the men rapidly become accustomed to wearing short pants or loincloths, and these have become very popular trade items. Men who wear pants stop tying their penises, an indication that not all the customs of a culture are enjoyed by the practitioners—a topic for anthropological research that deserves pursuing.

Needless to say, the Yanomamö were astonished to learn that most of the men from my kind of culture have their foreskins cut off. I was delivered by my grandfather, in my mother's bed at home, and he was an old-fashioned French-Canadian country doctor who left foreskins as they were, so this part of me was not peculiar to the Yanomamö. Toward the end of my first year, however, I was joined by a group of medical researchers, all of whom had been circumcised. The Yanomamö were incredulous when they saw them naked, bathing in the river their first day in the field. As it happened, I had had a bad day—my medical colleagues had run me ragged making sure they had enough Yanomamö patients to examine, measure, weigh, and take blood, stool, and saliva samples from. The Yanomamö turned to me and asked incredulously:

"What happened to their foreskins?"

"They were cut off."

"Why were they cut off?"

"Well, in our village we punish people who commit incest by cutting off their foreskins."

I never did tell my medical colleagues why such a large, curious, and cynical crowd of Yanomamö gathered around them whenever it was bath time. My guess is that the incident will eventually work its way into some Yanomamö myth, the metaphorical vehicle through which they rationalize contradictions in mortal experience.

Most of the cultivated cotton is used in making hammocks. A continuous strand of spun cotton yarn is wrapped around two upright posts until it reaches the proper width for a finished hammock, and then cross seams are plaited vertically every few inches to hold the strands in place (photo 20). When this is done, the posts are taken out of the ground and the ends of the hammock tied with stronger cotton yarn. A finished hammock is about five or six feet long. Everyone wants a permanent cotton hammock, but since hammocks are often acquired in trade, many people make do with a flimsier, less comfortable version made of vines.

The women use cotton yarn to make a small waistband that is pretty but covers nothing. Cotton yarn is also used to make armbands and a loose, multistring, halterlike garment that the women wear crossed between their breasts and extending to the middle of the back. The men sometimes wear a fat cotton belt that looks like a giant sausage, to which they tie their penises. Men, women, and children wear single strands of cotton string around their wrists, ankles, knees, or chests. Apart from these garments, they wear no other clothing.

Finally, in some villages a variety of magical plants are cultivated. Most are associated with the casting of spells—harmless spells, like the female charms called *suwä härö*. Men use tiny packets of a dusty powder wrapped in leaves to seduce young women. The charm is forced against the woman's nose and mouth, and when she breathes it she swoons and experiences an unsatiable desire for sex—so say both the men and the women. Women in some villages also cultivate magical plants that allegedly cause the men to become calm and tranquil. The charm is thrown on them to make them less violent when they are acting quarrelsome.

In villages to the north of Bisaasi-teri, people allegedly cultivate an especially harmful plant that can be blown on enemies from a great distance or sprinkled on unwary male visitors while they sleep. A particularly feared class of this plant, called *oka*, is said to be blown through tubes at enemies, causing them to sicken and die. Kaobawä's group does not use *oka*, but they insist that their enemies do. The enemies, in turn, deny this but claim that Kaobawä's group uses it. It is one of those harmful practices that you are sure your enemy employs but you do not—completely consistent with the Yanomamö's belief that all unexplained deaths in their own village are the result of harmful magic or spells cast on them by their enemies.

Slash-and-Burn Farming

Each man clears his own land for gardening and usually starts this lifetime activity as soon as he is married. Adult brothers generally clear adjacent plots,

20. *Cotton hammocks are made from a continuous strand of yarn wrapped between two upright posts. Cross woofs are plaited in every few inches.*

and, if their father is still living, his garden will be among theirs. Thus, the connections between males that are important in Yanomamö social relationships are also significant in the distribution of garden plots and land usage. The size of a plot is determined in some measure by a family's size and kinship obligations, but some of the men are poor planners and underestimate how much land their family needs. In fact, one might call the Yanomamö underproducers. I once overheard a headman vigorously scolding one of the inmarried men in his village who regularly had to borrow food. "This isn't big enough for your wife and children," the headman warned. "You will have to beg plantains from others if you don't make it bigger. See that tree over there? Clear your garden out to there, and you will have enough—and you won't have to beg from the rest of us later." His tone of voice made it clear that future begging would not be tolerated. One mistake might be overlooked, but the same ones again and again would not.

Headmen tend to make larger gardens than the other men, for they bear a considerable responsibility in entertaining the periodic groups of visitors that must be fed. They also contribute more food to the feast given when all the members of an allied village arrive for a visit of several days. Kaobawä's garden is much larger than those of the other men of his village. His younger brothers help with the heavy work, and so does his wife's brother, who has no wife or dependent children—largely because he is something of a brute and rather stupid and unattractive. He is, however, an unflinching supporter of Kaobawä and works indefatigably in his garden. This man's "son" (his dead brother's son) has also helped in Kaobawä's garden; he was eligible to marry any of Kaobawä's daughters, a relationship that put him in the position of owing Kaobawä favors. That young man is Bäkötawä, the guide who abandoned me in the headwaters of the Mavaca River on my journey to make first contact with Sibarariwä's group.

When the garden plot is cleared and ready for burning, the brush and smaller branches are stacked in piles and ignited, with other brush added as it is ripped from fallen trees. A man might have several of these fires going at once, and the burning is done at the most convenient time for the gardener. Sometimes fires are placed around large fallen timbers to dry them out and make them easier to split into firewood.

The collection of firewood is almost entirely the women's task, and the quantities needed are staggering. I had not anticipated that firewood could be such a major concern of the Yanomamö, or of any tropical forest society, but huge amounts are consumed—for cooking, for keeping warm at night, for cremating the remains of the deceased. The women expend much energy every day collecting firewood. A fallen tree in the garden plot—especially a species that splits easily—is jealously guarded. Over time, the best of the large trees are gradually split, broken, and chopped into firewood by the women, and the garden gets cleaner as it matures. A woman must not take firewood from the garden plot of a neighbor unless invited to do so. Firewood is not only a valuable resource for the Yanomamö, but in many other parts of the world as well, somewhat to my surprise, it is a strategic resource. The worldwide availability of firewood has been the subject of serious investigations by such scientifically reputable organizations as the National Academy of Sciences.

Planting the newly cleared and burned garden proceeds in one of two ways. If the site is at a considerable distance from the village, a great deal of planning is involved in determining the mixture of crops and the maturity of the cuttings that are to be transplanted. If the new garden is simply an extension of the old one, planning for the planting of seeds and cuttings is a small matter.

Settlement Patterns

Micro Movements of Villages and Gardens

A Yanomamö garden lasts about three years from the time of the initial planting. As it becomes overrun with scrub vegetation and thorny brush and the output declines, an extension is added by clearing the land around the periphery. The old garden, no longer able to produce, is referred to as an "old woman," and the new extension, called the "nose," is added to the "old woman" part (sometimes called the "anus") as the latter falls into disuse. This is the first and simplest scenario for making a new garden.

During the 1950s and 1960s, when the theory of cultural ecology first began to have a major impact on studies of cultural adaptation, some anthropologists advanced the argument that slash-and-burn gardens in tropical forest regions, such as those of the Yanomamö, were abandoned solely because the crops had exhausted the soil and new, fresh land had to be found. As the argument went, local villages in the tropical forest could not exceed a certain size, and complex cultural developments were therefore impossible, because the poor quality of the soil demanded chronic movement and relocation.

In the 1950s, an anthropologist named Robert L. Carneiro decided to put the argument to an empirical test, using his meticulous field research among the Kuikuru of the Brazilian Xingu area. His work literally overturned the "poverty of the soil" argument as the primary reason for village relocations in a tropical forest environment. By measuring crop yields in the Kuikuru gardens, testing soil samples for declining fertility, and noting several measurable variables—such as acreage required to support an average family or an individual, distance from the garden to the village that cultivators were willing to travel, and how long it took an old garden to regenerate new forest after being abandoned—he showed convincingly that tropical forest villages larger than 500 people were quite feasible, that villages were not forced to move because of soil depletion, and that a high level of horticultural productivity could be maintained in the lands immediately surrounding a typical village. In short, he argued, whatever it was that lay behind the relocations of tribes like the Kuikuru, exhaustion of soil nutrients was not a very persuasive explanation. Moreover, soil exhaustion was not a convincing explanation for the failure of villages to exceed a population of 500 or for a cultural inertia due to low productivity. Indeed, Carneiro was able to show that the Kuikuru produced more calories per acre than the Inca farmers had, and with far less labor. Few experts today still argue that settlement relocation in the aboriginal societies of the Amazon tropical forest can be reduced to a matter of soil poverty; we have learned that the issue is far more complex than that, with many variables involved in the decisions that lie behind the movement of villages.

The small relocations of the Yanomamö gardens—micro movements—entailing the extension of an existing garden or the clearing of a new one a few hundred meters away, are easily accomplished, for nothing has to be carried very much farther. The reasons the Yanomamö give for these relocations are similar to those Carneiro found among the Kuikuru and are also documented for other Amazonian cultivators: the vegetation that grows up in maturing gardens is dense and usually thorny, and therefore unpleasant to clear and burn, especially by people who wear no clothing. If you have ever had to make your way in the buff through such vegetation, you will understand immediately. And another reason the Yanomamö do not like to work in old gardens is the snake problem.

The illustration entitled "Micro Movements of Bisaasi-teri" depicts the way one Yanomamö village moved over a period of several years and brought adjacent new land under cultivation. Instead of rethatching the *shabono* every

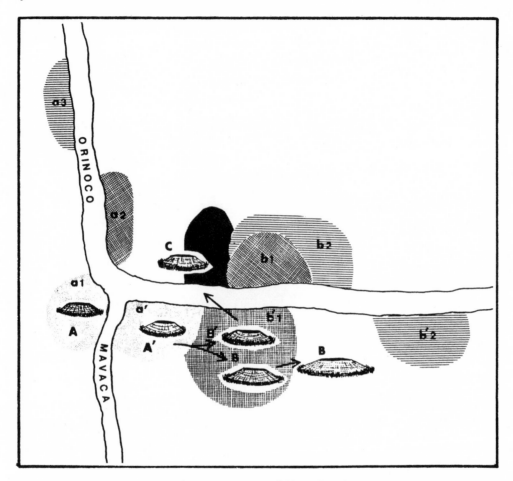

Micro Movements of Bisaasi-teri

*These movements of the village between 1960 and 1968 show how new gardens were added close to, or as extensions of, older ones. When the Bisaasi-teri moved here, there were two **shabonos** on opposite sides of the Mavaca River, just a few hundred feet from each other (A and A´). Kaobawä's group (A´) decided to make two new **shabonos** (B and B´) when they extended their gardens, the first sign of a fission. (The lowercase letters and numbers—b1, b2, etc.—indicate the sequence of the new gardens.) Eventually one group (B´) moved across the Orinoco to begin a separate existence (C). Kaobawä's group remained behind (B) and just a few hundred feet from the two other **shabonos**.*

two or three years, the movement of a garden might also serve as a reason for moving it, too—as well as to keep it located conveniently near the food crops.

The Yanomamö prefer to remain in one general area a long time, especially if it has a reliable source of game nearby. My research has revealed many instances of villages remaining in one area for sixty to eighty years—leaving only when military pressures became overwhelming.

Another reason for remaining is to stay close to the prized *rasha*, the domesticated peach palm tree, which produces large crops of tasty fruits every year and continues to produce well long after the garden is abandoned (photo 21). This palm is an exception to my earlier generalization that it takes a great many palm fruits to fill one's belly. Peach palm fruits have a fairly small seed (some have none at all) and a large amount of mealy flesh, about the texture of boiled potatoes. They are rich in oil and very tasty. Families usually plant one or more of the trees every time a garden is cleared, and eventually there is a large stand of them near the village. The fruits ripen all at once, in February and March, although some trees also produce a smaller crop in June and July.

Sometimes the fruit is so abundant that it has to be "wasted." Rather than let it rot, however, the villagers harvest it, boil it, pound it into a mash, mix it with water, and stage gluttonous drinking bouts with members of neighboring villages. They will quaff up to a gallon of the brew, vomit it out, and go back for more, repeating the process until it is all consumed. They will pick out a visitor, chase him around the village, catch him, and force him to down such a quantity of the beverage that finally it comes back out in large gushes. The visitors, of course, pick their own victims and do the same. It is colorful, but nauseating even to watch. On the other hand, many a beer party in my own culture fits the same description.

Plantains, bananas, and manioc are cultivated by the generative process, that is, through transplanting cuttings rather than sowing seeds. As a plantain tree matures, it sends out underground suckers that sprout, each of which can grow into a productive new tree. A mature plantain tree produces one bunch of fruits, often a very large one (depending on the variety). When the bunch is cut, the plant is useless, and it, too, is cut to the ground to make room for the growing suckers, the next generation of the tree. It takes about four months for a large sucker to yield a ripe bunch of plantains, perhaps six months for a small sucker. Plantains can be transplanted when they are quite small—a few inches high—or when they are several feet high. The larger they are, of course, the heavier they are to move—but the sooner they will yield their fruit. A man who wants an early new crop of plantains will transplant large suckers, each weighing ten pounds or more. But one usually does not want all the plantains to mature at the same time, and a good garden will have them in various stages of growth, to ensure a reliable supply all year long (photo 22). Probably 80 percent of the calories the Yanomamö get from cultivated foods are from plantains, and the gardens reflect that in the proportion of land devoted to plantain cultivation.

Macro Movements of Villages and Gardens

Warfare waxes and wanes throughout all of the Yanomamö areas. In some regions, such as those on the periphery of the tribe, years may go by with no intervillage conflicts. But for villages surrounded by neighbors on all sides, as in Kaobawä's area, active wars occur periodically. In the first place, long periods of tranquillity between villages are rare; several years might pass without a shooting incident with a neighboring group, but any length of time beyond that is not common. Second, once hostilities between villages have erupted and someone has been killed, the contestants are locked into a mortal relationship for many years, during which they do not have the option of migrating into a new, totally unoccupied area far away, as do the villages on the periphery of the tribe. In essence, this means that villages such as those in Kaobawä's area have no choice but to develop political alliances with neighbors. They cannot reach distant land to escape, and it is unwise to leapfrog over neighbors, for other, less familiar Yanomamö may lie beyond, who might prove more difficult to deal with than one's immediate neighbors. However, the distances between villages are great enough in Kaobawä's area that moves of an intermediate length can sometimes be accomplished—four or five days' walk—in order to escape from enemies and start a new garden.

I have characterized this situation as "social circumscription," similar in effect to what Carneiro calls "geographic circumscription." Carneiro argues that the world's major civilizations—Egypt, Mesopotamia, the Incas, and so on—all developed in regions that were geographically circumscribed by deserts, the sea, or other natural features that restricted expansion and therefore encouraged an increasing intensification of land use within the developing region, which led in turn to an increased complexity in social organization. My argument about social circumscription is similar, for the Yanomamö villages whose ability to move is limited by the presence of neighbors on all sides seem to be somewhat more complex in their organization and have much larger populations than villages on the tribal periphery, whose ability to migrate is unimpeded.

21. *Rerebawä climbing a* **rasha** *tree to harvest the fruit. He rests on one "A-frame" and pushes a second one up higher, climbs onto that, and then pulls the lower one up. In this fashion he painstakingly reaches the top of the 75-foot tree and lowers the bunch of fruit with a vine.*

22. *Plantains are transplanted by cutting suckers from a larger plant. These produce within a few months if they are large, but the larger they are, the heavier. Transporting them over a long distance takes a high expenditure of energy.*

The longer moves of the Yanomamö are not prompted by horticultural techniques, or by the demands of gardening, like crop type, soil, and the maturity of a garden, or by the deterioration of the *shabono*. They are motivated by politics and warfare, and must be understood in that context. I call these *macro movements*. Their most relevant ecological variable is human neighbors, rather than technology, economic practices, or inherent features of the physical environment. It will become increasingly clear why the establishment of alliances with neighbors is a kind of cultural adaptation that gives the Yanomamö some flexibility in dealing with—adapting to—intervillage warfare and conflict. (Chapter 6 describes the pattern in the context of a specific war and the relocation of a settlement.)

The first phase of many macro moves is each man's fear that the present village or area will become involved in violent fighting—with clubs, machetes, axes, or arrows—in which one of his close relatives or friends (or the man himself) may be badly injured or killed. Such fear might unite all the members of a village into making a collective move. Enemies from other villages may have begun raiding the group regularly, taking a small toll per raid but a significant one over time. The constant fear that raiders are lurking will have increased the level of anxiety and tension in the village and disrupted everyday life. Nobody will leave the village alone. Even the women, who must collect firewood and water daily, have to be escorted the short way to the garden or stream by armed men, who nervously keep their eyes peeled for telltale movements in the jungle and listen carefully for the disturbance of birds in the distance, while fidgeting with their nocked war arrows. During such times, people are afraid to leave the village even to defecate; they do it on leaves, which are thrown over the palisade. Several weeks or months of this is exhausting, and life would be easier if the village lived farther away from the known enemy.

In other cases, factions within a village might become increasingly hostile toward each other and increasingly violent in their arguments and duels, usually over sexual trysts and infidelity. Once started, such arguments tend to be aggravated by snide comments, thinly veiled insults, or any one of a host of trivialities that ruffle someone's feathers. As villages grow larger, internal order becomes more difficult to maintain, and factions inevitably develop: kin take sides, and social life becomes strained. There appears to be an upper limit to the size a group can reach and remain cooperatively organized by the principles of kinship, descent, and marriage, the integrating mechanisms characteristically at the disposal of primitive peoples—a fascinating subject, to which we will return. Suffice it to say here that kinship-organized groups can get only so large before they begin to fall apart and fission into smaller groups. The size limit appears to be determined as much by the inherent properties of kinship and marriage alliance as it is by the availability of strategic resources—the material things that sustain people and permit them to live in large social groups that are sedentary and fixed.

One might, in this vein, view the long history of our hunting and gathering ancestral past, as well as our more recent shorter history as cultivators, as a struggle to overcome the limitations on group size imposed by the traditional principles of organization that have marked most of our history—a struggle to transcend kinship and add new kinds of organizational principles. Many discussions of our social past as hunters and as early cultivators allude to the "magic numbers" of fifty to one hundred as the community size within which our recent cultural and biosocial evolution has occurred, a maximal size that was transcended only in the recent historical past—within the last several thousand years.

Thus, large Yanomamö villages eventually break apart and subdivide into smaller ones, usually in a bifurcation of the large group into two similar-sized smaller villages but occasionally into three. One of the groups retains possession of the existing garden—or the portion of it that belongs to that group's families—and the other faction must move away to clear, burn, and plant a new garden.

The distance between the fissioned groups can be small or large, depending on the nature of the confrontation that caused the fission. They may simply build two separate *shabonos* only a few yards apart and live *he borarawä*, side by side. This is the case when locating the two small new villages some distance apart would make them easy prey to hostile neighbors. Such a solution is not possible, however, if someone has been killed in the final confrontation that led to the split. Then, despite the number and resolve of external enemies, the village *must* fission into two parts, and one of the new groups must move far away and begin a separate garden.

Making a new garden from scratch while keeping the group adequately fed is not easy, especially if an existing productive garden has been abandoned without warning. If, for example, 100 people from a village of 200 must suddenly pull up roots and leave, because a fight has ended in someone's death, they have two choices. Either they can flee to a neighboring village that has been friendly in the past and live off those people for several months, or they can tough it out by trying to live off wild foods, supplemented by periodic visits to friendly villages, where they rest, gorge on the hosts' cultivated foods, and take away with them as much cultivated food as they can carry or their hosts are willing to part with. Meanwhile, they are busy clearing a new garden and attempting to get it producing as soon as possible.

Here is where a cost-benefit decision has to be made about what cuttings and seeds to bring along from their old garden plots. The question is whether an early crop is needed, in which case they would carry away fewer but larger plantain cuttings, or whether the longer-term security of a dependable food supply is more desirable, in which case they would bring a larger number of small cuttings. Maize affords a compromise of sorts. It is less desirable than plantains, but its lightweight seeds make it easily transportable, and the maturity time is short—two to three months. One can quickly get an abundant, early, low-effort crop of maize into the ground and have plenty of food while waiting for the plantains to mature. I have seen Yanomamö gardens that were established this way, and they are quite different from the standard garden in that the greatest part of the new garden is devoted to maize. In time, as plantains are transplanted, the composition of the garden shifts from mostly maize to mostly plantains.

Another important variable in one of these moves, also a function of the Yanomamö dependence on garden produce, is the precise location of the new site. Neighbors who are friendly will usually provide a new group with plantain suckers for transplanting, and if it will be impossible to return to the old garden for cuttings, the new garden must be located within a reasonable distance of a friendly neighbor. But the combination of variables can get quite mixed and complex. For example, an increase in tensions within a village might have prompted some members of the group to begin clearing a new garden elsewhere in anticipation of a fight that will lead to fission. In other words, under some circumstances the people can predict a disaster and plan for it by getting a new garden under production in advance. If the disaster never comes, the new garden may become a good place to camp out.

A more common combination of variables entails a pattern of the sort schematically represented in the illustration entitled "Macro Movements of Several Villages." A newly formed fission group can exploit several human and

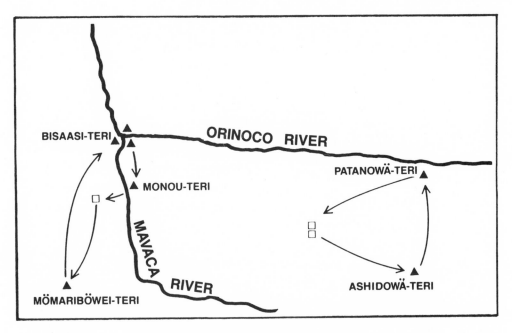

Macro Movements of Several Villages
How new gardens and villages are established at some distance from the old garden and
village in a series of macro movements.

natural resources in sequence. The people periodically return to their old garden to rest, fill up on the ripe crops, and collect food and cuttings to take to the new site. They camp out in the new garden while they clear and plant it, living off the foods from the old garden and seasonally available wild foods and game. They might even send young men back to the old garden for food periodically, or to a friendly neighboring village to beg supplies. The group follows a cycle of working in the new garden, moving en masse to the village of an ally for a fortnight or so, visiting their old producing garden, and then back to the new one.

However, the pattern involves several risks. The first is the risk of being attacked at the old garden or getting into a fight there with the members of the group who have stayed. The second risk is the new group's dependency on the allies who are providing food, refuge, or both. The Yanomamö are quick to take advantage of those who are vulnerable, and the cost an ally is likely to extract is the right of sexual license with the new group's wives, sisters, and daughters during their visits to the allied village. Disadvantaged groups expect this, and they can resist it only up to a point. If they cannot ignore the chronic attempts of the hosts to seduce the women of their guests, the new group will no longer be welcome in the allied village. The best solution is to make the visits to allies as short as possible, to extract the maximum amount of economic and political aid in that time, and then to repair either to another ally or to one of the gardens.

In general, the Yanomamö—and many other tribal peoples who subsist on hunting and gathering or on slash-and-burn agriculture—achieve an adequate, if not an abundant, subsistence with very few hours of work a day. So noticeable is this aspect of primitive economies that one distinguished anthropologist has referred to hunters and gatherers as the "original affluent society," in the sense that the difference between what they need and the means required to achieve it is very small. Hunters and gatherers like the Bushmen of the Kalahari Desert provide for themselves on only a few hours of work per day, and the Yanomamö productive efforts are about the same. By comparison, market forces have condemned those of us living in industrial societies to a lifetime of hard labor and overtime hours. One should remember this whenever grim economic statistics about certain peoples are presented to evoke our sympathy or our contributions. The Yanomamö are below anyone's definition of poverty if poverty levels are measured in dollars. Yet they can be considered affluent by other measures.

Long-Term Dispersal of Villages

The micro and macro movements of Yanomamö villages distribute the population and the villages thinly over the landscape. Immediate concerns about warfare and alliances tend to fix the villages in relation to each other for a time. The people seek to optimize their garden and village locations by staying as far away as possible from active enemies but close to current allies. With each village move, they also try to remain close to their abandoned gardens, primarily to harvest the peach palm trees. And they do not want to make moves that will entail severe deprivation—such as the extra labor of transporting cuttings a great distance, or a catastrophic flight that may lead to excessive dependence on an ally. Finally, some of the choices, as well as the timing of movements, are a function of the demographic composition of the village, especially the number of active, healthy adult males there will be in the new village.

The longer-term patterns that result from such decisions can be determined only by interviewing scores of old people about all the villages they have lived in during their lifetimes and the major events that transpired there. Two of the most important kinds of events are the enemy-ally patterns and the fissioning of larger groups. This information, when added to the genealogical data that link individual to individual by kinship and marriage ties, results in a settlement history encompassing a number of villages whose members are related historically and genealogically.

The illustration entitled "Long-Term Movements of Seven Yanomamö Groups" shows the historical movements of several blocs of Yanomamö, based on approximately 250 garden relocations, over a period of about 150 years. It is only a fraction of the information on garden relocation in my data files, but it is sufficient to illustrate the dynamic relationship between population growth in local villages and the dispersal of both the populations and the villages into which they subdivide. The figure summarizes this schematically, showing that it is possible to identify discrete population blocs and describe the long-term migration pattern each has followed. The illustration identifies seven such population blocs (labeled A through G). It is possible that as many as thirty or forty blocs could be identified through additional field research along the same lines.

Only two of the seven population blocs are the focus of most of the discussion in this book—the bloc to which Kaobawä's group belongs and the bloc that I have called Shamatari. I have designated Kaobawä's bloc as Namowei-teri, the name of an ancient site where the ancestors of his group and the villages related to his lived more than a hundred years ago.

New Findings on the Migration of Villages

In 1990, 1991, and 1992, I began new field research in several Yanomamö areas I had not been able to visit previously because of the extreme difficulty of reaching them by river or on foot. I finally was able to reach these remote areas via helicopters of the Venezuelan Air Force, and I will be making detailed field studies there over the next few years.

The trips enabled me to spend seven months in villages whose names and residents I had known about only from informants in nearby groups (photo 23). What I learned on the trips gave me new perspectives on Yanomamö settlement patterns and warfare, which I present here as preliminary findings, to be documented more extensively in the field research I am now doing. They are exciting findings, I believe, and will probably help explain why the known

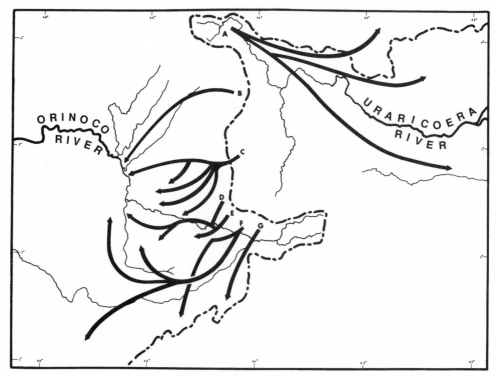

Long-Term Movements of Seven Yanomamö Groups
*The movements of seven groups over a 125-year period. Populations grow and fission
and move into new areas. In time, a given region will have as many as a dozen
interrelated villages that derived from the same mother village many years back.
Kaobawä's population bloc is labeled "D"; his Shamatari neighbors are "F."*

variations in warfare intensity and in fighting over women are so extreme from
one Yanomamö region to another.

On the seven trips I made into these areas in 1990, 1991, and 1992, I used,
for the first time, what are called GPS (global positioning systems) instruments—small, hand-held instruments that receive signals from a network
of satellites launched by the U.S. Department of Defense in the past several
years (photo 24). With the GPS instruments, an object's position (latitude and
longitude) anywhere on the surface of the earth can be pinpointed to within
approximately 30 meters—or within inches, by following a more complex
procedure. Such instruments are rapidly gaining commercial and scientific ap-
plications, for example as precise navigational aids for yachtsmen and in scientific
research focused on remote, poorly mapped areas of the world. For the first
time in my twenty-seven years of field research, I have been able to identify
the actual locations of major rivers, mountains, and, most important, many of

23. *Two Yanomamö headmen from remote Siapa Basin villages I contacted in 1990, the villages of Doshamosha-teri and Shokoburuba-teri. The two men are brothers, and their villages separated from each other in the recent past. I had heard about both these men from the groups I studied in the 1960s, but I did not actually meet them until 1990.*

24. *Taking a GPS fix in a remote Yanomamö village with a Trimble Navigation GPS instrument. Two Yanomamö headmen look on as Charles Brewer-Carías, my Venezuelan collaborator, and I determine the latitude, longitude, and elevation of this village.*

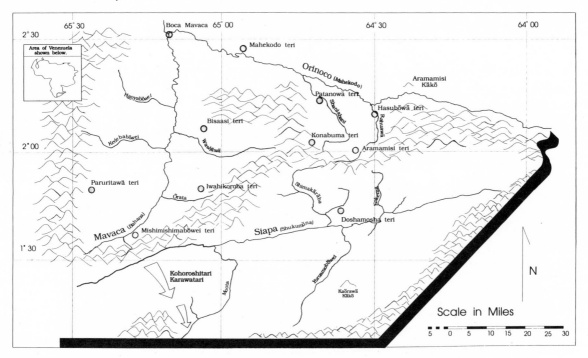

Schematic Map of Important Rivers, Mountains, and Village Locations
in the History of Bisaasi-teri

the 500 or so ancient gardens that were established in the area where Kaobawä's people originated over a century ago.

The map entitled "Schematic Map of Important Rivers, Mountains, and Village Locations in the History of Bisaasi-teri" is a schematic representation (not a geographer's map) of the large area whose current and former residents figure prominently in the history of Kaobawä's village. The Yanomamö population of Brazil and Venezuela is currently estimated to be 20,000. If that is accurate, approximately 25 percent of all the living Yanomamö live now or have recently lived in this region.

In the map, the major rivers—the Orinoco, the Mavaca, and the Siapa —are accurately represented, but the mountainous areas separating them are shown somewhat schematically, for the purpose of clarifying my findings for the reader. In addition, the identifications of the Yanomamö villages are approximations of their location and membership in the recent past, when their present social, political, and military patterns took form. For example, Kaobawä's village is shown as being located in the Mavaca Basin and is identified as Bisaasi-teri. In fact, when he and his immediate ancestors lived in that region, the group contained people who have subsequently fissioned away and are now known by other village names. Similarly, the group shown as Iwähikoroba-teri is today distributed among four different villages in other locations. The same applies to all the other groups shown.

The area has several important geographical and ecological features. First, there are large expanses of low-lying flat plains that are traversed by the three large rivers and their major tributaries. The Yanomamö can easily cross most of the tributaries at most times of the year, but they have considerable difficulty crossing the lower reaches of the Orinoco, the Mavaca, and the Siapa at almost any time of the year. They generally avoided settling in those areas until recent times, when missionaries arrived and introduced canoes, after about 1965. The low, flat areas in regions where the rivers are small and easily crossed are what Kaobawä's people—and many other groups—appear to have favored as their settlement locations for the past hundred years or so. The areas are dotted with more than 500 long-abandoned gardens.

The low-lying areas also appear to be richer than other areas in the kinds of natural resources the Yanomamö traditionally utilize—game animals, plants for food, construction, and manufacturing, and well-drained, easily cultivated land for gardens.

Mountainous terrain and rugged hills lie adjacent to the low-lying lands, and these, too, are occupied by Yanomamö groups. My 1990 and 1991 field research was largely focused on some of the groups living in this very distinct highland ecological zone. In these highland areas, crossing the rugged terrain, making gardens, and finding game animals and other resources are all more difficult. Just collecting firewood and hauling water each day takes much more energy than in the lowlands; the women have to walk up and down steep slopes to get to and from the river or their sources of firewood. And the men, to make the gardens, have to climb up and down the slopes, fell trees on them, pile up the brush there—all much costlier in energy terms than doing the same work on level ground. In general, it is considerably harder to make a living here.

These ecological and geographical differences seem to lie behind the social, political, demographic, and historical differences between the villages of the two areas. One immediately noticeable difference is the size of villages. Almost all those in the lowlands have been larger, occasionally reaching populations of 300 to 400. Mishimishimaböwei-teri, for instance, had nearly 300 residents when I first contacted the village in 1968, and that was shortly after it had fissioned from a group numbering well over 100. By contrast, villages in the rugged foothills and mountainous regions are much smaller, around 40 to 80 people—although, under special circumstances, some occasionally reach 100 people.

A startling discovery was the degree to which violence and warfare—and their consequences—distinguish the highland and lowland groups from each other. Warfare is much more highly developed and chronic in the lowlands. The men of lowland villages act pushy and aggressive; the men from the smaller highland villages seem sedate and gentle. Not unexpectedly, alliance patterns are more elaborate in the lowlands, and dramatic feasts are a regular occurrence, events to which a large group invites its current allies for dining and trading. Larger numbers of abducted women are found in the lowland villages—women taken from weaker neighboring villages and from highland villages. By contrast, highland villages have fewer abducted women, and those they have are usually from other small highland groups, not from the more bellicose, larger, and more powerful lowland villages. In addition, fewer of the adult men in the highland villages are *unokais*, men who have participated in the killing of other men.

While my research in the highland villages is just beginning, I can report a number of preliminary findings for eight villages I worked in during late 1990 and much of 1991. Some of these findings are summarized in the table entitled "Selected Sociodemographic Features of Refugee Villages in the Siapa/Shanishani Drainages." Three of the eight have only recently moved to the highlands from the lowlands, and, for this reason, some of their statistical attributes are possibly artifacts, or remnants, of the conditions they lived in prior to seeking refuge in the highlands or nearby foothills. However, the three villages (numbers 64, 71, and 72 in the table) all have relatively high percentages of *unokais*, compared to their highland neighbors, and one of them has a very high proportion of abducted females. My projected studies of uncontacted highland groups that have lived there a long time are likely to show more dramatic contrasts than I can offer at this early stage.

Some comparative data for the larger villages in the adjacent lowlands are instructive. There, the average percentage of adult males who have participated in the killing of another person is over twice as high (44 percent), but the average number of victims killed per *unokai* is only slightly higher—1.13 in the lowland villages compared to 0.96 in the highlands. The percentage of females who have been abducted is significantly higher in the lowland villages: 17.0 percent, compared to 11.7 percent in the highland villages.

Village	Size	Number Men Polygynous	% Abducted Women	% *Unokai* Men
69	53	1	14.3	7.7
71	43	1	33.3	36.4
64	99	2	14.5	27.6
72	28	1	0.0	57.1
59	81	2	0.0	21.4
57	81	1	15.0	15.4
68	54	1	14.3	0.0
67	40	0	0.0	12.5
Totals:	479	9	—	—
Averages:	59.9	1.1	11.7	21.2

Selected Sociodemographic Features of Refugee Villages
in the Siapa / Shanishani Drainages
Villages pursuing a refugee strategy are generally smaller, have lower rates of
polygynous marriage, and have fewer abducted women and fewer unokais.

Bellicose and Refugee Strategies

My recent field studies have also begun to reveal patterns of settlement location and relocation for both the highland and the lowland villages that seem to be coming together in the following scenario.

Groups that live in the lowlands have to be large and bellicose in order to control the large, desirable, and wide-open ecological niche they live in. They seem to keep their neighbors at a comfortable distance through extremely bellicose strategies that entail frequent raiding and chronic attempts either to abduct women from their neighbors or to coerce weaker neighbors into giving them a larger number of women than they give back via marriage alliances. For the strategies to be effective, they must maximize village size—in numbers there is military strength and credibility. But, since Yanomamö villages can become only so large before they fission—because kinship, descent, and marriage alliance principles seem to set limits on village size and the solidarity required to hold groups together—all the villages eventually subdivide into smaller groups, often making them more vulnerable to their enemies. At that point, several alternatives seem to have been followed among the groups I have studied.

(1) The two newly formed groups live *he borarawä*, that is, they locate their

two new *shabonos* side by side while continuing to maintain their previous gardens. This enables them to act as a unit in military conflicts, but it separates the group into smaller units in which intra-*shabono* arguments and conflicts are greatly reduced. Over time, both groups grow, and they might move farther and farther apart, depending on how many large neighbors they have, who has alliances with whom, and who is actively raiding whom. Some of them become large enough to hold their own against the other large villages of the lowlands.

(2) One or both of the groups become "peripheralized" and have to move out of the more desirable lowlands and into the foothills or the mountains for refuge. They may spend a generation or two there, until political circumstances in the lowlands make it possible for them to return. Meanwhile, their numbers grow, making it increasingly difficult for them to subsist in the less bountiful highlands and, for economic reasons, more logical for them to return to the lowlands. Some of the highland groups I have recently been studying are in this situation today. One of them, the Narimöböwei-teri (indicated on the map on page 104 as the Aramamisi-teri), are living *he borarawä* because their total population, in two groups, has reached approximately 200. They made one attempt to move back into the more productive lowlands, the Siapa Basin in this case, but became embroiled in wars with stronger neighbors and were forced back to the highlands again.

(3) The groups pioneer new, unoccupied areas of nearby lowlands whose ecological features are similar to those of the regions in which they originated. An excellent example is found in the history of the upper Mavaca Basin, shown on the map as being occupied by the Mishimishimaböwei-teri, the Iwähikoroba-teri, and the Paruritawä-teri. These groups all originated in the area along the Orinoco shown as being occupied by the Patanowä-teri, the Hasuböwä-teri, and the Konabuma-teri, and all can be traced back to a single large village. Another example is Kaobawä's group. Forced out of the Patanowä-teri region, it crossed the foothills separating the tributaries of the Mavaca from the tributaries of the Orinoco, especially the branch of the Orinoco indicated as Shanishani. But the group did not remain long in the new area, because of wars with the Iwähikoroba-teri, who also had been expelled from the Shanishani drainage area.

The upper Mavaca River has been the route followed by other Yanomamö groups forced out of the Shanishani drainage area that are only remotely related to the villages shown on the map. Two previous waves of migrants, the Kara-watari and the Kohoroshitari populations, had done the same thing, probably around the turn of the century. Most of the Yanomamö groups living in Brazil immediately to the south of the area covered by the map are contemporary descendants of these two groups; the remainder are recent migrants related to the villages shown—an indication that the migration process from Venezuela to Brazil is still going on.

In a sense, the Shanishani drainage basin appears to have been (and continues to be) some kind of demographic "pump" that spews rapidly growing, relatively warlike groups of Yanomamö into adjacent areas. Those groups that have remained there over long periods of time, such as the Patanowä-teri— represented in 1991 by several large and belligerent groups living close to each other—seem to have managed to do so by adopting a decidedly antagonistic stance toward all their neighbors. The groups that have been forced out appear to fall into two types afterward, in terms of their military attributes. If they are forced into the highlands, they become rather docile, nonmilitant refugees. If they pioneer into the ecologically similar lowlands, they carry on the tradition they know from their past: they continue to be large, militant, and belligerent villages.

A few caveats must be stated regarding this scenario, or model. One is that the Siapa Basin, essentially unexplored and anthropologically unknown at this point, has a number of cultural-ecological peculiarities not found in the Orinoco or Mavaca basins. The most significant of these is that it is approximately 300 to 350 meters *higher* than immediately adjacent areas of the Mavaca and Orinoco drainages—it is a high valley. Thus, while it is large, generally flat, and low-lying, it may not be as ecologically rich as the adjacent drainages, and therefore less desirable as a place to make a living.

I expect to resolve the question during the research I have just initiated, but there are several reasons to suspect that my speculations are correct. One is that, in general, species abundance and diversity tend to diminish with altitude. Because the Siapa Basin is higher, game animals and other useful species might be less abundant here. Groups that migrate into the Siapa Basin seem to remain for relatively short periods, especially in the western portion, where only one village is found today—Yeisikorowä-teri, with a population of approximately 220. And recall that two earlier populations—the Karawatari and the Kohoro-shitari—fled from the Macava Basin but moved far to the south, across this drainage area, to settle in Brazil. A second possible reason that the Yanomamö who have moved into or through the lower Siapa have not remained there might be that the rivers are too large for them to deal with. The Siapa itself, immediately south of the Mavaca headwaters, is a large, fast, and deep river, difficult for the Yanomamö to cross most of the year, and its major tributaries in this general region are also large. However, the upper reaches of the Siapa (starting at and running east from the village shown as Doshamosha-teri) are occupied by a number of Yanomamö villages that have not yet been studied. I will be visiting them to document their political and ecological attributes.

A third reason, also to be explored in my upcoming research, has to do with the outsiders who have moved close to the Yanomamö territory from the Brazilian side, as opposed to those who have moved in from the Venezuelan side. It is possible that the outposts of modern Brazilian culture—missions, government Indian posts, criollo (Creole) communities—were an attraction to the Yanomamö who had penetrated the Siapa from the north. The non-Yanomamö were a source of desirable items like machetes, metal cooking pots, and axes. These items appeared slightly earlier in Brazil than they did in Venezuela, and it is possible that once the Yanomamö in the Siapa Basin discovered these foreigners, the Yanomamö settlement patterns and the direction of their movements were dramatically influenced by them. A gripping story of one person's experiences in this region is that of Helena Valero, a Brazilian girl who was captured by the Kohoroshitari Yanomamö in 1935 just south of the area shown on the map and who spent most of her adult life as their captive, mostly in the Shanishani drainage basin. Her story is recounted by Ettore Biocca in *Yanoáma: The Narrative of a White Girl Kidnapped by Amazonian Indians.*

The area covered by the map, then, contains two broad types of Yanomamö villages. One kind is the traditionally large communities whose members are very bellicose, who have historically been heavily involved in warfare and the coercion or abduction of women from their allies, and whose mortality patterns show a high frequency of death due to violence. Kaobawä's people belong to this group. The second kind might be described as refugees who have fled from the larger groups and sought safety in the rugged highland terrain, where life is more difficult but political security is higher and predation lower. These groups are smaller, less bellicose, and gentler, and they have fewer males who are good warriors, lower rates of polygyny (multiple wives), fewer abducted women, and lower rates of death due to violence.

Anthropologists who work in different regions of the same tribal population frequently report data that show patterns or statistical frequencies that are at variance with each other. Responsible anthropologists generally take these as valid pieces of information that illustrate variabilities within the tribal group—

variabilities that they must explain. For reasons unclear to me, my well-documented statistical information on frequencies of death due to violence and high rates of abductions of females, in an area I have been studying for twenty-seven years, has not been received charitably by some French and Brazilian anthropologists, who subsequently did field research in other Yanomamö areas and found much lower frequencies. A number of these researchers have publicly claimed that I invented the data, exaggerated the violence, or am unable to tell a "symbolic" death from a "real" one. What I believe are the motivations behind such remarks (the tragic events surrounding the 1987 gold rush in Brazil, and the unrealistic "noble savage" view some anthropologists endorse) are discussed at greater length at the end of this book.

If the ecological differences I have been discussing have wider applicability in other Yanomamö areas, many of these disputed variations in levels of violence and warfare may prove to be explainable in long-term cultural-ecological processes.

The "Protein Debate"

My research and publications on the Yanomamö have provoked a number of debates on theoretical issues in anthropology and evolutionary ecology. One such theory, known in anthropology as the "protein hypothesis," argues that the cause of warfare among tribes like the Yanomamö is a shortage of high-quality animal protein; that is, the people suffer from a dietary protein shortage and are fighting over the scarce supply. I disagree with that theory.

Around the time I began my fieldwork with the Yanomamö in the mid-1960s, many anthropologists were endorsing new theories about the interrelationships between ecology and human cultures, theories that were a partial synthesis of anthropology and ecology, which is a biological science. One of the central anthropological questions in this synthesis was to find an explanation of the causes of tribal warfare.

One reasonable assumption behind the synthesis was that because the material resources on which all forms of life depend are finite, an abundance or shortage of particular material resources must play some kind of role in any explanations of human social behavior. This much I agreed with; indeed, this assumption lay behind the design of my research when I first arrived to study the Yanomamö. I soon had to modify my thinking, however, for I quickly discovered that Yanomamö conflicts were frequently provoked by sexual jealousy, illicit affairs, infidelity, and other matters having to do with sex. I concluded that my anthropological colleagues were borrowing only half of the toolbox of ecological theory and ignoring the half that dealt with reproductive competition—competition over members of the opposite sex. I decided to borrow the *whole* tool kit from ecology, including theories about both material resources and sexual competition. It was as if these colleagues were trying to calculate the area of a rectangle from its height alone, while ignoring its width.

To them, contesting violently over women evidently seemed inadmissible in explanations of warfare or fighting—women were not material resources. Women and men as organisms were too biological, and apparently biological factors were not valid explanations of cultural phenomena. One distinguished anthropologist with whom I was corresponding after I published some of my early papers said, in one letter, "Women? Fighting over women? Gold and diamonds I can understand, but women? Never."

As the synthesis developed, I would summarize it in this argument: In the Amazon tropical forests, large game animals and large herds of them were scarce and were easily eradicated by hunting. The Amazon Indians probably did not have enough protein in their diets, and somehow they knew that they needed it. Therefore, if there was fighting among them, and if fighting is a conflict over shortages of a material resource, and if protein in the form of game animals is in short supply, the fighting and warfare must be a competition over protein. The conclusion was that the Yanomamö were short of protein. The supporters of this theory went so far as to argue that other tribal institutions, such as female infanticide, were related to the protein shortage; by destroying female babies at birth, the population could be kept from growing larger than its available protein resources could sustain.

As my work became more widely known, it became more and more a noisome problem for the advocates of this theory. I was seemingly becoming some sort of villain to those who believed that the only scientific explanation for warfare among Amazon natives was that they were fighting over dwindling protein resources—a materialist explanation.

So prominent did this debate become in anthropological circles, in part because of my work (or an alleged lack of proper focus in my work), that in 1974 I made the investigation of Yanomamö protein consumption one of the prime objectives of a major four-year research project. I recruited three graduate students, gave them six months of special training at my university, obtained for each one about $20,000 in research support, brought in as advisers two consultants who were both familiar with and sympathetic to the protein hypothesis, and accompanied them all right to the Yanomamö villages they would be working in. The students were to collect data on several issues central to the project, the results of which we would publish as coauthors, and would also collect data for their own Ph.D. dissertations. I even provided them with all the genealogies and ID photographs I had of the people they were to live with.

On the day before our departure for Venezuela, we met in New York with the principal and most vociferous anthropological champion of the protein theory, Marvin Harris, then of Columbia University, and several of his protégés. We discussed what kind of data would be needed to prove that one of us was wrong. My hope was to settle the issue scientifically. Harris declared that if the Yanomamö could be shown to consume 30 grams of protein per person per day, he would "eat his hat." We left for the field the next day.

A large number of astonishing incidents—defections, denunciations, lies, unprofessionalism, chicanery, dirty tricks, and so on—happened after that, a few of which are still going on, and I will address them elsewhere.

As it turned out, the Yanomamö had very adequate levels of protein intake, as did many other tropical forest peoples who were subsequently investigated. Ironically, the data accumulated so far on human protein consumption seem to indicate that if one insists on a narrow cause-effect relationship between warfare intensity and protein consumption, a much stronger case could be made that those peoples who have the highest levels of protein consumption are the ones who are most warlike.

My position was that warfare was too complex a problem to reduce to a single cause, like an alleged protein shortage, and that many variables had to be considered. Harris did not eat his hat: he changed his position. After our data were published, he argued that he had not really meant to say that the Yanomamö were suffering from a protein deficiency as such (though his published statements were quite clear on that point); what he had meant to say was that they *perceived* that they had a shortage of protein. He basically recast his position into an untestable form: if they are fighting, and if it can be shown that they have lots of protein in their diet, they must be fighting because they perceive that what they have is not enough.

When I explained to the Yanomamö what Harris had said about the causes of their fighting—that they fought over animal protein, or meat—they looked incredulously at each other. Then one of them said, "*Yahi yamakö buhii makuwi, suwä käbä yamakö buhii baröwo* [Even though we like meat, we like women a whole lot more]."

During the period when the debate was in full swing, I stopped publishing anything on Yanomamö infanticide. I did so because a Venezuelan official had only recently learned that there were Indians in her country who occasionally killed babies, and she wanted a full investigation to determine the identities of the culprits and punish them for murder. I was asked to file an official statement with the government about Yanomamö infanticide, and I said in it, very truthfully, that I had not actually seen a Yanomamö woman kill a baby. Marvin Harris has taken my subsequent silence on this topic as concealing data that support his theory. Let me simply suggest that few biologists or ecologists can seriously believe that a woman would take the life of her infant in order to make the jungle more abundant in monkeys or peccaries so that some future Yanomamö would have more protein.

In 1985, Ray Hames, one of the three graduate students on the project, who was then an anthropology professor (and is now the director of the Cultural Anthropology Program of the National Science Foundation), and I were visiting with a Ye'kwana Indian who had grown up in a village that included both Yanomamö and his own people. He was fluent in the Yanomamö language and knew their culture intimately. He knew nothing of the "protein debate." As we spoke (in Spanish), he told us about having recently attended an anthropology conference in Caracas at which Jacques Lizot, a French anthropologist, had given a paper on the causes of Yanomamö warfare. He was unaware that I knew Lizot, who disagrees with many of my theoretical positions. He said he had listened intently to the paper, but was surprised and disappointed when Lizot finished. The paper was supposed to be about the causes of Yanomamö fighting and warfare, and he had been waiting for Lizot's explanation, which, to him, never came. He said he was embarrassed to ask a question, because his Spanish was not sophisticated, but he could not let the topic end where Lizot had left it. He nervously got up, raised his hand, and was permitted to speak. He said something like "I was very impressed with all of Lizot's sophisticated words and sayings, but he missed the most important thing. What he forgot to say is that the Yanomamö fight over sex and women."

While this is not the whole answer, it is a big part of it—so large a part that it is ludicrous to claim, as some of my anthropological critics do, that it is irrelevant.

It is also a major cause of fighting in our own culture. Some Saturday night just visit a hard-hat bar where fights are frequent. What are the fights usually about? Are they about the amount of meat in someone's hamburger? Or study the words of a dozen country-and-western songs. Do any of them say, "Don't take your cow to town?"

Chapter Three

Myth and Cosmos

The simplicity of the Yanomamö's material culture contrasts sharply with the richness and ingenuity of their beliefs about the cosmos, the soul, the mythical world, and the plants and animals around them. One fascinating dimension of their intellectual world is the extent to which individuals can manipulate and elaborate on ideas and themes, although within certain limits demanded by orthodoxy and by local versions of the Truth. Not only can individuals experiment as artists and creators, but there is room for poetic and literary expression as well.

Despite the lack of a written language, the Yanomamö language affords them considerable leeway in turning a clever phrase or stating something in a sophisticated manner. Some of them play with their rich language and work at being what we might call literary or learned. The conception of primitive peoples as having gruntlike languages whose small vocabularies require lots of hand gestures is far wide of the mark. The working vocabulary of most Yanomamö individuals is probably much larger than the working vocabulary of most people in our own culture (usually no more than 6,000 or 7,000 words). While it is true that the number of words in the English vocabulary greatly exceeds the number in the Yanomamö vocabulary, it is also true that we know fewer of them than they do of theirs. If you do not have a written language, you have to store more in your head. One might even suggest that our possession of writing and dictionaries has made us lazy, for we can always look it up and don't have to remember it. In this context, the often heard Yanomamö comment that "I possess the Truth" makes a great deal of sense. To make the point as a Yanomamö might, if we're so smart, why don't we have a word for that part of the body between the forearm and the bicep, rather than saying "inside the elbow." The same for the "back of the knee." I can't imagine words that would be more useful.

The Yanomamö have a rich vocabulary and a complex language, and they

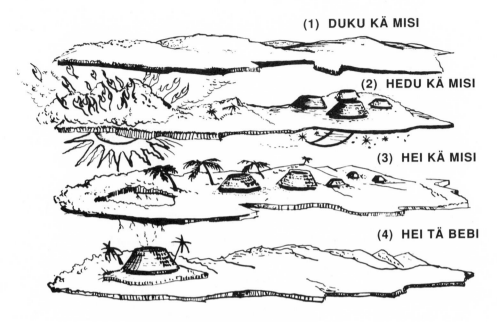

(1) DUKU KÄ MISI

(2) HEDU KÄ MISI

(3) HEI KÄ MISI

(4) HEI TÄ BEBI

The Yanomamö Cosmos

delight in making poetic use of them in their marvelous stories and sagas of the cosmos and humanity's place in it.

The Cosmos

The illustration entitled "The Yanomamö Cosmos" depicts four parallel layers, lying horizontally and separated by an undefined but relatively small space. The layers of this cosmos are something like inverted dinner platters—gently curved, round, thin, rigid, and with a top and a bottom surface. The edges of some of the layers are thought to be "rotten" and rather fragile, as if to walk on them might be like walking on the roof of a deteriorating building where your feet periodically sink through. Many magical things happen out in this region, a mysterious and dangerous netherland dominated by spirits. The best geographers and sailors in our own recent historical past had conceptions not markedly different. Magellan was mightily relieved when his ships didn't fall off the edge of a supposedly flat earth some 475 years ago.

The uppermost layer of the four (there might be more, according to some Yanomamö) is thought to be "pristine" or "tender": *duku kä misi*. At present this layer is void (*broke*), but many things originated there in the distant past —in the Yanomamö cosmos, things tend to fall or descend downward to a lower layer. Sometimes the uppermost layer is described by the term "old woman," like the abandoned, nonproducing gardens. This layer does not play much of a role in the everyday life or thoughts of the Yanomamö, not even in their shamanism or myths. It is just there, having once had some vague function.

The next layer down is called *hedu kä misi*, the sky layer. The top surface of *hedu* is invisible but is believed to be similar to earth—it has trees, gardens, villages, animals, plants, and, most important, the souls of the deceased Yanomamö, who are in some sense similar to mortals. They garden, hunt, make love, eat, and practice witchcraft on each other. Everything that exists on earth has its counterpart in *hedu*, as if *hedu* were a mirror image of human life.

The underneath surface of *hedu* is what we on earth actually see—the visible sky. Stars and planets are somehow attached to this surface and move across it on their individual trails, east to west. Some Yanomamö think the stars are fish, but their astronomical ideas are undeveloped and they have nothing that we would call named constellations. The underside of *hedu* is conceived to be relatively close to the earth, for I was repeatedly asked if I bumped into it when I was in an airplane. (Airplanes were only rarely seen in 1964, when I began my fieldwork, for there were no airstrips in the upper Orinoco region at that time. Today planes and helicopters are commonly seen, even in the most remote villages.)

Humans—Yanomamö—dwell on what is called "this layer," or *hei kä misi*. "This layer" was created when a chunk of *hedu* broke off and fell down. As everyone can plainly see, "this layer" has jungle, rivers, hills, animals, plants, gardens, and so on, and it is occupied by people who are slightly different variants of the Yanomamö and speak a dialect of Yanomamö that is "crooked," or wrong. Even the non-Yanomamö here (*nabä* or, in some dialects in Brazil, *kraiwä*) are believed to dwell in *shabonos*, for foreigners are thought to be nothing but degenerate copies of the real humans, the Yanomamö. In fact, the Yanomamö thought I was a reincarnated version of a Yanomamö, and they frequently asked if I had drowned and come back to life. The logic behind the question was that in one of their myths a great flood had occurred, and some Yanomamö had escaped drowning by grabbing onto logs. They floated downstream, were not seen again, and presumably had perished. But some are now returning, floating on logs (canoes), who look different and speak "crooked"—foreigners. A spirit named Omawä fished them out of the water downstream, wrung them out, brought them back to life, and is returning them home.

Finally, there is the surface below "this layer," the *hei tä bebi*, which is almost barren. A peculiar variant of Yanomamö live here, a people called Amahiri-teri. They originated a long time ago when a piece of *hedu* broke off, crashed down to "this layer," knocking a hole in it, and continued to fall. The piece hit "this layer" at the place where the Amahiri-teri lived and carried them and their village down with it. Unfortunately, only the garden and the *shabono* of the Amahiri-teri were carried down, but not the jungle where they hunted. Thus, they have no game animals and have turned into cannibals. They send their spirits up to "this layer" to capture the souls of children, which are carried down and eaten. In some Yanomamö villages, the shamans contest regularly with the Amahiri-teri, attempting to thwart their cannibalistic incursions.

The Yanomamö have an almost morbid fear of becoming cannibals. It is almost as though they think humans are close to having an inherent predisposition to devour members of their own species, an act they find repugnant but a possibility that is very real to them and therefore must be constantly opposed. Whenever I was hunting with them and we shot a tapir, I would cut off a thick juicy slice of tenderloin and fry myself a rare-cooked steak dripping with delicious red juice. This so disgusted the Yanomamö that they could not even watch me eat, and they would accuse me of wanting to become a cannibal or a jaguar, which to them is a disgusting eater of raw human flesh. For their part, they overcook their meat so badly that one can almost drive nails with it.

The Amahiri-teri lived at the time of the *no badabö*, the original humans. These original humans are distinct from living humans in that they were part spirit and part human, and most were also part animal—many of the myths explain how the transformation into humans occurred. When the original people died, they turned into spirits, or *hekura*. The term *no badabö* means "those who are now dead." In the context of myth and stories of the cosmos, it means "the original humans" or "those who were here in the beginning of time."

Myths

The Beginning of Time and the No Badabö

It is almost impossible for the Yanomamö to explain how the first beings were created. They seem to assume that the cosmos began with them already present. Most of the *no badabö* had specific roles in the creative events that transpired after they were in existence—events that, for example, explain the origin of certain animals or plants. The *no badabö* figure prominently in these myths, and many bear the names of plants and animals, both useful ones and those of little consequence. The *no badabö* are the spirits of these living things, although there is little correlation between the mythical importance of some of the spirits and the usefulness of the plant or animal whose name they bear.

Some of the characters in Yanomamö myths are downright hilarious, and some of the things they have done are funny, ribald, and extremely entertaining to the Yanomamö. They love to listen to the men telling stories as they prance around the village, "tripping out" on their hallucinogens and adding comical twists and nuances, to the sidesplitting delight of the audience. Everybody knows, for example, how Iwäriwä (Caiman Ancestor) was tricked into sharing his fire with everyone—an obscene act made him laugh, and the fire escaped from his mouth. That part of the story cannot be changed. But the description of the act, what gestures and comments he made, his tone of voice, and other details are subject to considerable poetic license, and it is this that entertains and amuses the listener. Occasionally an inspired narrator will go beyond what is acceptable, a violation that his own villagers might good-naturedly forgive but that people in another village might not. I realized this when I tape-recorded some of the narratives and invited people in other villages to comment on them. "He's got it wrong. He's lying. It wasn't that way at all," they would complain, adding that if I wanted the Truth I should ask them. Usually the degree of objection was related to the degree of contempt they held for the other village—war and the orthodoxy of myth run on parallel lines. Most of it was simple ethnocentrism and chauvinism: nobody does anything as well as "my people," a sentiment all peoples exhibit to some degree.

With a filmmaking colleague, Timothy Asch, I have produced several films that record the telling of specific myths and the variants of some of them. The films capture something of the humor and wit of the storyteller, not to mention the humorous content of the myths themselves. They also reveal the high dramaturgical skills of a storyteller like Kaobawä and illustrate how different the impact of a documentary film is, as compared to the written word. It would be very difficult to capture the humor, subtlety, and wittiness of Yanomamö myths without using motion-picture film, a distortion of reality no more severe than writing the myths down on paper. Advocates of the latter are sometimes too quick to criticize the use of film as a distortion. While we have filmed a large number of myths, only a few of them have been included in final films as yet. I am therefore focusing here on themes and stories that are not available in the finished films.

Sex plays a large part in Yanomamö myths—general relationships between men and women, on the one hand, and their biological attributes, on the other. Sex is also an important part of everyday life among the Yanomamö, as it is elsewhere, and much of their humor, insults, fighting, storytelling, and conceptions about humans revolves around sexual themes. If I were to illustrate the dictionary I have been patiently compiling on my field trips, it would be, as one of my graduate students once commented, very good pornography. The Eskimos are said to have thousands of words for snow, the point being that a culture's vocabulary often reflects what is important in that culture, and one would expect the Eskimos to have a lot of words for snow. The Yanomamö, of course, have no words for snow, but if one had a dictionary of the Yanomamö language, one would have no difficulty concluding that sex is their equivalent of snow.

The stories of the *no badabö* provide a good sampling of the wit, humor, and themes of Yanomamö intellectual life. Some of the stories seem to have morals or lessons, and others purport to explain or justify why things are as they are in the real Yanomamö world today. Still others seem to have no discernible point, such as the simple story of the Armadillo Ancestor and the Jaguar Ancestor exchanging their sets of teeth, which reverses their roles and their original natures.

One of the themes that crops up regularly has to do with relations between men and women. The Yanomamö consider men not only different from women but superior to them in some regards—an idea that is not unique to the Yanomamö. And, as is sometimes found in the myths of other peoples, a peculiar intellectual struggle is implicit in such myths. Claude Lévi-Strauss, the eminent French anthropologist who devoted much of his brilliant career to the study of mythical themes as a key to how the human mind works, dealt repeatedly with the male-female problem in his writings. To him, the problem was broader than just the relationship between the sexes; it had to do with the working out via myths of certain irreconcilable human beliefs and concerns. The distinguished British anthropologist Edmund Leach assessed Lévi-Strauss's views in a masterly summary that ran something as follows: We often phrase, in ideological terms, the general proposition that men and women are more or less equal, no matter what other beliefs and attitudes we might have about the relative importance of males and females. But we also explicitly condemn the practice of incest within the nuclear family. We have in these two statements the making of a contradiction that is hard to avoid and difficult to reconcile. If men and women are in fact equal, they must have parents who are equal. Most creation stories begin with two individuals whose offspring people the earth, but the only way those first two can be absolutely equal is if they are siblings, are brother and sister. If they are brother and sister, then all humans are the consequence of an original act of incest, of a brother and a sister mating. That is pretty distasteful in most cultures, but only some of them solve the problem by having separate creation myths for women and for men. It avoids the incest problem, but it runs smack into a different one: if they are created separately, they are not absolutely equal.

That is how the Yanomamö have solved the problem: they have separate origin myths for women. Leach points out that our Bible opts for the other solution: Eve was created from a portion of Adam's body, his rib, and then the pair set about creating the rest of us. A pre-biblical account might have been chosen but wasn't—the legend that Adam set about his procreative work with a mate named Lilith, who was part human and part fabulous animal. As the Leach summary concludes, the authors of Genesis had a tough choice, but they gave us the incest version.

One of the Yanomamö myths on the creation—the story of Moon-blood—is itself ambiguous, for some Yanomamö claim that only men were created, and others say that both men and women were. In the Moonblood story, one of the Ancestors shot Moon in the belly. His blood fell to earth and changed into men, but men who were inherently *waiteri*, or fierce. Where the blood was the thickest, the men were especially ferocious and nearly exterminated each other. Where only droplets of blood fell or where the blood became mixed with water, the men fought less and did not kill each other—that is, their inherent violence seemed to be more controllable. Because of Moon's blood, however, all humans are *waiteri*. The "time of Moonblood" is a phrase the Yanomamö frequently use to indicate something like "the beginning of time." In collecting genealogies, I would eventually get to the most distant ancestor known to my informant, and further questioning would often be met by this answer: "Whaa! Those people lived at the time of Moonblood," or too far in the past for anyone to know.

Those Yanomamö who maintain that only males came from the blood of Moon say that females came from a kind of fruit called *wabu*. The males created by Moon's blood, having no women with whom to copulate, were very horny. They went out collecting vines one day, and as they were pulling them from the trees the headman noticed that one of the vines had a newly opened *wabu* fruit attached to it. The fruit had what appeared to be eyes. The headman thought to himself, "Ummm, I'll bet that's what women look like," and he tossed the fruit to the ground. It changed immediately into a woman, who developed a large vagina. The men continued collecting vines, not aware that the fruit had turned into a woman. As they dragged the vines home, the woman, keeping her distance, would step on the ends of the vines whenever she caught the men off guard, but would hide behind a tree when they turned around to look. Finally she stood on one of the vines, bringing the men to a halt. They turned and saw her. They were startled to see that she had a vagina—a long and extremely hairy (*weshi*) one. They stared at it and were overcome with lust. They rushed to her, and all took a turn at copulating frantically with her. They brought her back to the village and let all the men there have a turn. Eventually she had a baby—a daughter—and then another and another. As the daughters came out, all the men copulated with them, and eventually there was an abundance of females, all descended from the *wabu* fruit. And that is why there are so many Yanomamö today.

Jaguar Myths

A theme that appears repeatedly in Yanomamö myths is Man's relationship to Jaguar. In earthly form, the jaguar is an awesome and much feared beast. It is as good a hunter as the Yanomamö are, and is one of the few animals in the forest that hunts and kills humans—as the Yanomamö themselves do in their wars. The jaguar is in that sense like men, but, unlike men, it is part of Nature, not Culture. The distinction is fundamental in Yanomamö thought, for the Yanomamö hold themselves apart from the animals, pointing out, as proudly as we do, that humans have Culture and the animals do not. It is another instance of their division of the world into *urihi tä rimö* ("of the forest") and *yahi tä rimö* ("of the village"); the former are Nature, the latter Culture.

It is tempting to speculate about the nearly universal distribution of this nature-culture opposition. Where does it come from and what does it mean? Too often, the concepts appear to be fixed at two opposing poles, rather than being viewed as on a continuous scale of "more natural" or "more cultural." There is probably no one reading this who has not been confronted with arguments pitting learning against instinct or the cultural against the biological. The polarization is "in our heads," and it takes considerable effort to translate it into something more sophisticated than a simple Culture-versus-Nature dichotomy. There is considerable evidence that cultures must be very special and work very hard to break down the dichotomy. Cultural anthropologists in particular seem to have a severe case of being in the grip of the dichotomy; most are adamantly opposed to using biological concepts to help understand human behavior, which they take to be completely determined by culture and education.

Be that as it may, the Yanomamö pit Culture against Nature, as we often do, and in many contexts they see the cosmos as an either-or division into equal halves. An animal killed in the wild is "of the forest," but when brought alive into the village, it becomes "of the village" and somehow different, for it is then part of Culture. For the Yanomamö, to eat forest animals that have become pets—such as monkeys, birds, and rodents—would be an act similar to cannibalism: eating something "cultural" and therefore humanlike. Nothing disgusted the Yanomamö more than my casual comments on our eating of domestic animals like cattle and sheep, and many a missionary gave up in frustration any attempts to raise chickens at the mission posts and expect the Yanomamö to eat them. The Yanomamö liked the roosters because they crowed at dawn and kept them for that aesthetic reason (if they kept them at all), but they refused to kill and eat a rooster. It was "of the village" and part of Culture. They did, however, have a different attitude toward hens' eggs and ate them with gusto, for the eggs were not quite the same as the chickens they produced. It is like the attitude many of us display when we discuss the moral and legal implications of abortion: we regard the fetus as different from the human being it will become, and in some circles we are prepared to treat it differently in law and in medical practice.

The jaguar is an ambiguous creature to the Yanomamö, for it combines several human capacities but at the same time is part of Nature. It is almost as if they both respect and fear jaguars, and this dual nature might be the kind of contradiction that Lévi-Strauss had in mind in his view of myths as the intellectual vehicle through which such contradictions are reconciled. The many stories the Yanomamö have about jaguars all seem to make the point, in one way or another, that Man is ultimately the master over Jaguar and can outwit him. Jaguar is usually portrayed as large, clumsy, stupid, and bungling, even if that is not so in real life.

Indeed, the Yanomamö are terrified at the prospect of having to spend a night in the jungle without fire, for they know that jaguars often hunt at night and that they are no match for the beasts then. I was awakened many times by villagers begging me to go looking for someone who had failed to return by dark. They knew the person had no fire drill or matches and were worried that jaguars might kill and eat him. I would have to take them out in my canoe, with flashlights, to find the wayward traveler, who was always grateful that we had found him before the jaguars did. I know how they feel, for I myself was stalked a number of times by jaguars, and on one occasion was nearly a meal for one. It had walked into our camp at about three A.M., after the fire had gone out, and was sniffing at me. Fortunately, one of my guides, who had my flashlight, awoke and shone the light on the beast, which retreated quickly into the jungle as the guides hissed frantically into my ear, "Jaguar! Jaguar! Jaguar!" It is a Yanomamö word that I will never forget, for the hot breath and the fearsome size of the animal are forever linked in my mind with its name, *öra*. Jaguars are also occasional daylight hunters. In August 1990, a large male attacked a party of armed Yanomamö men in the village I was then studying and killed three of them before a single arrow could be fired. He dragged one of them off and ate most of him before the others found the body and cremated what was left. Several years earlier, a crazed jaguar walked into a large Yanomamö village and attacked in broad daylight. The men speared him to death with bowstaves before he could kill anyone, but he left a lot of ugly claw scars behind.

The mythic Jaguar, however, is consistently portrayed as a stupid brute, constantly being outwitted by Man and subjected to scathing, ridiculous, and offensive treatment. But some stories are more oblique than others in this regard.

In the story of the jaguar named Kashahewä, or sometimes Hoo, he is destroyed by men using a palm-wood club called *himo*. Such clubs, long, heavy, and sharpened at the upper edges, are made from a dense, black, heavy palm wood called *shidibasi*. The circular shaft is slightly thicker than a broom handle for most of its length, but it widens at the top into a kind of skinny canoe paddle with very sharp edges. The Yanomamö sometimes have duels with these clubs, which can deal a severe and often fatal blow because of their weight and sharpness; the idea is to hit the opponent on the head with the sharp edges forward.

In one story in which Jaguar is known as Hoo, he had already exterminated most of humankind. An old man in one of the remaining villages was asleep, snoring loudly. Jaguar entered the village and carried off his son, who screamed that Jaguar was treating him like a common game animal. The members of the village—Shidibasi-teri (from the wood used in the club)—decided to go with a *himo* club to their neighbors, the Beribosihi-teri, knowing that Jaguar had been devouring them. When they got there, they found that the village had already been wiped out by Jaguar and that enormous buzzards were finishing off the human remains that Jaguar had left. It was growing dark, and they became frightened. They fled to a nearby tree and climbed it, for they heard Jaguar roaring and whining in the jungle. At the top of the tree, an *arausi*, they scraped the bark off the trunk, got out their fire drill and set the bark afire, attached the fire to the tree, and sat in the highest branches to wait for Jaguar.

The brother-in-law of the man whose son was taken had the *himo* club. He also had a vine hammock, slung between the branches, and stood in it watching for Jaguar. (Only in a myth can one stand in a hammock to swing a club.) Jaguar arrived, sniffed around, and started to climb the tree. When he got near the top, the man with the club walloped him soundly on the head, forcing him out of the tree and knocking him unconscious. When Jaguar regained consciousness, he climbed up again, and again he was clouted on the head with the *himo* club. Up and down, up and down, all night long. Meanwhile, the men huddled close around the fire and blew on it to keep it burning. Jaguar could not make them out and climbed close, peering at them, perhaps blinded by the fire. They smacked him with the club, and he fell to the ground. Near dawn, Jaguar climbed the tree once more. He got almost up to the men and stretched his claws out toward them. They hit him on the bridge of his nose with the sharp edge of the *himo* club. He fell again and lay motionless. It got light and the forest was absolutely silent. Jaguar did not move. One of the men climbed down cautiously and examined Jaguar to see if he was breathing. Blood was oozing from his nostrils, and bees were beginning to come for the blood. "Whaaa! He is dead. We got him," the men exclaimed, and with that they departed. And that is how the people of Palm-wood Village got Jaguar with a palm-wood club.

In another story, Jaguar had not yet come around to eating humans—he acquired the taste gradually. The story is interesting as well in that it tells of red peppers being used as a sort of chemical weapon. The tactic is also described by the early Spaniards, who observed tropical forest peoples smoking out their enemies by burning red peppers upwind of them; the drifting smoke and toxic vapors would drive the coughing and gagging residents from their village. The present Yanomamö do not use red peppers in this fashion, but the myth indicates that they are fully aware of its potential.

Jaguar's name keeps changing, and in this story it is either Käyäkäyä or Kräyäkräyä. In the story, Jaguar's son-in-law (or nephew) actually began the dastardly practice of eating humans. And, since Jaguar mysteriously becomes human, it is in fact an act of cannibalism. The son-in-law, Siroroma, saw some humans out hunting one day. He caught some game, approached the wife of one of the humans, and gave her the meat. Then he copulated with her and got her pregnant. Her husband began to suspect that he had not caused the pregnancy and grew very suspicious. His wife told him that a bird named Kawamari had given her the meat, for she wanted to conceal the fact that she was pregnant by a jaguar. The husband went hunting, and when he returned, he discovered that his wife had more meat—another turkey. "What the hell is going on here?" he said to himself. He began watching her more carefully, and eventually he heard a noise in the forest. It was Jaguar's son-in-law, Siroroma. The husband immediately concluded, "Haaa! He's the one who has gotten her pregnant." The husband decided to get rid of Siroroma and spent all day collecting firewood. He made a huge bonfire in the village, and then he approached Siroroma, grabbed him in a tight bear hug, and threw him into the fire to roast. But Siroroma turned into a liquid and quenched the fire. Then he attacked the husband, squirting a stinging liquid into his eyes in the form of spit. The husband was blinded and fled in agony, rubbing his hands in his eyes. Siroroma, scorched by the fire, peeled off his skin with his fingernails, skinning himself on the spot. He took his own pelt home and hung it on his roof, where it hangs to this day.

Siroroma looked very different with no skin, of course. Seeing him, his father-in-law (uncle), Jaguar, thought, "Hooo! My nephew has sent a wild pig home for me to eat." Not knowing he was eating his own son-in-law, Jaguar devoured Siroroma and so developed a voracious craving for flesh. He decided to hunt only this kind of game, and from then on Jaguar hunted humans. But the humans soon caught on to his appetites and tried to stay out of his way.

Jaguar took to living in caves, where he reared his family and fed them on human flesh.

One day Jaguar went to a village called Wayorewä-teri, in the mountains, singing his hunting song as he approached—"Käyäkäyä, Käyäkäyä, Käyäkä-yä. . . ." In the village, he found that all the adults were gone. They were off hunting for *naö* fruits far away. Only an old woman, many children, and one pubescent girl going through her first menses confinement were there. Jaguar asked the old woman for water and complained, when he got it, that it was stagnant. The old woman, the mother of the pubescent girl, was feeling sorry for the girl, because she knew that the girl was hungry but could not eat because of the menstrual taboos. Jaguar set his pack basket down, and the children grew apprehensive. He asked the old woman why there were no adults around and was told that they were out foraging for wild foods.

The story becomes very funny here, but there is no way to convey the sophistication of the humor in a literal English translation. I will change the names of the fruits and animals, to make them recognizable—at the expense of accuracy. I will also change a few of the body parts, for the Yanomamö have a different view than we do of what parts are important. (The liver is more important to them than the heart, but, for example, "liverthrob" doesn't come across as well as "heartthrob" in a romantic passage, and "my liver and shadow" doesn't mean to us what "my heart and soul" does.) In addition, there is no way to easily render the allusions to the forehead and the complexion that appear in Yanomamö insults. These are the foulest of insults in their lan-guage—like our saying "Fuck you."

Jaguar proceeded to address the old woman, insulting her viciously with his caustic remarks.

"What kinds of food are they seeking?" Jaguar asked.

"They went collecting peaches," said the old woman.

"Hrumph! That will cause them to have fuzz all over their asses if they do that," said Jaguar.

"Well, they also mentioned that they wanted hard-shell crabs," said the old woman.

"Hrumpf! Their tits will turn into armor plating if they eat them," said Jaguar.

"Well, they also were after crayfish," said the old woman.

"Hrumpf! Their peckers will turn pink and curl up if they eat any of them," said Jaguar.

"And they wanted to catch a few bullhead fish as well," said the old woman.

"Hrumpf! That will cause them to have stringy tentacles growing from their foreheads," said Jaguar.

"Moreover, they plan to catch some striped fish," added the old woman.

"Hrumpf! Their skins will be striped like zebras if they eat them," said Jaguar.

"Some said they wanted a few eggplants," said the old woman.

"Hrumpf! They'll break their assholes trying to pass an eggplant," said Jaguar.

The old woman went to the river to get Jaguar some fresh water, leaving the pubescent girl and the children unattended. While the old woman was gone, Jaguar entered the girl's puberty hut and killed her. The old woman heard a noise and hastily returned, asking what the noise was. "I was just fanning the fire," Jaguar lied. Satisfied, the woman left, and Jaguar immediately set upon the children, killing them as fast as he could catch them and stacking their tiny corpses in his pack basket. He thought he had them all and was about to leave when he noticed two strange-looking creatures. They were children, too, but with their heads shaved clean because of lice. Jaguar, not very perceptive, thought they were dogs and decided to bring them along as pets. He put them in his basket on top of the dead children and left for his cave.

As he got close to the cave, he passed under a vine. The older of the two children grabbed the vine and swung off into the trees. Jaguar noticed the sudden change in the weight of his load and stopped. He tried to entice the child down, but the child would not come, so Jaguar left him there and went on to his cave. (Jaguar's cave was actually an armadillo den—recall the story about Jaguar and Armadillo exchanging teeth.) He entered the cave with his basket of dead children and began distributing them among his kinsmen.

The child who had escaped into the trees fled home and told the adults what had happened. The adults decided to go after Jaguar and kill him. They collected large amounts of red peppers and termite nest material, mixed these together, and set off for Jaguar's den. There, they covered all the entrances with dirt and brush, put the mixture of peppers and termite nest material at the entrances, and lit it. Inside the den, Jaguar was distributing the meat. "Ahhh! Father has brought us some wild pigs," exclaimed Jaguar's children. (Other tribes in the South American tropical forest use the term "wild pigs" as a euphemism for humans when they go off on war parties.) Jaguar's family then cooked and ate the dead children. As they were sucking the marrow from the bones and passing morsels back and forth—"This is for your sister." "This is for your brother-in-law." "This is for your mother."—the adults outside were blowing acrid smoke into the cave. Jaguar's family began to choke and cough. There was smoke everywhere, and they grew delirious and screamed in pain from the red-pepper smoke burning their lungs. Soon they were all dead, and flashes of lightning came from the entrances to the den.

A giant basket remained on the mountain, like the one Jaguar carried the dead children in, with many red peppers growing around it. The basket made noises like the spirits do: "Dei! Dei! Dei! Dei!" That is the story of how Kräyäkräyä began to eat humans. Today, when the Yanomamö chant to the spirits, only the spirits of the Kräyäkräyä come, for the original ones—the *no badabö*—were all exterminated by the poisonous fumes.

The story that best captures the cynicism and ambiguity the Yanomamö have for Jaguar is the poignant story of *misi*, the tortoise. Tortoises and turtles are virtually helpless, of course, when their feet are off the ground. Some South American Indian groups "store" turtle meat by capturing large numbers of the creatures, turning them upside down, and leaving them to squirm helplessly until it is time to kill and cook them. *Misi* was similarly helpless in the story, but it has a different ending.

The Original Beings from the village of Manakae-teri were traveling through the forest, hunting and collecting. They were delighted when they came upon a tortoise: it would be their pet, their "dog." Little did they know that Jaguar was systematically exterminating everyone and that they would soon become his victims. When Jaguar neared their village, they fled. But before they went, they tied *misi*, their tortoise, to a vine and suspended him from the roof, as they always did with special possessions, to keep them dry and clean. Dangling from the cord, the helpless *misi* was unable to do anything but move his legs and head randomly and ineffectually. Jaguar entered the deserted village looking for someone to eat. He slowly wandered around the periphery, but the houses were empty. Then he came to the house where *misi* was dangling from the rafters. *Misi*'s head waved from side to side, and he was making a pathetic noise that sounded like "beek, beek, beek. . . ." Jaguar approached to sniff at him, and *misi* grabbed Jaguar's snout in his jaw. As Jaguar struggled to get free, *misi* held on firmly, tightening his grip the more violently Jaguar struggled. *Misi* hung on until Jaguar weakened and collapsed. They both fell to the ground. *Misi* released his grip, and Jaguar gasped, his eyes dulled, and he died.

Misi then packed his belongings—this is a story, remember—and set off on a camping trip. On the way he came to the big river where his owners had made a palm-wood bridge and crossed. He caught up to them, and they were overjoyed to see their "dog." They examined him and discovered that he had been in a fight, for there was blood around his mouth. When they went back to the village and found the dead Jaguar, they exclaimed, "Whaaa! Just look how big he is." On hearing that, *misi* dropped dead. His mourning owners, grateful to him for killing Jaguar, decided to cremate his body and eat his ashes, reciting his exploits as they wept for him. Word reached other people that *misi* had died, and all requested gourds of his ashes so that they, too, could honor him by eating his ashes. The spirit of the dead Jaguar now roamed the forest, hungry for meat. He is said to eat only agouti today.

The irony of the story is that a simple, helpless tortoise had destroyed Jaguar, the king of Amazonian beasts—a stupid king of beasts, but only in myth.

The Twins: Beauty and the Beast

Several of the stories the Yanomamö tell involve two paired male ancestors, Omawä and Yoawä (or Yoasiwä). The two perform many feats and are involved in the creation events that gave rise to many familiar plants, animals, and Yanomamö customs. The two characters are something of complementary opposites. One is smart, beautiful, competent, and admirable, while the other is stupid, ugly, a boob, and contemptuous. Sometimes there is a switch of identities in the stories; the dumb one becomes the smart one and vice versa.

Of all the fabulous events and situations in which these two Original Beings appear, the story of the Origin of Copulation is the most humorous. In some versions of the story told by the Shamatari, in which Omawä is the attractive one and Yoawä the stupid one, Yoawä the Ugly went fishing one day. He tied bait to his fishing line and cast it into the river. (The Yanomamö claim that they used to fish with lines made of native fibers. They would tie a piece of bait to the string, wait for a fish—usually a small one—to swallow it, and then pull out the fish. I never saw them fish this way.) As Yoawä fished, he saw in the water a beautiful maiden, Raharaiyoma, the daughter of the giant river monster Raharariwä. No women existed at that time, and Yoawä wanted to capture the river maiden so he could copulate with her. She was in the water spinning cotton into yarn—and he noticed she was very sexy. "Wow! A real female. She has a beautiful vagina. I'd like to try it. I'm horny as hell," he said to himself. He knew she would not cooperate, so he decided to change into a small bird and lure her to the surface, where he could catch her. Changing into a bird with a long beak and a combed head, he fluttered above her trying to be seductive. But he was so stupid that he didn't know how and managed to do everything wrong. The maiden dismissed him with insults, saying he looked ugly with such a long snout and that ridiculous appendage growing out of his forehead. Then he changed into a spotted, flecked bird and hovered above her again. She continued to insult him—now his skin was blemished with spots. He tried several other bird guises, but each time he was dismissed by her biting insults. Frustrated and angry, he went home in a huff, threw his catch of fish onto the smoke rack, and went to bed in disgust.

In the morning, his beautiful brother asked him why he had let his fish cook to a black, charred, inedible mess and why he was so moody. Yoawä explained that he was horny because he had seen his first woman and could not seduce her. The sympathetic Omawä devised a plan to catch the woman, for he had grown horny himself just thinking about it. He asked Yoawä to take him to where the maiden was, and the two of them set off. She was still in the river, this time casually delousing herself. Again Yoawä transformed himself into a small bird, but she dismissed him because he had ugly blemishes all over his body. He changed into another bird and was dismissed because his skin was too dark. He changed into a hummingbird, and she dismissed him because his eyes were beady, he squinted, and his beak was too long. Yoawä now asked Omawä for help, and Omawä told him to change into a small, minnowlike fish. This Yoawä did, and hid in the water near the maiden. Omawä then changed himself into a beautiful small bird with scarlet feathers and hovered above her. She was attracted to Omawä and told her father that she wanted to catch this beautiful crimson bird and keep it as a pet. As she surfaced to reach for the bird, the two of them grabbed her, one on each arm, and dragged her screaming and struggling out of the water and onto land. Her father, the water monster, tried to come to her aid, but the two fled, dragging the woman with them. They brought their sexy trophy home, eager to copulate with her.

But their nephew, *Howashi*, the white (capuchin) monkey, lived with them, and when he saw her vagina and the provocative pubic hair, he was overcome with lust. "Let me have her first. Let me have her. I'm horny as hell, and just look at that fantastic vagina," he cried. So they let him have the first turn. He mounted her passionately and stuck his penis into her vagina with a mighty pelvic thrust—then screamed in agony as he withdrew a bloody stump. She had piranha fish concealed in her vagina, and they had bitten off the end of his penis. He screamed and howled and fled into the forest, holding what was left of his bloody penis. That is why *howashi* monkeys have penises that look like tenpenny nails—straight and with a flattened head.

Yoawä removed the fish from the maiden's vagina with a barbed arrow, and then he mounted her. He was consumed with lust and made long, passionate pelvic thrusts. His penis went in deep and came out rhythmically, making a foul, disgusting noise: "Soka! Soka! Soka! Soka!" Omawä threw up his arms in despair, for such clumsy copulating, such foul noise, would anger anyone who might overhear. He demanded that Yoawä cease and dismount, so that he could demonstrate the proper manner. Omawä mounted as Yoawä watched. He copulated with slow, discreet pelvic thrusts, making no noise. "See? That is how to copulate properly, so nobody can hear your penis going in and out," he said. From that time on, the Yanomamö have been able to copulate discreetly.

Spirits and Drugs: The War for the Soul

The Soul

Yanomamö concepts of the soul are elaborate and sophisticated. The true, or central, part of the soul is the will, the *buhii*. At death, this turns into the *no borebö*, which escapes up the person's hammock ropes and rises to the next layer of the cosmos. When it reaches that upper layer, it follows a trail until it comes to a fork. There, the son of *Yaru* (Thunder), a spirit named Wadawadariwä, asks the soul if it comes from a person who has been generous or stingy during mortal life. If the person has been stingy, Wadawadariwä directs the soul along one path, leading to a place of fire: *Shobari Waka*. If the person was generous, the soul is directed along the other path—to *hedu* proper, where a tranquil semimortal existence ensues.

The Yanomamö do not take this very seriously—that is, they do not fear the possibility of being sent to the place of fire. When I asked why, I was told, "Well, Wadawadariwä is kind of stupid. We'll just all lie and tell him we were generous, and he'll send us to *hedu*." I suppose, if they are ever Christianized, they will have the same attitude toward Saint Peter.

Another portion of the soul, the *no uhudi* or *bore*, is said to be released during cremation. It wanders around on earth and lives in the jungle. Some

Yanomamö claim that children always change into *no uhudi* and do not have a *no borebö* because their wills (*buhii*) are *mohode*—innocent, unaware. It would appear that to them the soul experiences an ontogeny paralleling human development, that a certain amount of living has to occur before parts of the soul develop. Some of the wandering *bores* are malevolent and attack travelers in the jungle at night; they have bright glowing eyes and beat the mortals with clubs and sticks. In 1968, I took Rerebawä to Caracas for a few days—a hilarious but informative experience for him—and he saw automobiles for the first time. As we drove along at night, the oncoming cars with their bright headlights terrified him. He thought they were a constant stream of *bore* spirits rushing past him at an incredible speed.

The most critical component of the soul is known as the *möamo* and lies inside the thoracic cavity, near (perhaps inside) the liver. This portion can be lured out and stolen, and it is very vulnerable to supernatural attack if removed from the body. A person who has lost his or her *möamo* will sicken and die, and the daily shamanistic attacks during the illness are usually directed at the *möamo* portions of the souls of the sick one's enemies, or are directed toward recovering this soul and returning it to its owner.

In addition to their multifaceted souls, all Yanomamö individuals have an animal counterpart, an alter ego known as the *noreshi*. It is a dual concept, for the *noreshi* is both an animal that lives in the forest and an aspect or component of the person's body or psyche. It is possible for people to lose their *noreshis*.

A male inherits his *noreshi* from his father, while a female inherits hers from her mother. Male *noreshis* are said to "go above" and female *noreshis* to "go below." Thus, certain monkeys and hawks found in high places are male *noreshi* animals, whereas snakes and ground-dwelling creatures are female *noreshi* animals, which travel low—a sexual superior/inferior equation. Kaobawä, for example, has the black spider monkey, *basho*, as his alter ego, which he and all his brothers inherited from their father. "We are of the *basho mashi*," they would say—of the lineage of the spider monkey. Bahimi, Kaobawä's wife, has the *hiima*, the dog, as her *mashi*, which she and her sisters inherited from their mother. This up/down, superior/inferior, male/female duality occurs in other contexts, including very mundane ones. Men tie their hammocks high, and women sleep in hammocks below them; when the campfire gets low, a man dangles a foot over the edge of his hammock and nudges his wife, who grunts and sleepily throws another piece of wood on the fire.

Noreshi animals duplicate the lives of their human counterparts. When

Kaobawä or Rerebawä goes hunting, so does his *noreshi* animal. When they sleep, so do their *noreshis*. If they get sick, the *noreshis* do, too. A two-day trip for the man is a two-day trip for the *noreshi*.

While humans and their *noreshis* theoretically live far apart and never come into contact, it is said that misfortunes occasionally occur, as when a hunter accidentally shoots and kills his own *noreshi*—and thus dies himself. Moreover, if another hunter kills a man's *noreshi*, the man dies. In a sense, the hunting of game animals is akin to the hunting and killing of humans, for some of the animals are the *noreshi* of humans.

The close association the Yanomamö make between loss of the soul and sickness is best exemplified in the shamanistic practices of the men. Those who are shamans spend several hours each day chanting to their tiny *hekura* spirits, enjoining them either to attack the souls of enemies or to help recover souls that people in the village have lost. It is a constant battle, and the men take their hallucinogenic snuff—*ebene*—daily to do contest with their enemies through the agency of their personal *hekura*.

But apparently not all aspects of the soul are equally vulnerable. For example, when I showed the Yanomamö pictures of themselves or others, they called the photographs *noreshi*. Tape recordings, though, were *no uhudi*. They seemed, at first, quite anxious over photographs and cameras and were very annoyed by my photographic attempts in the beginning. They would throw dirt and stones at me and, on one occasion, threatened to club me with red-hot firebrands grabbed from the hearth. After about a year, however, they pretty much ignored the cameras, except for a grumble or two from time to time. But they never objected to hearing tape recordings of their own voices. In fact, they liked them so much that they would make me play them back over and over again.

Endocannibalism

Anthropologists distinguish between two kinds of cannibalism: the eating of people who are not members of one's group, or exocannibalism, and the eating of one's own people, or endocannibalism. Neither form requires that the whole body be consumed, and, in fact, most cannibalism entails the consumption only of selected parts. Most documented cases of cannibalism, except in such extreme circumstances as the infamous Donner incident of our own pioneer days, indicate that it is highly ritualistic and occurs for religious or mystical reasons. Advocates of the protein theory have argued that the cannibalism widespread among some peoples, such as the Aztecs, was a response to an acute protein shortage. My response to that argument centers on the ultimate explanation, the function, of a hypothetical event. For example, a valiant warrior overcomes his equally valiant enemy in a mortal hand-to-hand contest. In celebration of his victory, he rips out his enemy's heart and ritually devours a portion of it, to honor the enemy and perhaps also to acquire some of his valor. Is the triumphant warrior short of protein, or is he, more logically, performing a symbolic gesture? Perhaps the best way to drive home the argument is to ask whether the taking of Holy Communion in the Christian religion is evidence of a calorie shortage or is a symbolic, mystical—and ritually cannibalistic—act of eating the body and drinking the blood of a man called Jesus Christ. Holy Communion falls into a special category of cannibalism called theophagy, or the eating of gods, and it makes little sense if explained in terms of calorie or protein shortages. The same is true of most anthropophagy—the eating of humans.

The Yanomamö are endocannibalistic anthropophagers—a mouthful in both senses. They eat portions of *their own deceased*: the ashes and ground-up bones that are left after a body is cremated.

When someone dies, say an adult, his or her body is carried to the clearing in the village and placed on a pile of firewood. More wood is stacked up around and on top of the body, and the fire is ignited. Children and those who are ill are sent away from the village, for the smoke from the burning corpse can contaminate them. The men often wash their bows and arrows after a cremation, to rid them of contamination, and I once saw the villagers wash all the smoked meat their hunters had brought back for a feast. Someone attends the fire to make sure the body is entirely burned, especially the liver. If the liver does not burn well, it is taken as a sign that the person committed incest during his or her life.

When the ashes have cooled, they are carefully and solemnly sifted. The unburned bones and teeth are picked out and placed in a hollowed-out log especially prepared for the occasion. A close kinsman or close friend of the deceased then pulverizes the bones by grinding them with a short stout pole about five feet long. This powder is carefully poured onto a leaf and transferred to several small gourds, each with a small opening. The dust and ash that remain in the hollow log are rinsed out with boiled ripe-plantain soup and solemnly drunk as the assembled relatives and friends mourn loudly and wildly, rending their hair with their hands and weeping profusely. The log is then burned. The ash remains are often obliquely referred to as *madohe*, a word meaning "possessions," or in this context "human remains." The gourds containing the ashes are carefully and tenderly stored in the roof of the kin's house, after being plugged shut with white down, and are saved for another, more elaborate ash-drinking ceremony, which might be attended by kin from distant villages. At this second ceremony, large quantities of boiled ripe-plantain soup are made, and the ashes are poured into gourds full of the soup. The gourds are passed around among the close kin and friends of the deceased, who solemnly drink while the onlookers weep and mourn. A joyous feast follows.

Children's corpses produce much less ash and bone, of course, and their remains usually are consumed by the parents alone. Important adults who have many kin and many friends get more elaborate ceremonies, with many people partaking of their ashes. Normally, all the remains are consumed in a single ritual. However, men who have been killed by enemy raiders are treated in a special fashion. Only the women drink their ashes, and they do so on the eve of a revenge raid. Thus, the ashes of a man who has been killed by his enemies may remain in his village for several years until his kin feel that his death has finally been avenged. One prominent man I knew, the headman of his village, was killed by raiders in 1965. (The full story is told in chapter 6.) Ten years later, the gourds containing his ashes were still in the rafters of his brother's house, and his group continued to raid the villagers who had killed him—despite the fact that they had already killed several men in revenge.

If many people die at one time, as during an epidemic, their bodies, wrapped in bark and wood, are taken into the jungle and placed in trees. After the bodies have decomposed, any remaining flesh is scraped from the bones, the bones are burned, and the ashes are stored in gourds, to be drunk later.

Finally, as the myth of *misi* suggested, some prized pets are cremated, especially good hunting dogs, but the bones are buried afterward, not eaten. The bodies of ordinary dogs are discarded a short distance from the *shabono*, sometimes even before the dog is dead.

Shamans, Hekura, *and Drugs*

The word *shaman* comes from the language of a Siberian tribe, the Chuckchee, and has been widely applied to the men and women of any tribal society who manipulate the spirit world, cure the sick by magic, sucking, singing, or massaging, diagnose illnesses and prescribe magical remedies, and in general intercede between humans and the spirits in matters of health and sickness (photo 25).

25. *Three shamans chanting to the* **hekura** *while curing the sick.*

Among the Yanomamö, only men become shamans. It is a status to which any man can aspire if he so chooses, and in some villages a large percentage of the men are shamans. They are called *shabori* or *hekura* in the Yanomamö language, the latter word also applying to the myriad tiny humanoid spirits the shamans manipulate.

One must, however, train to be a shaman, as priests must in many religions. This entails a long period of fasting, a year or more, during which time the novice loses an enormous amount of weight. He may literally be skin and bones at the end. An older man or men instruct the novice in the attributes, habits, songs, mysteries, and fancies of the *hekura* spirits. During the period of fasting, the novice must also be sexually continent, for the *hekura* are said to dislike sex and to regard it as *shami*—filthy. The novices must attempt to attract particular *hekura* into their chests, a process that takes much time and patience, for the *hekura* are fickle and likely to leave a human host. The inside of a shaman's body is thought to be a veritable cosmos of rivers, streams, mountains, and forests where the *hekura* can dwell in comfort and happiness. But only the more accomplished shamans have many *hekura* inside their bodies, and even they must strive to keep the *hekura* contented. Once a man is on good terms with his *hekura*, he can engage in sex without having his spirits abandon him. I sometimes suspect that the older men are putting one over on the younger men when they say that it is good to be a shaman and all of them should try it—and then telling them that they have to forsake women for an extended period of time. It is an effective way to reduce sexual jealousy, one of the chronic sources of social disruption in a village, and to allow the older men more opportunities for copulation. Some young men have told me in confidence that they did not want to go through the shamanism training because of the sexual continence requirement.

There are hundreds—perhaps thousands—of *hekura*. They are all small, varying in size from a few millimeters to an inch or two for the really large ones. Around the heads of male *hekura* are glowing halos called *wadoshe*, a kind of palm-frond visor that the Yanomamö themselves sometimes wear. Female *hekura* have glowing wands sticking out of their vaginas. All the *hekura* are exceptionally beautiful, and each has his or her own habits and attributes. Most are named after animals, and most came into existence during some mythical episode that transformed an Original Being—one of the *no badabö*—into both an animal and its *hekura* counterpart. The *hekura* are said to be found in the hills or high in trees, often suspended there, but they can also live under rocks or even in the chest of a human. Many of them have special weapons for striking or piercing the soul. Some are physically hot and some are *naiki*—meat hungry and cannibalistic. Some are both hot and meat hungry, and these are often the ones sent to devour the souls of enemies.

All the *hekura* have individual trails that they follow when their human hosts call to them. The trails lead from the sky or the mountains, or even from the "edge of the universe," to the human host's body. There, the trail enters the feet of the human and traverses the body until it reaches the thoracic cavity, where the symbolic villages, forests, and mountains are found. The *hekura* come out of these mountains and lairs, reeling and dancing, glowing as they come, fluttering around in ecstasy, like a swarm of butterflies hovering over a food patch. Once they are in the body, they are subject to the designs of the human host, who sends them out to devour enemy souls—especially children's souls—or to help the host cure sickness in his village.

The shamans have to take hallucinogenic snuff—*ebene*—to contact the spirits, but highly experienced shamans need very little. A pinch is enough to get them singing the soft, melodic, beautiful songs that attract the *hekura* spirits. Since the *hekura* require beauty, most shamans decorate their chests and stomachs with red *nara* pigment, don their best feathers, and make themselves attractive before they call to the *hekura*. The *hekura* have their own intoxicant, a magical beverage called *braki aiamo uku*, that they take when their human counterparts are snorting *ebene*.

As the *ebene* takes effect, the shamans begin to sing louder and louder, often screaming, but always melodically and expertly. They recite the deeds of the *hekura*, the time of their creation, their songs and habits, and tell of many marvelous and fabulous events. Since this performance happens almost every day, most of the people in the village appear to be ignoring it, but, consciously or not, they are listening. Someone might interrupt to correct a slurred or inaccurate statement of "mystical truth," or to remind the shaman that he left out a particular gesture when he got to a certain point in his mythical account. This is generally the way the stories of mythical times are circulated, and often just snippets of the story are told, but all know the whole story. Sometimes an inept younger man will take too much hallucinogen and "freak out," as if he had overdosed. Some men take *ebene* only because they like to get high and have no interest in trying to control the *hekura*. In the villages I lived in during the earlier years of my fieldwork, the men took *ebene* almost every day. More recently, I have lived in villages where its use is less common.

Taking *ebene*, which is noisy, exciting, and dramatic—but is also unpleasant because of the vomiting and profuse discharges of green mucus—can sometimes be dangerous as well. The trances are often the occasion for a man to relieve any frustrations that have been building up. The Yanomamö attitude seems to be that a man is not fully responsible for his acts when he is in communion with the *hekura* and high on *ebene*. One occasionally sees a timid man become boisterous and, at times, violent—running around in a stupor, wild-eyed, threatening to shoot someone with an arrow or hack someone with a machete.

I have always suspected that one of the primary functions of the daily *ebene* round is to give the men a quasi-acceptable means of working off their pent-up antagonisms and of showing, if only briefly, an intense emotion they might not otherwise be able to express. When a man becomes *waiteri* on drugs, the others pay attention to him, chase and disarm him, attempt to calm his temper, entreat him to calm down and stop being fierce. Mostly they allow their concerned peers to calm them, for they appear to be aware that they may carry things too far. But for a moment the timid can be fierce and can display a passion that they probably would not show when sober. Violations of some of the most stringent avoidance taboos are overlooked when the violator is intoxicated on *ebene*. For instance, a son-in-law can touch, talk to, or caress his father-in-law, something that would be unthinkable if both were sober. It is a sort of psychological release valve for the pent-up strains of a workaday life.

But the *ebene* taking can get out of hand. In a village to the north of Kaobawä's, a man intoxicated on *ebene* decapitated another with a single blow of his machete, precipitating a violent fission in the village and a long war between the two groups. In my estimation, it is not irrelevant that the decapitated man was a chronic opponent of his killer and that there was a long history of argumentation between them. I myself was nearly shot by a wild-eyed young tough high on *ebene*, a man with whom I had had a disagreement earlier in the day.

The Yanomamö cosmos, then, parallels and reflects the mortal world that humans know and dwell in. When the humans die, they repeat life elsewhere, in the cosmic layer above, hunting, collecting, gardening, making love, making war. In *hedu* as it is on earth.

Daily Life, the Family, and Society

This chapter will consider the daily social life and social organization of the Yanomamö from several vantage points. But my primary focus will be on the fascinating phenomenon of village fissioning among the Yanomamö.

Fissioning reflects the breakdown of solidarity in the village, its inability to hold together through ties of kinship, marriage, and descent from common ancestors, supplemented by the authority of a headman, like Kaobawä. It appears that primitive societies can grow only so large at the local level—the village in this case—when internal order is provided solely by these common integrating mechanisms. The issue is not an arcane one, of interest only to specialists in anthropological kinship theory. It is one of the big questions about our very social nature. If we are smarter than animals, why did it take us so many hundreds of thousands of years to develop the ability to live in groups larger than fifty? Modern humanity has existed in its present morphological form for several hundreds of thousands of years. (Some physical anthropologists would say nearly 2 million years, depending on how one defines modern morphology; upright posture, bipedal locomotion, and brain size in excess of 1,000 cubic centimeters are nearly 2 million years old in our species.) Yet it has been only in the last 8,000 years or so—a flicker of the eyelash in social evolutionary time—that we have been able to live in large groups, and only in the past few score of years that we have achieved cities of a million people. Why?

I think that a big part of the answer has to do with how difficult it has been for our ancestors to cast off the heavy yoke of nepotism—the evolutionary tendency to depend on blood relatives for support, paired with the tendency to be suspicious of nonrelatives and strangers. By focusing on the practices of the Yanomamö, I hope not only to describe their society but to shed some light on the novelty and newness of our own.

My approach will counterpose two points of view that are widely found in the field of anthropology. One is the structural approach, which constructs ideal models of societies based on their general rules of kinship, descent, and marriage. But these models, while simplified and, in scientific parlance, "elegant," do not address the actual behavior of individuals in their day-to-day roles or the reasons they cannot always follow the rules. The second is the statistical models approach, which is based on large numbers of verifiable behavioral and genealogical facts but yields a less elegant and simplified model. However, the statistical model conforms more to reality, and I prefer it for the way it can lead to a better understanding of individual variations and therefore the ability to predict some social actions.

To employ the statistical approach, of course, one must know what the ideal patterns are that people are deviating from. Think of the two approaches in terms of two studies about homicide. The ideal model approach will tell you "thou shalt not kill." The statistical approach will tell you the grim realities of how, who, where, when, and why people kill. If you are interested in scientifically predicting homicides, you will follow the latter approach. Or take the principle—the ideal model—that everyone is equal before the law, and statistics showing that the probabilities of being convicted, being sent to prison, serving out a full term, and being given the death penalty are several times higher for Americans who are not of Anglo-Saxon origin.

I once heard the distinguished French anthropologist Claude Lévi-Strauss tell this anecdote to justify his lifetime interest in ideal models and structures. He likened social and cultural anthropology to the scientific study of mollusks. It is legitimate, and even meritorious, he said, to concern oneself with the shell of the organism—its structure. He himself preferred to study the shells, because they are attractive, symmetrical, pleasant to handle and to think about. But, he acknowledged, there are other ways of studying this life form. One could focus on the slimy, amorphous, rather unpleasant oyster or snail that lives in the shell. That, too, is a legitimate and meritorious endeavor, he said, and he had no objection if others chose to pursue it. The point, of course, is whether the shell and the amorphous animal inside it make much sense when considered separately. My own view is that the animal inside the symmetrical shell is not as amorphous as it appears and itself has some structured integrity. I also believe that there has to be a causal relationship of some sort between the animal and the type of structure—the elegant shell—it generates.

The shell in this analogy is social structure. The amorphous animal inside it is social behavior. Once we pose the question of what causes the animal to produce the elegant, symmetrical shell, a great variety of possible answers and theoretical issues comes into play. In terms of human society, the questions we pose are about individual behavior—the acts, thoughts, and relationships of individuals in particular cultures—and how that behavior is shaped by and reflects such realities as demography, physiological differences between males and females, and the evolved nature of the organism itself. And, of course, how culture and learning affect behavior in specific environments.

Daily Life Among the Yanomamö

Males and Females

A number of distinctions based on status and physiology are important in Yanomamö daily life. Perhaps the most conspicuous and most important of these are the distinctions between males and females—what each sex goes through in growing to adulthood and what their roles are after achieving it.

Yanomamö society is decidedly masculine—male chauvinistic, if you will. One hears many statements like "Men are more valuable than women" or "Boys are more valuable than girls." Both men and women say that they want to produce as many children as they can, but they especially want boys. This was impressed on me in many ways, but the incident that I have found most striking combined two closely related sentiments.

For the ten-year period between 1976 and 1985, I was prevented from visiting the Yanomamö by the intense opposition of a group of Venezuelan anthropologists. When I finally was able to return, in 1985, one of my first objectives was to visit Kaobawä's village, to see him and my other good friends there. It was a joyous occasion for us all. Eventually Shadadama, one of Kaobawä's younger brothers, got around to the sensitive matter of inquiring how things were with my family. He carefully phrased his questions so as not to hurt me if any of them had died since we met last. Once he had determined that my wife, son, and daughter were all alive and well, he was visibly overjoyed and pressed me for more news. His first question was:

"Have you sired any new children since I saw you?"

"No."

"Ahh! Your wife is now *patayoma* [beyond childbearing age]."

"No."

Not knowing how to phrase the next question, for fear he would be asking about children who had not survived, he fumbled around for a moment, so I volunteered the answer:

"Even though she is not *patayoma*, we have decided not to have any more children. Two are enough for us."

He was annoyed, even outraged, at this. "Whaaa! Don't ever say things like that. You should *always* want to have children. Some of them will be sons, and when they grow up, they will avenge you."

Female children assume responsibilities in the household long before their brothers are obliged to perform domestic tasks. At an early age, girls are expected to tend their younger brothers and sisters and help their mothers with such chores as cooking, hauling water, and collecting firewood (photo 26). By the time girls have reached puberty, they have learned that their world is decidedly less attractive than that of their brothers. And most of them have been promised in marriage by then.

Yanomamö girls—and to a lesser extent boys—have almost no voice in the decisions of their older kin as to whom they will marry. They are largely pawns for their kinsmen to dispose of, and their wishes get almost no consideration. A girl is often promised to someone well before she reaches puberty, and sometimes the husband-elect takes over her rearing for part of her childhood. Boys seem better able to initiate the marital process and to have their older kin make the first inquiries. But the males marry later than the females do, so these boys are really young men, and the girls they are interested in are much younger, often just children. Girls do not participate as equals in any of the political affairs of the corporate kinship group, and they seem to inherit most of the duties without enjoying any of the privileges, largely because the husband is older than she is at first marriage and thus has a higher status.

Marriage does not automatically enhance a girl's status or even change her life much. There is no marriage ceremony as such; public awareness of it begins with no more than a comment like "Her father has promised her to so-and-so." The girl usually does not start living with her husband until after she has had her first menstrual period, although she may have been officially married for several years. Her duties as wife require her to continue the laborious tasks she has already been performing, such as the daily collecting of firewood and fetching of water.

Collecting firewood is hard work, and the women spend several hours each day scouring the neighborhood for suitable wood. There is an abundant supply in the garden for about a year after the land has been cleared, but this

26. *A woman and her young daughter returning with loads of firewood. Girls become economically useful earlier than boys do and contribute significantly to the labor of the household.*

disappears in time. Then the women must forage farther afield, sometimes traveling several miles every day. The women can always be seen leaving the village at about three or four in the afternoon and returning at dusk, usually in a procession, bearing enormous loads in their pack baskets (photo 27). If one of them happens to find a good supply of wood near the village, she will haul away as much as she can and store it, rather than let it be taken by anyone else. And it is a lucky woman who owns an ax to lighten her work.

Women are expected to respond quickly to the wishes—sometimes the demands—of their husbands and even to anticipate their needs. It is interesting to watch the women's behavior when their husbands return from a hunting trip or a visit to another village. The men march proudly across the village and retire silently to their hammocks, especially when they have brought home some choice item of food. The women, no matter what they have been doing, hurry home and quietly but rapidly prepare a meal. If the wife is slow about it, she may be scolded or even beaten.

Most physical reprimands take the form of kicks or blows with the hand or a piece of firewood, but a particularly nasty husband might hit his wife with the sharp edge of a machete or ax or shoot a barbed arrow into some nonvital area, such as the buttocks or a leg. Another brutal punishment is to hold the glowing end of a piece of firewood against the wife's body, producing painful and serious burns. Normally, however, the husband's reprimands are consistent with the perceived seriousness of the wife's shortcomings, his more drastic measures being reserved for infidelity or suspicion of infidelity. It is not uncommon for a man to seriously injure a sexually errant wife, and some husbands have shot and killed unfaithful wives.

I was told about one young man in Monou-teri who shot and killed his wife in a rage of sexual jealousy, and during one of my stays in the villages a man shot his wife in the stomach with a barbed arrow. She suffered extensive internal injuries, and the missionaries had her flown to the territorial capital for surgery, but by then the wound had become infected and she was near death. Another man chopped his wife on the arm with a machete; some tendons to her fingers were severed, and it was feared that she would lose the use of her hand, but eventually the wound healed.

A club fight involving a case of infidelity took place in one of the villages just before the end of my first field trip. The male paramour was killed, and the enraged husband cut off both of his wife's ears. A number of women have had their ears badly mutilated. The women wear short pieces of arrow cane in

27. *Women returning from the garden at dusk with loads of firewood.*

their pierced earlobes; these are easily grabbed by an angry husband—and, once in a while, jerked so hard that the earlobes are torn open.

There is one somewhat rare way for a woman to escape the anguish of marriage to an especially unpleasant husband. The Yanomamö even have a word for it, *shuwahimou,* and the word is applied to a woman who, on her own, flees from her village to live in another village and find a new husband there. It is rare to do this because it is dangerous. If the woman's own village is stronger than the one she flees to, the men will pursue her and forcibly take her back—and mete out a very severe punishment to her for having run away. They might even kill her. Most of the women who have fled have done so to escape particularly savage and cruel treatment, and they try to flee to a more powerful village.

But a woman can usually count on her brothers for protection against a cruel husband. If the husband mistreats her too severely, the brothers may take her away from him and give her to another man. Women dread the possibility of being married to men in distant villages, because they know that their brothers will not be able to protect them.

Some women—provided they have not been too severely treated—even seem to measure their husbands' concern for them in terms of the minor physical damage they have sustained. On several occasions, I have overheard young women examining each other's scalp scars and remarking, for instance, that a woman's husband must really care for her, since he hit her on the head so frequently. Both husbands and wives often laugh and joke with each other about past incidents in which the woman received a serious wound.

A woman who has married a male cross-cousin may have the best of it, for she is related to her husband by blood ties of kinship as well as by marriage. Bahimi, for example, is Kaobawä's mother's brother's daughter, and their marital relationship is very tranquil. He reprimands her occasionally, but never cruelly.

I am sometimes asked what the Yanomamö idea of love is. They have a concept, *buhi yabraö,* that at first I thought could be translated into our notion of love. I remember being very excited when I discovered it, and I ran around asking lots of questions like these: "Do you love so-and-so?"—naming a brother or sister. "Yes!" "Do you love so-and-so?"—naming a child. "Yes!" "Do you love so-and-so?"—naming the man's wife. A stunned silence, peals of laughter, and then this: "You don't *love* your wife, you idiot!" One could go so far as to say that, if love in their culture is restricted to the kind of feelings they have toward close blood relatives, then they are more likely to have those feelings toward a spouse if, as in Kaobawä's case, the spouse is a blood relative—a first cousin—as his is.

The women tend to lose their shapes by the time they are thirty, because of the children they have borne and nursed for up to three years each and because of their years of hard work. They seem to be much more subject to bad moods than the men are—moods in which they display a sullen attitude toward life in general and men in particular. To an outsider, the older women appear to speak constantly in what sounds like a whine, punctuated with contemptuous remarks and complaints. When the women are happy or excited, the whining tone disappears, and they laugh gleefully, make wisecracks, and taunt the men, or each other, with biting insults and clever—usually bawdy—jokes.

A woman gains increasing respect as she ages, especially when she becomes old enough to have adult children to look out for her. The oldest women occupy a unique position in intervillage warfare and politics. Immune from the incursions of raiders, they can go from one village to another in complete safety, and they are sometimes employed as messengers and, occasionally, as the retrievers of dead bodies. If a man is killed near the village of an enemy, old women from the slain man's village are permitted to recover his body, or old women from the killers' village may take the body back to his kinsmen.

All women except the very old live in constant fear of being abducted by raiders when their village is at war. Whenever they leave the village, they take their children with them, particularly the younger ones, so that if they are abducted, the child will not be separated from its mother. The fear of abduction gives the women a special concern with the political behavior of their men, and they occasionally try to goad the men into action against an enemy by caustic accusations of cowardice. The men, of course, cannot stand being belittled in this fashion, and they may be badgered into acting.

Children and Grown-ups

Although the children of both sexes spend much more time with their mothers, it is the fathers who, largely by example, teach the boys their sex-specific roles and masculine attitudes. The distinction between male and female status develops early in the socialization process. The boys, encouraged to be fierce, are rarely punished for hitting their parents or the hapless girls of the village. Kaobawä, for example, would let his son, Ariwari, beat him on the face and head in a fit of temper, laughing and commenting about the boy's ferocity.

Although Ariwari was only about four years old at the time, he had already learned that an acceptable expression of anger was to strike someone with his hand or something else, and it was not uncommon for him to smack his father in the face if something displeased him. He was frequently egged on in this by the teasing and good-natured attitude of his mother and other adults in the household.

When Kaobawä's group was traveling, Ariwari would emulate his father by copying him on a child's scale. For example, he would erect a temporary hut made of small sticks and leaves and would play happily in his own camp, while his sisters were pressed into helping their mother with domestic tasks. Still, young girls are given some freedom to play, and they have their moments of fun with their mothers or other children—such as the merry games of tug-of-war with long vines in the village plaza, especially when it is raining hard.

But a girl's childhood ends sooner than a boy's. Her game of playing house fades imperceptibly into a constant responsibility to help her mother. By the time a girl is about ten years old, she has become an economic asset to her mother and spends much of her time working. Boys, by contrast, spend hours playing together, and many manage to prolong their childhoods into their late teens or early twenties—by which time a girl will have married and may have a child or two. The young men (usually unmarried) called *huyas* are a social problem in almost all Yanomamö villages; their attempts to seduce the young women, almost all of whom are married, are the source of much sexual jealousy. Their equivalent in our culture is teenage boys who are juvenile delinquents or gang members.

A girl's transition to womanhood is obvious because of its physiological manifestations. At first menses (*yöbömou*), Yanomamö girls are confined to their homes and hidden behind a screen of leaves. Their old cotton garments are discarded and replaced by new ones made by their mothers or by older female friends. During this week of confinement, the girl is fed sparingly by her relatives, and the food must be eaten with a stick, as she is not allowed to come into contact with it in any other fashion. She speaks in whispers, and then only to close kin. She must also scratch herself with a second set of sticks. After her puberty confinement, a girl usually takes up residence with her promised husband and begins her life as a married woman.

Women in our culture often ask me, "What do the women do during their menstrual periods? What do they wear for sanitary napkins?" The Yanomamö word for menstruation translates literally as "squatting" (*roo*), and that

is a fairly accurate description of what the pubescent females, and the adult
women, do. They remain inactive, squatting on their haunches and allowing
the menstrual blood to drip on the ground, usually into a shallow hole scraped
out for the purpose. The Yanomamö women do not use the equivalent of
tampons or sanitary napkins, and herein lies an important difference between
our "environment" and theirs. Sanitary napkins are a useful invention for those
who need them regularly, but the Yanomamö women menstruate with relative
infrequency because for much of their adult lives they are either pregnant or
nursing infants. But that kind of life did not strike me as strange. I will forever
remember the remarkable thing my own mother said to me, when I was about
twenty-two years old and accompanying her on a trip to Detroit. We were in
a crowded downtown bus when she suddenly turned to me with an anxious
look and whispered, "My menstrual period is starting. This is the first one I've
had in ten years." My mother bore twelve children—the last one after my own
son was born—and she breast-fed them all until they were about two years
old.

The male transition into manhood is not marked by any ceremony. Nevertheless, one can usually tell when a boy is attempting to enter the world of
men. The most conspicuous sign is his resentment at being called by his name,
since it is a mark of an adult male's status *not* to be called by his personal name.
Young men, more than others, are touchy about their names and quick to take
offense at hearing them spoken. To get around the problem of how to address
people, the Yanomamö use kinship terms, but when the kinship usage is ambiguous, they employ what is called *teknonymy*. Thus, in a certain context the
appropriate kinship term for Kaobawä might not distinguish him from his several
brothers; he would then be referred to teknonymously as "father of Ariwari."
However, as Ariwari gets older, he will try to put a stop to this in an effort
to establish his own status as an adult. A young man has been recognized as
an adult when people no longer use his name in teknonymous references. Still,
the transition is not abrupt or marked by a recognizable point in time.

Finally, Yanomamö children differ from adults in their presumed suscep-
tibility to supernatural hazards. A great deal of Yanomamö sorcery and myth-
ological references to harmful magic focuses on children as the targets of
malevolence. Shamans constantly send their *hekura* to enemy villages to secretly
attack and devour the vulnerable portions of children's souls, causing much
sickness and death, and the shamans spend equal amounts of time warding off
enemy malevolent spirits. The children are especially vulnerable because their

souls are not firmly established within their physical beings and can wander out
of the body almost at will—most commonly escaping through the mouth when
the child cries. A mother is quick to hush her bawling baby in order to prevent
its soul from escaping, usually by sticking one of her nipples in its mouth. A
child's soul can be recovered by sweeping the ground around the place where
the soul probably escaped, sweeping with a particular kind of branch while
calling for the soul. I helped several times to lure the soul of a sick child back
into the child's body by such calling and sweeping. But I also contributed a
dose of medicine for the child's diarrhea.

Daily Activities

Kaobawä's village, typical of most Yanomamö villages, is oval shaped. His
house is located among those of his agnatic kinsmen (those related through the
male side), who occupy a continuous arc along one side of the village. Each
built his own section of the village, and each house is owned by the family that
built it. Shararaiwä, Kaobawä's youngest brother, helped build Kaobawä's house
and shares it, as he also shares Koamashima, Kaobawä's younger wife. The older
wife, Bahimi, hangs her hammock next to Kaobawä's most of the time, but
when there are visitors and the village is crowded, she ties her hammock under
his so she can tend the fire during the night.

Children sleep with their mothers until they are given their own hammocks
at the age of five or six. The parents are afraid small children will fall into the
fire at night if they are allowed to sleep alone. Indeed, that happened to a baby
in Kaobawä's village. It slipped from its mother's arms while she slept and fell
into the glowing embers below her hammock. The mother did not awaken, and
the infant died of its burns. The mother also died tragically, from a snake bite,
not long after. (She is pictured in photo 10, in chapter 1.)

Daily activities begin early in a Yanomamö village. One can hear children
crying and people chatting lazily long before it is light enough to see. Often
they are awakened by the cold just before daybreak and go back to bed after
building up the fire, but many stay up to converse about their plans for the
day. Everyone is awakened around dawn by the procession of people leaving
the village to relieve themselves in the nearby garden, noisily going in and out
through the brush-covered entrances.

The village is very smoky at this time of day from the smoldering of newly
stoked campfires. The air is usually still and chilly, and the ground damp from
the dew. The smoke is pleasant and seems to drive away the chill. The morning

serenity may be punctuated with loud thumps—wood striking flesh—immediately followed by the painful howl of a dog caught snitching its master's food.

Clandestine sexual liaisons often take place at this time of day. The lovers may have arranged the previous evening to leave the village, on the pretext of relieving themselves, and meet at a predetermined location. They return separately, by different routes.

During periods of active war, early morning is when raiders strike, so anyone who leaves the village at dawn must be cautious. If there is reason to suspect that raiders are around, the people do not go outside the confines of the log palisade surrounding the village until full light, and then they go in armed groups. I have seen villages whose members cleared every blade of grass and every shrub within thirty or so yards of the village, to make sure raiders could not sneak close for an easy shot, and left the village only when accompanied by nervous men usually with arrows already nocked in their bows.

By the time it is light enough to see, everybody has started preparing breakfast. This generally consists of green plantains, peeled and placed on the glowing coals of the family fire—similar to our breakfast toast. Any leftover meat is taken down from the roof, where it has been dangling over the hearth on a vine, and shared, with the men getting the tastiest portions.

Men who have made plans to hunt that day leave the village before it is light. *Paruri*, a kind of wild turkey, can be easily taken at this time of day because they roost in conspicuous places. During the dry season, the *hashimo*, a kind of grouse, sing before dark, by which the men locate them and then return to stalk them at dawn, when they sing again.

The chewing of tobacco starts as soon as people begin to stir. Those who have a fresh supply soak the new leaves in water and add ashes from the hearth to the wad. If someone is short of tobacco, he will request a share of someone else's already chewed wad or simply borrow the entire wad when its owner puts it down. Tobacco is so important to the Yanomamö that their word for poverty, *hori*, literally translates as "being without tobacco." If I tried to justify my reluctance to give them something of mine on the basis of my poverty, using the word *hori*, they often would respond by spitting out their wads and handing them to me contemptuously. The act implied something like "If you are *that* poor, then take my tobacco from me. At least one of us is generous and willing to share." They respond to each other's requests in the same way.

Work begins as soon as breakfast is over, to take advantage of the morning coolness. Within an hour after it is light, the men are in their gardens clearing brush, felling large trees, transplanting plantain cuttings, burning off dead timber, or planting new crops of cotton, maize, sweet potatoes, or cassava, depending on the season. They work until about ten thirty, when it becomes too humid and hot for strenuous work. Then most of them bathe in the stream and return to their hammocks for a rest and a snack—they are inveterate snackers.

The women usually accompany their husbands to the garden and help with the planting and weeding. This is one way the men have of preventing the women from engaging in affairs. I have seen young men force their newly acquired wives to stay within eyesight almost all day. They assume, not without reason, that an unguarded mate is bound to be approached by other men for sexual favors and that she might well succumb, a concern that is equally well grounded.

The children spend a lot of time exploring the plant and animal life around them, and they are accomplished naturalists at an early age. Most twelve-year-old boys, for example, can name twenty species of bees and describe their anatomical or behavioral differences, and they know which ones produce the best honey. Like people everywhere, they seem to focus on the things that are important at certain ages; I'm sure that most adult males in our culture remember all their lives details about the kinds of cars that were desirable when they were in high school but care far less about the cars being produced in their middle age. Among the Yanomamö, such preoccupations tend to revolve around the natural world and the creatures in it. An eight-year-old girl once brought me a tiny, unidentifiable egg for us to watch together. Presently it cracked open and numerous baby cockroaches poured out, as she described for me the intimate details of their reproductive process.

The younger children stay close to their mothers, but the older ones have considerable freedom to wander about the garden and play. Young boys hunt for lizards with miniature bows and tiny featherless arrows. If they capture one alive, they bring it back to the village, tie a string around it, anchor the string to a stick in the village clearing, and boys chase the lizard around, shooting scores of tiny arrows at it (photo 28). Since lizards are very quick and little boys are poor shots, the target practice can last for hours. Usually, however, the fun terminates when an older boy, to show off his archery skills, puts an end to the unhappy lizard by killing it with his adult-sized arrows.

The game that I found most ingenious was the get-the-bee game. The children catch live bees, tie light cotton threads to their bodies, and set them loose dragging the strings. The bees can't fly well and move very slowly, with

28. Little boys practicing archery on a lizard tied to a string.

the draft from their frantically beating wings holding the string straight out behind them. The children then chase the bees and knock them down by throwing sticks or other objects.

Sometimes the older men lead the children on a mock raid. The children sneak up on an effigy made of leaves, shoot it full of arrows at the men's command, and then flee from the scene.

One kind of game that I have seen in many different villages occurs when a hapless small bird gets trapped inside the thatched roof of the *shabono*. The frantic bird flies around under the roof, sometimes making three or four complete circles before finding a way out. Meanwhile, everyone—men, women, and children—excitedly and noisily tries to knock it down and kill it by throwing things or batting at it with long sticks or arrows as it whizzes by their houses. This can be very unnerving when one sees it for the first time: with no warning, the whole village is standing up screaming and violently throwing things.

The village is often almost empty at midday, with most people off collecting, hunting, or doing other tasks. The few who remain rest in their hammocks during the heat of the day.

If the men return to their gardens, it is at about four o'clock, and they work until sundown. Prior to (and often instead of) that, they gather in small groups around the village to take their hallucinogenic snuff and chant to the *hekura* spirits. This usually lasts for an hour or two, followed by a bath to wash off the vomit and nasal mucus from the snuff.

Whatever the men do for the afternoon, however, the women are invariably off searching for firewood, and haul heavy loads of it back to their houses just before dark.

The evening meal is the biggest one of the day. The staple is plantains, but other kinds of food are often available as a result of the day's activities, usually some form of protein, such as small game animals or birds, a monkey, crabs, fish, snakes, or even insect larvae. It is a happy occasion if someone has killed a bigger animal, such as a tapir, for then a large number of people will get a share, depending on their kinship ties. Hunters who kill tapirs are expected to give all the meat away, keeping none of it for themselves. They usually give it to their brothers-in-law or father-in-law, who take charge of the sharing. Both sexes do the daily cooking, although the women do more than the men. (The men do all the cooking for ceremonial feasts.) But food preparation is not elaborate, rarely requiring much labor, time, or equipment.

As a rule, they eat in their hammocks, using their fingers. If a meal cannot be eaten from a reclining position, the members of a family squat in a circle around the common dish. For example, a large quantity of small fish is cooked by wrapping the fish in leaves and roasting them in the hot coals. Then the steaming package is spread open and everyone squats around it and shares the contents, alternating with bites of roasted or boiled plantain, and with a great display of finger licking, spitting out of bones, tossing away of inedible portions, and satisfied sighs.

Animals are never skinned before cooking, but are simply put over the fire, after the entrails have been removed, and roasted—head, fur, claws, and all. Most of the fur is singed off during the cooking process, or sometimes a fire is made outside the village to singe off the fur, after which the animal is gutted. Most small animals are cooked whole; larger ones are cut up with knives or machetes before being smoked or roasted. The head of a monkey—one of the more common meats—is prized for the brain, considered a delicacy. Certain parts of other animals are reserved for the women, like the heads of wild turkeys, and the old women often eat the flesh of some animals that the younger people disdain, such as deer in some areas—a reflection of these women's low status when it comes to the sharing of choice foods.

It is nearly dark by the time supper is over. Now the fires are prepared for the night; if a family has allowed its fire to go out during the day, someone borrows two glowing brands from a neighbor and rekindles the hearth. The dry brush at the entrances to the village is put in place, so that prowlers cannot enter without raising an alarm and so that harmful spirits will stay outside. Before retiring to their hammocks, the Yanomamö sit in them and wipe off the bottoms of their feet by rubbing them together to knock off the debris that has accumulated during the day. I got into this habit, too, and unconsciously do it at home now before I jump into bed, to the amusement of my wife, who, like most wives, must find it odd to see a grown man rubbing the bottoms of his feet together before going to bed. I do several other odd things I have picked up in the field, like getting very jumpy when someone behind me unexpectedly reveals his or her presence, clicking my tongue when something pleases me, or smelling my food before putting it in my mouth—or blowing on it to remove the imaginary dirt.

Everyone sleeps naked and as close to the fire as possible. Despite the inevitable last-minute visiting, the village is usually quiet by the time it is dark.

But it does not always stay quiet. If someone is sick, a shaman will chant to the spirits most of the night to exorcise the sickness. Or, should someone be mourning a dead kinsman, he or she will sob and wail long after the others have fallen asleep. Occasionally a fight will break out between a husband and wife, and soon everybody in the village will be screaming and expressing an opinion about the dispute. The shouting may continue sporadically for hours, dying down and then breaking out anew as someone gets a fresh insight into the problem. Once in a while, someone, usually one of the more prominent men, will give a long, loud speech in the wee hours voicing his opinions of the world in general. The Yanomamö call this *patamou* or *kawa amo*—to act big. Interested parties sometimes add their own comments, but mostly the audience just grumbles about the noise and falls asleep. The more proficient I became in the language, the more I tried to emulate the Yanomamö, and I have adopted the practice of making nocturnal speeches myself, to the village at large, telling everyone, in elaborate detail, what I plan to do the next day and what gifts I will be giving out. This helps the people schedule their own activities, since if I will be working with women informants, the men know there is no point in their hanging around the village hoping for gifts, and vice versa. I have received many compliments on my *kawa amo* speeches.

Leaders and Followers

Daily activities do not vary much from season to season, except for those that involve gardening, collecting, and visiting neighbors. Most of the variations that do occur are a function of age or sex. Also, certain status differences account for some variations in the activities of particular individuals.

Rerebawä, for example, was an outsider to Kaobawä's group and had no intention of joining the village permanently. He intended to return to his own village with his wife as soon as his bride service was over. Consequently, he did not participate in the gardening activities and had considerably more spare time than other married men his age, time he spent hunting to provide for his wife and her parents, one of his obligations as a son-in-law. He was dependent on them, however, for the bulk of his diet, the plantains and other produce from the garden. While quick to call attention to his hunting skills and his generosity with meat, he was able to avoid making a garden because of his status as a *sioha*, an inmarried son-in-law. But his in-laws, who have no sons, wanted him to stay permanently, to provide for them when they got old. They even promised Rerebawä their second daughter if he would remain, and they prevented him from taking Shihotama, his first wife, and her children away by keeping at least one of the children with them when Rerebawä went to visit his own family. They knew that Shihotama could not bear to be separated permanently from the child and that Rerebawä would eventually bring her back.

By the Yanomamö's standards, he had done enough bride service and deserved to be given control over his wife. Also, by their standards, he had lived in the village so long that he should have been compelled to make his own garden. But he had been in a position to continue refusing to do so because he had discharged his son-in-law obligations well beyond what was expected of him.

Kaobawä's activities, by contrast, are governed by his special status as headman, by his twenty years' seniority to Rerebawä, and by his many more obligations to his larger number of kin. Rerebawä, for instance, thought nothing of taking week-long trips to visit friends in distant villages, leaving his wife and children with her parents—a casual attitude toward the children that was quite different from Kaobawä's. Kaobawä was coming with me to Caracas once, for example, to see how "foreigners" lived, until Ariwari began to cry. At this appeal to his paternal sensitivities, Kaobawä stepped out of the canoe, took off the clothing I had loaned him for the trip, and picked up Ariwari. "I can't go with you," he explained. "Ariwari will miss me and be sad." Such paternal solicitude can even cross generations. On a 1991 field trip, I invited a knowledgeable seventy-five-year-old man to accompany me by helicopter to a nearby village and help with my genealogy work there. He agreed at first, but then he backed out. He wasn't afraid of the helicopter, he said, but was concerned that his five-year-old grandson would miss him and be sad.

Kaobawä seems to think for the others in the village, many of whom are unable to see the less obvious implications of a situation. He is the most politically astute man in the group, but he exercises his influence so diplomatically that the others are not offended. If a person is planning something that is potentially dangerous, Kaobawä will simply point out the danger and add parenthetically, "Go ahead and do it if you want to, but don't expect sympathy from me if you get hurt." Shararaiwä, his youngest brother, once planned to go with me to a distant village that, I knew, was not on particularly good terms with his but was not actively at war with it, either. Kaobawä came over to my canoe as we were about to depart and asked me not to take Shararaiwä, explaining that the people we planned to visit might possibly molest him and precipitate hostilities between the two groups. Shararaiwä had been willing to take a chance that my presence would be sufficient to deter trouble, but Kaobawä would not risk it.

On another occasion, three men from Patanowä-teri arrived to explore with Kaobawä the possibility of peace between their two villages. The men were brothers-in-law to him and were confident that he would protect them from the village hotheads. But one of the more ambitious men in Kaobawä's group saw an opportunity to enhance his prestige and laid plans to kill the visitors. This man, Hontonawä, was cunning, treacherous, and jealous of Kaobawä's position as headman, a position he wanted for himself. (He told me privately to address *him* as the headman.)

Kaobawä let it be known that he intended to protect the visitors, however, and for the better part of a day the village was in a state of suspense. Hontonawä and his followers were nowhere to be found; a rumor spread that they had painted themselves black, were boasting of their fierceness, and were well armed. Kaobawä and his supporters, mostly his brothers and brothers-in-law, deliberately remained in the village all day, their weapons close at hand. Late in the afternoon, Hontonawä and his men appeared in their black paint and took up strategic posts around the village. He himself, carrying an ax, strutted arrogantly over to the visitors, holding the ax over his head as if ready to strike. The village became very quiet, and most of the women and children fled. Neither Kaobawä nor the Patanowä-teri visitors batted an eyelash at Hontonawä's menacing actions, although the younger men were visibly anxious and sat upright in their hammocks. It was a showdown. But instead of striking at the visitors with the ax, Hontonawä brought it back down to his side and aggressively invited one of the visitors out to chant with him. Within seconds, all three visitors were paired off with members of Hontonawä's group and were fervently chanting with them, explaining the reasons for their visit and their justification for the current state of hostilities. Kaobawä's implied threat to defend the visitors with force had averted a crisis.

But a number of the men in Hontonawä's group were from Monou-teri, whose headman had been killed a few months earlier by the Patanowä-teri. When Hontonawä failed to go through with his plan, these men left in a rage, hoping to recruit a raiding party in their own village and ambush the Patanowä-teri visitors when they left for home. Realizing this, Kaobawä came to see me that night and asked me to take the visitors back to their village at dawn in my canoe. He knew that I was planning to go there in a day or so and wanted me to accelerate my plans. When I agreed, he proceeded to instruct me not to stop at any of the villages along the upper Orinoco, for all of them were at war with the Patanowä-teri and would shoot my companions on sight. He also had me take along all my tarps, with which the Patanowä-teri men, lying on the floor of the canoe, could cover themselves when we neared these villages. As we passed by, the men on the bank shouted curses at me for not stopping to visit or give them trade goods. At the time, the Patanowä-teri were being raided by about a dozen villages, and we had to proceed with equal caution over the distance we had to cover on foot. The men pointed out one spot where a Hasuböwä-teri raiding party had killed a Patanowä-teri woman about a fortnight earlier. This safe-conduct Kaobawä had arranged got the visitors safely back to their home village.

Kaobawä also keeps order within the village when things threaten to get out of hand. Hontonawä, for example, is extremely cruel to his four wives and beats them severely at the slightest provocation. None of the wives have brothers in the village to protect them, and hardly anyone else dares to interfere with Hontonawä. On one occasion, Kaobawä was preparing a feast for the members of an allied village, an effort being duplicated by Hontonawä in an obvious attempt to show that he was a leader, too. Some of the visitors, arriving early, gathered at Hontonawä's house, and he commanded one of his wives to prepare some food for them. When the woman moved too slowly to suit him, Hontonawä went into a rage, grabbed an ax, and swung it wildly at her. She ducked and ran screaming from the house. He recovered his balance and violently threw the ax at her as she fled, but he missed. Kaobawä had seen the ax go whizzing over the woman's head and raced across the village to wrest a machete away from Hontonawä. Before Kaobawä could disarm him, however, Hontonawä hit the woman twice, splitting open between two fingers the hand she was holding up to protect her head. On another occasion, one of Kaobawä's brothers became violent from taking too much *ebene*. He staggered to the center of the village, shooting at random with his bow and arrows, while people ran frantically out of their houses to avoid being hit. Kaobawä was able to disarm him and hide his weapons.

During the several club fights that took place while I was in the village on my first field trip, Kaobawä stood by with his bow and arrows to make sure that the fighting remained relatively innocuous. (Photo 38, in chapter 6, shows a club fight.) In one chest-pounding duel, he succeeded in keeping the fight from escalating into a bloodier confrontation. (The fight is described in chapter 5.) After the duel was over, Kaobawä coolly discussed the fight with the leaders of the opposing group, stating that he would not raid them unless they raided first. But a number of men in the village, notably Hontonawä and some of his followers, shouted threats that they would shoot their departing opponents on sight the next time they met. Although Hontonawä frequently made such threats, he rarely put himself in a position that was actually dangerous. Later on, he ran into a party of hunters from this group while he was leading a raid against the Patanowä-teri. Instead of carrying out his threat to shoot on sight, however, he traded arrows with them and rapidly retreated toward home. He boasted in the village about having terrified the men, but they told me later that Hontonawä was the one who had been terrified. They had simply resumed their hunting after he fled.

Kaobawä's personality is the opposite of Hontonawä's. The former is unobtrusive, calm, modest, and perceptive; the latter is belligerent, aggressive, ostentatious, and rash. Kaobawä has an established status in the village and numerous supporters, whose loyalty comes in part from kinship ties and in part from his wise leadership. Hontonawä wants to share the leadership, but he has not established his position. It is obvious who the real leader is. When visitors come to Upper Bisaasi-teri, they seek out Kaobawä and deal with him, no matter how ambitiously Hontonawä attempts to imitate him. Hontonawä does not have as many living brothers in his group as Kaobawä does, so his natural following is somewhat limited. In addition, two of his brothers are married to actual sisters of Kaobawä and have some loyalty to him. Hontonawä, left with fewer kinship ties by which to establish his position, is given to using bluff, threat, chicanery, and treachery instead. This he does well, and many of the young men in the village seem to admire him for it. He has gained the support of a few by promising them his wives' yet *unborn* daughters. Remarkably enough, some believe such promises and are willing to do his bidding. He is, in short, a successful manipulator.

Finally, one of Kaobawä's most unpleasant tasks is to scout the neighborhood of the village when signs of raiders have been found. This he does alone, since it is dangerous and is avoided by the other men. Not even Hontonawä will do it. A surprisingly large number of Yanomamö headmen are killed by raiders because they voluntarily expose themselves to this risk.

Kaobawä has definite responsibilities as headman and is occasionally required by the situation to exercise his authority, but he tends to exert it only for the duration of the incident. After it is over, he goes about his business like any other man in the group. Even then, though, he sets an example for the others, particularly in his efforts to produce large amounts of food for his family and for the guests he must entertain. Most of the time he leads purely by example, and the others follow if it pleases them to do so. They can ignore his example when they wish, but they almost always turn to him in a difficult situation (photo 29).

The Larger Society and Rules

It takes many months of living with a people like the Yanomamö to learn the abstract rules and principles they follow in their social interactions. And it is difficult to say precisely how an anthropological fieldworker learns them, except that it is a gradual process, much like the way we learn the rules of our own culture. Most of us cannot, for example, explain precisely how or when we came to know that having sex with a sister or brother is bad, but we do know it. Anthropologists are aware, however, that tribal societies have rules about proper behavior and that these rules are usually expressed in the context of (a) kinship, (b) descent, or (c) marriage. So at least we know where to start.

Take one such rule, about who should marry whom. It was difficult to get the Yanomamö to state this as a general principle, and so I tried to establish it indirectly, by asking individuals such questions as "Can you marry so-and-so?" The answers, when pieced together, allowed me to formulate a general rule so self-evident to them that they could not imagine anyone not knowing it. Answers to the question might take the form of: "What? No, I can't marry so-and-so. She is my *yuhaya* [the daughter of my child or sister, or my grand-daughter]." Or; "No, she is my *tääya* [my daughter or my brother's daughter]." Eventually I learned all the kinship terms that both the men and the women used for their kin and which of these terms indicated a prohibited spouse. In this fashion, I also learned that men could marry only those women they put into the kinship category *suaböya* and, by reciprocal extension, that women could marry only the men they put into the category *hearoya*. By collecting genealogies that showed exactly how one person was related to another, I was able to specify a man's "nonmarriageable" and "marriageable" female kin. As it turned out, a man (woman) could marry only those women (men) who fell into the category of kin we call cross-cousins. For a man, these are the daughters of his mother's brother and the daughters of his father's sister.

By contrast, parallel cousins are a person's mother's sister's children or father's brother's children. The sex of the linking kinsmen is parallel; that is, the father and the father's brother are the same sex. The Yanomamö call parallel

29. *Kaobawä, the quiet, unpretentious headman.*

cousins by kinship terms that mean brother or sister, and, quite understandably, they forbid marriages between these cousins. The biblical discussions of the levirate may help clarify this—the rule that says a man should marry his dead brother's widow. In such a case, the woman's children by her dead husband would call her new husband "father." The Yanomamö simply institutionalize this by calling both men—the father and the father's brother—by the term meaning father, whether or not both men have married the mother. They do the same on the mother's side: the mother and the mother's sister are called by the word meaning mother, and a woman can marry her dead sister's husband. The rule is called the sororate—the mirror image of the levirate. It is quite logical to the Yanomamö that parallel cousins should be classified as brothers and sisters.

The rule, therefore, is that the Yanomamö marry bilateral (from both the father's *and* the mother's side of the family) cross-cousins. In their words, the rule is: "Men should marry their *suaböya*." In a sense, it is like saying, "We marry our wives," for the men call their wives *and* their female cross-cousins *suaböya*. Thus, to ask them the general question "Whom do you marry?" strikes them as peculiar. They marry their wives, as everyone does.

It is important to note that this marriage rule is embedded in the kinship terminology: men marry women they call *suaböya*. The Yanomamö kinship system literally defines who is and who is not marriageable to whom, and it has *no* terms that are limited to what we call in-laws. In a word, everyone in the Yanomamö society is called by one or another kinship term that we would translate as the term for a blood relative. To be sure, the Yanomamö extend kinship terms to those who are nonkin; Kaobawä calls Rerebawä by a kinship term, although they are not related. One fascinating aspect of their society is that *all* neighbors are some sort of kin, and therefore all their social life takes place in a kinship matrix of real and fictive kin. Nobody can escape it, not even the anthropologist. Kaobawä calls me *hekamaya*—nephew (sister's son)—and Rerebawä calls me *aiwä*—older brother. Everyone gets placed in some sort of kinship matrix, which, to a large degree, defines how one is expected to behave toward specific categories of one's kin. Both Kaobawä and Rerebawä know that I am not his sister's son or his older brother, respectively, but I must be put into *some* kinship category in order to establish a general basis of proper social behavior. To be outside the Yanomamö kinship system is, in a very real sense, to be inhuman or nonhuman: all humans are some sort of kin. This is what anthropologists mean when they say that a primitive society is largely organized and regulated by kinship. Remember it when you read a shallow account by some journalist or traveler telling how "the natives liked me so much that they adopted me." The natives were simply putting him or her into a kinship category, whether or not they liked the outsider. And it was probably the most exploitable category, that is, the one that would bring in the most gifts for the largest number of people. It is exactly what the Yanomamö did to me.

Here are two humorous examples of how kinship dictates expected forms of behavior, both involving the Yanomamö's rule that it is very inappropriate for a man to be familiar with the mother of a woman he can marry or has married. Indeed, they describe such behavior as *yawaremou*, or incest. A man should not look into the face of his mother-in-law, say her name, go near her, touch or speak to her.

On one occasion, I was mapping an empty village with the help of two young men. As we proceeded around the village, we came to a hearth. One of the young men walked out to the middle of the village, took three or four steps in the direction we were headed, and came back and stood on the other side of the abandoned hearth. When I asked why he was acting in such a strange way, the other man whispered in embarrassment, "His mother-in-law lives there." Then both of them blushed.

Some time later, I decided to have a little fun with this taboo. The Yanomamö term for mother-in-law is *yaya*, but the same kinship term also applies to one's father's sister or one's grandmother, women who need not be avoided to the same degree. While visiting my wife's family in northern Michigan one year, I had a photograph taken of me hugging my wife's mother and kissing her on the cheek. On my next field trip, I brought along this photo and many others of my family and my wife's family to show to Kaobawä's people, who were fascinated by them. When we got to the photo of me hugging my mother-in-law, they recognized me and asked, "Who are you hugging?" I responded, "My *yaya*." Chuckles and giggles followed. Then one of them asked, "Is she your father's mother?" "No," I replied casually. (It is all right to be somewhat familiar with a grandmother.) "Ahh. She must be your mother's mother." Again I nonchalantly said, "No." Murmurs and whispers followed, and their smiles changed to looks of apprehension—there was only one legitimate choice left. "Ahh. She is your father's sister." I paused, to extend the suspense, and then I said offhandedly, "No, she's my wife's mother." Embarrassed laughter and protests exploded from the group. They were incredulous at my audacity and my flagrant violation of the incest avoidance prohibition—the more so because

I was carrying around photographic evidence of the misdeed. For several years afterward, visitors from distant villages would come to my hut and beg to see the photograph of me "committing incest" with my wife's mother, as if it were something pornographic. They even blushed as they looked at it.

The discovery of one principle often leads to the identification of others. I knew, for example, that the Yanomamö men held a warm affection for the men they called by the term *shoriwä*. These men, it turned out, are the brothers of the woman a man has married, will marry, or could marry—they are his male cross-cousins. Similarly, the obviously warm relationship between a man and his mother's brother (photo 30) is quite comprehensible in terms of the marriage rule: the man can marry the older man's daughter.

These general rules or principles also exist for notions of descent from remote, long-deceased ancestors, and the anthropologist discovers them in essentially the same way as kinship rules. For the Yanomamö, descent through the male line is more important than descent through the female line, especially with regard to general principles of marriage. Patrilineal descent defines as the members of a group—called a patrilineage—all those individuals who can trace their descent back to some male ancestor using only the male genealogical connections.

An easy way to grasp this is to relate it to the way in which our traditional American culture passes on family names to our descendants. If you are a man named Jefferson, your children are also Jeffersons, including your daughter. If she marries, say, a Washington, her children will be Washingtons. But your son's children will continue to be Jeffersons. Those who have the family name of Jefferson would be a patrilineage, distinct from the patrilineage of the Washingtons.

For the moment, let us assume that an entire village has only Washingtons and Jeffersons in it. The general Yanomamö rule about marriage, insofar as it can be phrased in terms of a descent rule, is that everyone *must* marry outside his or her patrilineal group: if you are a Jefferson, you should marry a Washington, and vice versa. This descent rule, plus the rule of marriage with cross-cousins, can be summarized in the form of a structuralist model of Yanomamö social organization, as shown in the diagram entitled "Ideal Model of the Yanomamö Social Structure." This model shows patrilineal descent and patrilineage exogamy (everyone must marry outside his or her group). Marriage with a cross-cousin is unavoidable if everyone follows these rules: all male Jeffersons have to marry female Washingtons who are approximately their own age, and

30. *Ariwari at play with his mother's brother. This is a very special kinship relationship among the Yanomamö.*

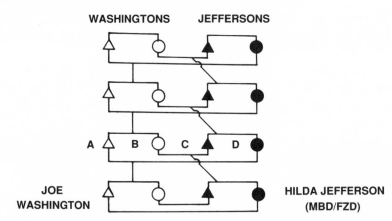

WASHINGTONS   JEFFERSONS

A   B   C   D

JOE WASHINGTON

HILDA JEFFERSON (MBD/FZD)

Ideal Model of Yanomamö Social Structure
The model shows how two lineages, the Washingtons and the Jeffersons, exchange marriageable
women. Each man marries a woman who is simultaneously
his MBD and his FZD.

all male Washingtons have to marry female Jeffersons, as the diagram shows. Over time, every Washington would be marrying a cross-cousin named Jefferson, as Joe Washington's marriage with Hilda Jefferson illustrates. Trace out the relationships for yourself: Joe's father is A and his father's sister is B. Hilda, the daughter of B, is therefore Joe's father's sister's daughter (FZD). Joe's mother is D and his mother's brother is C. Hilda, being also the daughter of C, is Joe's mother's brother's daughter (MBD) as well.

Structural anthropologists, such as Claude Lévi-Strauss, are fascinated by the ideal models they can draw to represent, in shorthand fashion, the social structure of a society like this one, using as the basis of the model abstract rules or principles of the sort just described: the society's rules about kinship, descent, and marriage. These are the nice, symmetrical shells I spoke of earlier.

But the real world is much less tidy, and people do not always follow their rules to the letter—usually because they cannot. The ideal model assumes something of a demographic paradise in which each parent has two and only two children, one a son and the other a daughter, the children all live to reproduce, there is no divorce, a brother always gives his sister to a man who gives his sister in return, and so on and on. In the real world, people die, get divorced, have five sons and no daughters, marry several spouses, give their sisters to someone they shouldn't, et cetera. These are the demographic realities that individuals have to contend with. They result in a statistical outcome very different from the one implied in the ideal model—the amorphous creature that is unpleasant to deal with.

The Demographic Basis
of the Yanomamö Society

Let me illustrate the statistical approach by focusing on the question of *solidarity* as it relates to the process of village fissioning, an extremely important and recurrent feature of Yanomamö social organization.

Anthropologists have long been concerned with the problem of social solidarity, a vague and ill-defined concept. It basically has to do with cooperation and the ability of groups of people to live cheek by jowl in the same community without incessant disagreements and conflict while simultaneously helping each other as members of the group. The argument is essentially this: what provides the binding force or cohesion in primitive societies, the attraction between individuals and groups that permits them to live together amicably? One might think of solidarity as the social glue that holds such groups together.

At the expense of oversimplifying, let us recast the problem in the language of the marriage arrangements just described. It is obvious that if the Jeffersons kept marrying the Washingtons generation after generation, they would all be related to each other. After a while, all the Jefferson men would be related to their Washington wives as cousins. If the two families live in the same village, the anthropological question becomes: are the Jeffersons and the Washingtons able to live together in peace and tranquillity because they keep *marrying* each other or because they are *related by blood* to each other? Where does the glue come from? Is it the marriage obligations between the families? Or does the altruism emanate from the fact that they are blood relatives? Does Ariwari Jefferson defend his uncle, Woodpecker Washington, because Ariwari married his daughter or because Woodpecker is his blood uncle?

While this seems a bit simplistic in the analogy developed here, it becomes more complex if the village has, in addition to the Jeffersons and the Washingtons, Smiths, Browns, O'Mearas, and Cunninghams, all of whom can marry each other's women—and are actively competing to do just that.

Yanomamö village fissioning can be viewed in this context. The villages grow to a certain size and then fission into smaller, more cohesive villages—the large village comes "unglued." One might even think of the process of village growth and fissioning as the failure of solidarity in a certain sense, for the forces or principles that keep a group together in a cooperative whole fail to do so beyond a certain size limit. While there are many variables that affect village size—geographical, ecological, demographic, military, and social—much of the internal cohesion of Yanomamö villages is generated through kinship relationships and marriage ties.

Now let us look at actual marriage patterns statistically and try to relate them to the problem of explaining why some Yanomamö villages are able to grow to a large size—300 people or more—while others seem unable to grow beyond 125 or so. Could it be that there is something about the patterns of marriage that helps explain this difference? If so, what should one look for in the marriages?

Let's assume that each individual marriage adds some glue and contributes something toward holding the village together. Thus, Kaobawä (Jefferson) married his first cross-cousin, Bahimi (Washington), and this marriage can be thought of as providing a little glue to the cohesion of Upper Bisaasi-teri. Rerebawä (Smith) married Shihotama (Jones), who was totally unrelated to him. This marriage probably added less glue to the cohesion of the village because it did not tie two already related families closer together: it was the first marriage between these families. Other men of the village (O'Mearas, Cunninghams, and so on) had other marriages, each of which we can examine in similar genealogical detail.

Such an approach allows us to see if there is a different kind of marriage pattern within large villages as compared to small villages. Both have the same overall system or set of rules, but individuals may apply the rules differently or may be better able to marry specific kinds of cousins simply because there are more of them to begin with.

Such an exhaustive statistical examination would have been almost impossible for me to do without the use of a computer. First I coded all the genealogical, marital, and reproductive data that I had collected in all the villages I studied. Then the computer searched each person's relationships and built up an exhaustive genealogy, or pedigree, from this field data. It compared each person to his or her spouse, spelling out all the genealogical connections and describing precisely how each person was genealogically connected to his or her spouse. The resulting printout was thick enough to stand on to change a light bulb in the ceiling.

In the villages that got the largest before they fissioned, more of the men tended to be related to their wives as first cross-cousins of both the FZD and the MBD types than did the men in the smaller villages. In other words, in the large villages the men were marrying *closer* cross-cousins.

What these data suggest is that the maximum size a village reaches might somehow be related to the fact that the men in that village tend to marry close cousins more often than do the men in smaller villages.

Polygyny, Genealogical Structures, and Close Kinship

The main reason men are able to marry first cousins has to do with how much polygyny (the practice of having multiple wives) there has been in previous generations. More precisely, if a man is particularly successful in obtaining several wives, his male grandchildren will have a large number of female cross-cousins as potential marriage partners.

Say, for example, the founding Jefferson had ten wives and five children by each, for a total of fifty children. Say also that all his wives were Washingtons. He would encourage his sons (whose names are Jefferson) to find Washington women to marry. Old man Washington, of course, gave old man Jefferson his five sisters, and he would like about the same number of women back so that he can have lots of children, too. They strike a long-term deal: I'll give you my sisters in exchange for yours, and when I have children I'll give my daughters to your sons if you give your daughters to my sons. So they carry out the deal, and in the next generation all the grandchildren are grandchildren of both men. And the grandchildren can fall into only four kinds of relationships with respect to each other: (1) brothers and sisters, (2) half brothers and sisters, (3) parallel cousins, who cannot marry, and (4) cross-cousins, who can.

Polygyny in a society with patrilineal descent has very different consequences for social organization than does polyandry (women with multiple husbands) in a society with matrilineal descent. One man with ten wives can have many more children than one woman with ten husbands, and these reproductive and physiological differences have profound implications for understanding the extent of a lineage and the interlineage marriage exchange practices of tribal societies like the Yanomamö. Polygyny and its reproductive and social consequences lie at the very heart of solidarity and traditional social organization in the tribal world, and it should be clear how devastating it is to such a society when missionaries or others forbid its men to have more than one wife.

Yanomamö polygyny can have remarkable reproductive consequences for some men. The Shamatari population of several generations back included a particularly accomplished man named Shinbone. Think of him as the original Jefferson of our analogy. Some of Shinbone's children are still alive today. He had eleven wives, by whom he had forty-three children. His children, of course, were all siblings or half siblings to each other, and therefore the males among them had many sisters to give away in marriage—in exchange for women that they (or their sons) could marry.

I was told of two or three other men like Shinbone who were around at the same time—Washingtons, Cunninghams, or Browns, men with many wives and many children—but none rivaled Shinbone in marital or reproductive performance. By entering into marriage alliances with these men and their sons, the members of Shinbone's patrilineage became bound to them in long-term marriage exchanges. Thus, many of Shinbone's grandchildren had many cross-cousins to choose among as potential spouses, and it was relatively easy for them to follow the rules of cross-cousin marriage.

One consequence of the marriage arrangements between members of the larger lineages such as Shinbone's is that their villages become characterized by higher levels of what we call inbreeding. Marriages between close cousins raise the degree of kinship relatedness between *all* individuals over time. As might be expected, the larger villages differed from the smaller ones in patterns of relatedness: individuals in larger villages had more relatives and were more closely related to those relatives than was the case in the smaller villages.

This is something we anthropologists still argue about. Does the solidarity come from *kinship* relationships or the *marriage* alliances? What is clear from Yanomamö marriage and kinship is that we cannot dismiss either as irrelevant. One, in fact, leads to the other.

But kinship relatedness, patterns of marriage, and obligations based on descent eventually seem to break down as solidarity-promoting mechanisms. Yanomamö villages appear unable to get larger than about 300 people before they fission into smaller ones. In fact, a human population group was rarely able to get above the "magic numbers" of 50 to 100 until we discovered ways to organize our communities along principles that went beyond kinship, marriage, and descent. Thwarting the power of nepotism on a society-wide scale may have been one of the most significant accomplishments in human history, for then we could develop the communities of today that reach into the millions of people.

But the power of nepotism is still real and still with us. Within those communities of millions, the persons to whom we are related tend to be our most dependable allies. If we need a reliable partner, associate, or accomplice, we ask a close kinsman. Few of us have friends who are as unflinchingly loyal as our brothers, sisters, parents, or children. The risks get a bit higher with cousins, nieces, nephews, uncles, and aunts.

In our contemporary society, many of us do have more reliable friends than we have distant cousins or shirttail relatives—nepotism can be extended only so far. The principles on which our modern society rests have, in general, gone far beyond nepotism. We have laws, police, courts, governments, and many other institutions to do things for us as individuals that in the evolutionary past only a kinsman would have done. It is even possible today to bring suit against one's brother, father, or cousin, something unthinkable in the evolutionary past. And our spouses and former spouses are popular targets of litigation in our world—among other reasons, because they are rarely our kinsmen.

Kinship Rules, Reproduction, and Rule Breaking

I mentioned earlier that many Yanomamö break their rules, especially the kinship and marriage rules. The arena in which their kinship rule breaking is most conspicuous is that of incestuous marriage. Recall that Yanomamö men define only one category of women as marriageable; all other marriages are prohibited, and sex or marriage with a person in the prohibited categories is considered incestuous, or *yawäremou*.

One reason for so much rule breaking in marriage has to do with the differences in the reproductive physiology of males and females. Women marry young and begin producing children while young. But their reproductive life spans are relatively short—twenty years or so. Men marry later and begin reproducing later, but their reproductive life spans are long. Shinbone, for instance, had children who were at least fifty years apart in age. One of my best Shamatari informants and closest friends, a man named Dedeheiwä, was about sixty-five years old at the time of the following incident. A girl of about eleven passed by and called him by a term meaning "older brother." When I asked him why she had addressed him by that kinship term, he explained that they were half siblings. His father had had many wives and had sired Dedeheiwä by one of his first ones. Fifty or so years later, he had sired this young girl by a different wife.

One consequence of all this is that the length of generations through females is relatively short compared to the length through males. Say that a sixteen-year-old girl has a child; if it is a female, she at sixteen might also have a child; if a girl, she at sixteen can have another, and so on. Their respective brothers in each generation are likely to be in their mid-twenties when they sire their first children. The net result is that the ages of individuals get out of synchrony with their generational identities, and, with older men marrying young women, people may have brothers or sisters who are younger than their grandchildren. Since the Yanomamö kinship classifications utilize generational position to define who is marriageable to whom, something has to give. Girls are ready for marriage at puberty and boys when they are in their early twenties, and no right-thinking Yanomamö will wait patiently for fifty years until his sister's daughter is old enough to marry one of his sons. What gives is the kinship classification. People *must* chronically reclassify some relatives in order to keep kinship classifications more or less in harmony with ages and generational identities; they *must* break the kinship rules to make the marriage practices work.

This finding is very far from what is implied in anthropological theory and in textbooks on kinship—that the kinship terms used by tribesmen for their relatives are learned once and remain inflexible during an individual's lifetime. My findings suggest that kinship relations are very dynamic and are constantly being changed to fit immediate marriage requirements.

The "Decay" of the Nuclear Family

The more I thought about the necessity for rule breaking, the more it led me into an investigation of another set of demographic problems. I will end this chapter with a brief discussion of these and what they mean for an understanding not only of Yanomamö social organization and social behavior but probably of what we would find in many other tribal societies and what possibly has characterized the entire course of human history. I offer this as an example of the way detailed information about one society can help us understand another society, even one in the ancient past, about which we are unable to obtain such information.

Yanomamö mortality patterns and birth rates lead to a characteristic distribution of the population into age and sex categories that can be graphically represented in a pyramid similar to the one shown on page 271 in chapter 7. Basically, there are many children, because of a relatively high birth rate, but many of them die before the age of ten, because of a relatively high death rate, causing the steplike narrowing of the pyramid. The biggest step is the reduction in the number of children between the first age category (the bottom bar) and the second one. Note, however, that the mortality rate is high enough at all ages to make the steps obvious and fairly large; that many young adults are dying as well, although at a lower rate. Our population's age/sex distribution looks very different, because our mortality rates and birth rates are much lower (the final chapter has a more extended discussion of this).

The Yanomamö age/sex distribution is characteristic of tribal populations in all parts of the world where introduced diseases and other exogenous forces have not radically altered the demography—and the distribution has probably been characteristic of populations throughout history. One of the predictions we can draw from this is that many children will be orphaned at an early age because of the premature death of one or the other of their parents. This is true of the Yanomamö, who have many orphan children.

Divorce also occurs among the Yanomamö, at a rate of approximately 20 percent—comparatively low by anthropological standards. This adds to the number of children raised by other than their two biological parents. Presumably divorce was also common in the ancient past.

What does this mean for an understanding of the Yanomamö nuclear family? Or for the nuclear family throughout our long history as hunters and gatherers or members of tribal societies? Several years ago both *Time* and *Newsweek* ran cover stories that interpreted the increasing rate of family dissolution as an alarming recent trend of our civilized world. My suspicion is that it has been characteristic of our entire history, but that the rates fluctuate within the same society over short periods.

I examined the composition of households in a large number of Yanomamö villages that had a total population of approximately 1,400. I asked these kinds of questions for each individual—or had my computer ask them: is the mother alive and in the same village? Is the father alive and in the same village? Are the biological mother and father both alive and living in the same village?

The results surprised even me. Most textbooks in anthropology refer to the nuclear family as the fundamental building block of all human societies, emphasizing how important it is in understanding social ties and how universal it is—while dutifully noting that one or two societies, like the Nyar, seem to be unusual in not having a nuclear family. One gets the impression from many textbooks that once the nuclear family is formed, it lasts forever. What my analysis indicated, however, was that by the time Yanomamö children reach the ripe old age of ten, only about one in three lives in a family including his or her still-married mother and father, and by the age of twenty only about one in ten comes from such a family.

There is good reason to believe that this has been true for most of our history, certainly for that vast period of it when our ancestors lived under circumstances similar to those found among the Yanomamö. The so-called fundamental building block of human society appears to have a very short half-life when it is examined statistically.

The issue becomes even more intriguing when we think about what it means for an understanding of the marriage practices and marriage systems of many tribal societies, especially those in which the parents, particularly the father, arrange their children's marriages.

Most Yanomamö men, when they reach marriageable age (the early twenties), do not have a living father. Who arranges their marriages? This raises yet other questions, and sometimes acrimonious anthropological debate. For example, I would predict that if a man had a biological son and a son he had adopted when he married a woman with children from a previous marriage, and it came time for him to arrange marriages for both, he would be more interested in the reproductive future of his biological son than of his adopted son, especially if marriageable girls were scarce. I get hissed and booed by some of my cultural anthropology associates for saying such things. Many of them argue that this is an unacceptable form of biological reductionism and, as an article of faith, suggest that this father would be equally interested in looking out for both sons. Kinship, they would say, has nothing to do with biology; father is a symbolic category; people's behavior is determined entirely by their culture and symbols.

A distinguished English biologist and dear friend of mine, who is often criticized by social scientists for the kinds of views I also hold, once mused over dinner, "If that is true, then I should imagine that the following kind of scenario is commonplace in pediatric wards. When the father comes in on the day he picks up his wife and new infant and goes to the nursery to ask, 'Which one is mine?' the nurse says, 'Take anyone you want. They're all the same.' So he takes the one closest to him."

The statistical information on the Yanomamö nuclear family suggests that most males, when they reach marriageable age, will not have their fathers around to help them find a wife and will have to rely on the assistance of other adult males.

Given these general facts, I was prompted to make the following predictions about kinship and genealogical knowledge by sex and how the kinship reclassifications—the rule breaking—might be patterned.

(1) The men have difficulty finding wives because women are in short supply—some successful men have many wives, but unsuccessful men have none. If a man cannot rely on having a living father to help him, he must pay attention to which other males might—and that means he must learn genealogies and kinship classifications thoroughly, because the information will be useful for his marriage possibilities and reproductive future. Yanomamö men should, in short, know more about genealogies and kinship than the women do, something that may be counterintuitive even to anthropologists, who would probably use the same argument that nonspecialists do: since it is the women who have the babies, they are the ones most likely to know more about kinship and relatedness.

(2) The women never have trouble finding husbands and are always (or almost always) married throughout their adult lives. No amount of knowledge about genealogies or kinship classifications will alter this.

(3) If kinship classifications have to be altered to keep age and generation in synchrony so that the marriage system works, and if men can marry only the women they classify as *suaböya*, then the men should show a bias in their reclassifications: men should tend to move women out of the maritally prohibited categories (sister, daughter, niece) and into the wife category whenever they have to reclassify them.

In 1985, I did an elaborate test of these predictions. I had 100 informants of both sexes and all ages in three different villages tell me what kinship term they used for everyone in the village. To make sure we both knew who we were talking about, I showed each informant a Polaroid picture of the person as I whispered that person's name into the informant's ear and asked, "What do you call so-and-so?" I tape-recorded and timed the 12,000 or so responses. I already knew, from many years of fieldwork in the same villages, how everyone was related, going back four or five generations, and I knew what the informants *should* be calling their kinsmen if they were following their ideal rules of classification.

The results were as I had predicted. The males were faster than the females at classifying their kin, suggesting that they knew more about the genealogy and kinship than the females. They had the information at the tip of their tongues, so to speak, while the females frequently had to do some genealogical algebra, like "Well, I call his father so-and-so and his sister such-and-such, so I suppose I'd call him husband."

When the kinship classifications of the adult males (seventeen and older) were analyzed, they showed a clear, statistically significant pattern of reclassifying more women into the wife category than into any of the other categories for female relatives. The bias was to move females out of reproductively useless categories and into the only reproductively useful category, that of wife. A detailed analysis of the women who were moved into this category showed that most of them were young and had a high reproductive value; they were not older women past their reproductive prime.

I learned a number of anthropological lessons in the course of this elaborate exercise. One of them was that the Yanomamö kinship system was quite dynamic, rather than being a crystallized set of terms for relatives that each person learned and faithfully recited for the remainder of his or her life. The people simply *had* to change their kinship usage to keep the marriage system working, since marriageability was defined in large measure by what kinship term a person used for those around him or her. I also learned that the initial rule-breaking manipulations were made by prominent men who had great confidence that their manipulations would succeed and would find support among their friends and kinsmen, many of whom would benefit from the manipulations: incest was, in a very real sense, a kind of political act that reflected the status and authority of the initiator. The overall result of the manipulations was that they usually had positive reproductive consequences for those who initiated them. This suggests that individuals ultimately manipulate their culture for gains that have positive reproductive benefits.

Rerebawä, predicting the future of Breakosi, his firstborn son, once said to me proudly, "He is a real fierce little guy. So fierce that when he grows up he will probably commit incest." What he was saying was that the boy would know the kinship rules and genealogies so well that if they got in his way he would break them and put someone into a marriageable category who did not belong there—would commit incest. In the Yanomamö culture, a man can do this successfully and predictably only if he is prepared to defend his rule violations, and his ability to do so depends largely on how believable his threats are—how fierce he is. The most flagrant cases of incest I have recorded—men marrying parallel cousins or, in one instance, a half sister—involve men who were not only headmen but headmen with reputations for ferocity. Breaking the rules to gain personal advantage is easier in any culture if the rule breaker has power, acquired or inherited. In the Yanomamö culture, power is partly acquired, via demonstrations of individual prowess, and partly inherited, by a man's having lots of kin who will endorse his manipulations and rule breaking, probably because they, too, stand to gain.

After I realized all of this, something else made sense to me. When I had showed the Yanomamö the picture of me hugging my wife's mother—"committing incest"—some of them had blurted out, "Wow! You are really fierce." I didn't understand at first why they equated incest with personal prowess or ferocity and tended to predict one from knowing the other. Now I saw that they probably had invented all sorts of fabulous activities I was engaged in to be able to get away with hugging my mother-in-law.

Chapter Five

The Art, Politics, and Etiquette of Entertaining Guests

Yanomamö feasts are political events. They are held whenever one sovereign group entertains the members of an allied group. To be sure, they have significant economic and ceremonial implications, but those are minor when compared to the feast's importance in the forming and maintaining of alliances. The chief purpose of entertaining allies is to reaffirm and cultivate intervillage amity in the intimate, sociable context of having a festive meal together. The allied group then feels obligated to reciprocate in its own village with another feast, and more intervillage amity. The feasts are an important element in reducing the possibility of warfare between groups.

Significant factors in the formation of alliances are trade, economic specialization, historical ties between groups, patterns of warfare, and intervillage marriage exchanges, all of which are intimately connected and interact with each other in the development of alliances.

I described in chapter 2 how the members of several villages cultivated friendships with each other and built up a loose network of allied villages. In chapter 4, I showed how Kaobawä's followers were related to him and how he was related to the members of several other villages. I will continue the story here by going into the political consequences of these ties and the way they shaped the relations between Kaobawä's group and others. To illustrate my points, I will describe a particular feast in Kaobawä's village in the context of the political ties, both historical and contemporary, that existed between his group and the guests at the feast. First, however, some comments on Yanomamö alliances in general.

Yanomamö Alliances

One of the benefits that the Yanomamö expect from an alliance is the obligation of the partners to shelter each other whenever one of them is driven from its village and garden by an enemy.

Sometimes the beleaguered partner has to remain in the host village for a year or longer—approximately the length of time required to establish a new garden and a productive base for an independent existence. The members of Kaobawä's group were driven from their gardens twice in their recent history and forced to take refuge in the village of an ally, where they remained for about a year. In both cases, the hosts seized the opportunity to demand a number of women from Kaobawä's homeless group without reciprocating in kind. The longer a group remains under a host's protection, the higher the cost in terms of the loss of women, so visitors always try to establish their new gardens and move as quickly as possible. Without allies, however, the members of a village would have to remain at their old garden, suffering the attacks of their enemies, or else break up into small groups and join other villages permanently, losing many of their women to their protectors. Living in the jungle is not a desirable option; it does not produce enough wild foods to permit a large group to remain in one place, and a small group would soon be overrun by its enemies.

The risk of being driven from one's garden is so pervasive in Kaobawä's area that no village can continue to exist as a sovereign entity unless it has alliances. The Yanomamö take the bellicose position that the stronger villages should always act ready to take advantage of weaker ones and to coerce women from them; to counter this, the members of all villages try to behave as if they are strong. The result of the constant military posturing is to make intervillage alliances desirable, but it also spawns an attitude that inhibits the formation of alliances: allies *need* each other but do not *trust* each other.

Alliances are usually the outcome of a sequence that starts with casual trading, goes on to mutual feasting, and finally leads to an exchange of women between villages to cement the alliance. The most intimate allies are those who, in addition to trading and feasting together, exchange women in marriage. A developing alliance may stabilize at the trading or feasting stage, without proceeding further, but these are weak alliances, serving mainly to limit the degree of fighting if relations turn hostile. The Yanomamö tend not to attack villages with which they trade and feast, unless a specific incident, like the abduction of a woman, provokes them. Allies linked by trade and feasting, for example, will rarely accuse each other of practicing harmful magic, often the trigger for war. Allies bound to each other by affinal kinship ties—relatedness created through intermarriage—are more interdependent, however, because they are under an obligation to each other to continue exchanging women. It is, in fact, through the exchange of women that historically independent villages expand their kinship ties.

Alliances almost always begin with trading between men from different villages, a phase that can last for years. Men go off to another village alone, leaving their women behind—but often making concealed camps in the forest for the women to hide in while the men are away. Indeed, suspicions may be so high that even after the trading phase has moved into feasting the men will continue to leave the women at home, for fear their new allies will appropriate some of them. Not until trust and confidence have developed will they bring their wives and children along.

Members of allied villages are usually reluctant to take the final step in alliance formation of ceding women to their partners, for they always worry that a partner might not reciprocate as promised. This attitude is especially conspicuous in small villages, whose larger alliance partners often try to pressure them into demonstrating their friendship by ceding women. The strong can and do coerce the weak in Yanomamö politics, forcing the weak into a posture of bluff and intimidation to make themselves appear stronger than they really are. Such behavior tells the larger partner that any attempt to coerce women will be met with an appropriate reaction, such as a chest-pounding duel or a club fight. Still, each partner in an alliance expects to gain women by it—indeed, enters it with this in mind—and each hopes to gain more women than it loses.

Hence, the long and difficult road of trading and feasting usually must be traversed before an occasional meeting of nervous groups of men from different villages can evolve into a stable intervillage alliance based on the reciprocal exchange of women. Suspicion must give way to confidence and to a period of reciprocal feasting. Only then does the intervillage relationship reach a point at which the partners may begin ceding women to each other, and even that is done cautiously.

The women who are exchanged are the ones who like it least of all, for in their new village they will have no brothers or other kinsmen to protect them from a cruel husband. And often their parents share the feeling. Shihotama's parents worried for her well-being every time Rerebawä threatened to move back to his native village with her and their children.

But this is only a thumbnail sketch of the necessary steps in the development of an alliance. Rarely do relations reach the stage at which women are actually exchanged, particularly if the two villages are approximately equal in military strength. Fights and arguments break out over women, food, etiquette, generosity, status, and the like, and the principals may withdraw on semihostile terms, perhaps attempting a rapprochement later on. Or, if the principals are obviously unequal militarily, the stronger of them will try to coerce its weaker partner into ceding women early on, taking advantage of its military strength but impeding the development of the alliance.

Whatever the specific sequence of events, the environment in which they take place is hardly conducive to the establishment of warm ties of friendship. Each of the principals attempts to demonstrate that it does not really need this political alliance to keep its enemies in check. Both groups brag about past military victories and their fierceness in club fights and chest-pounding duels, insinuating that one's own group is on the verge of exploding into a force so great that no combination of allies could overcome it. The smaller and more vulnerable the village, the harder it works to insinuate such a potential, especially if its members are trying to remain in a desirable ecological niche.

Political maneuvering in such a setting is both tricky and potentially hazardous. Each principal must establish the credibility of its threats, while taking care not to go beyond the point at which the partner's bluff will dissolve abruptly into action. It is a politics of brinkmanship, a form of political behavior in which each negotiator tries to expose his opposite number's threats as bluff, at the risk of inciting the opponent to violence—a club fight, immediately and honorably, or perhaps, later and treacherously, a feast during which the hosts descend on their guests in a deadly attack.

Trading and Feasting to Make Friends of Enemies

There is little in the way of natural encouragement for two groups to begin visiting each other. One group is always ready to take advantage of the other's weaknesses, especially when the alliance is just developing. Pride and status preclude open attempts to develop stable and predictable alliances. The Yanomamö cannot simply arrive at the village of a potential ally and declare that they are being harassed by a powerful neighbor and need help. To do so would concede their vulnerability and perhaps even invite a raid from the potential ally. Instead, they subsume the true motive for forming an alliance in the vehicles of trading and feasting, developing these institutions over months and sometimes years. In this way they retain their sovereignty and pride while working toward their objective of intervillage solidarity and military interdependence.

Three distinct features of Yanomamö trading practices are important in the context of alliance formation. First, each item traded must be paid for with a different kind of item, in a type of exchange called *no mraiha*. To the inexperienced observer, a person who gives something *no mraiha* appears to be giving it for free, as a gift. But someday the giver remembers it and uses it as a lever to ask for a gift in return. The delayed repayment is a second feature of the *no mraiha*. Taken together, these two features mean that one trade always calls forth another and gives the members of different villages both an excuse and an opportunity for visiting. And the trading tends to continue, for the members of one village always owe the members of the other some trade goods from their last meeting.

I was recently reminded of the reciprocity of the *no mraiha* when I traveled to a remote village that I had not visited for several years and found the people eagerly waiting for the gifts they knew I had brought. Preparing my meal the first night, I filled my small aluminum pot with water and looked around for a piece of vine or an old bowstring by which I could hang the pot from the low roof poles over my host's campfire. I noticed that an old woman in the next house had just what I needed, an old bowstring tied to a hook-shaped piece of wood made specifically to hang a pot over a fire.

"Can I borrow that cord next to you so I can hang my pot over the fire?" I called to her.

She grinned from ear to ear, untied the cord from her roof pole, and handed it to me.

I told her she was very generous and a good friend.

Still grinning, she whined, as old women do, "*No mraiha mai* [Just don't get the idea that this is a free loan]."

The third significant trade feature is a peculiar kind of specialization in the production of items for trade. Each village has one or more products that it provides to its allies. These might include dogs, hallucinogenic drugs (both cultivated and wild), arrow points, arrow shafts, bows, cotton yarn, cotton and vine hammocks, baskets of several varieties, clay pots, and, in the case of villages that have contact with outsiders, steel tools, fishhooks, fish line, and aluminum pots.

The specialization has nothing to do with the availability of natural resources to make the product. Each village is capable of self-sufficiency. (The steel tools and other products from the civilized world are the major exception.) The explanation for the specialization lies, rather, in the sociological aspects of alliance formation. Trade functions as a social catalyst, the starting mechanism by which mutually suspicious groups are repeatedly brought together in friendly meetings. Without these frequent contacts, alliances would be much slower to form and far less stable. A prerequisite to a stable alliance is repeated visiting and feasting, and the trading mechanism serves to bring about these visits.

Clay pots are a good example of how this specialization in trade promotes intervillage relations. The Mömariböwei-teri are a group allied to both Kaobawä's nearby group and the people of a distant Shamatari village who are mortal enemies of Kaobawä. When I first began my fieldwork, I visited the Mömariböwei-teri, about a ten-hour walk away, specifically to ask them about the making of clay pots. They all vigorously denied any knowledge of pot making, saying that they had once known how but had long since forgotten. They added that their allies the Möwaraoba-teri (Sibarariwä's village) made pots and provided them with all they needed. Besides, they said, the clay around their village was not suitable for pots. Later in the year, their alliance with the pot makers cooled, because of a war, and their source was shut off. At the same time, Kaobawä's group began asking them for clay pots. The Mömariböwei-teri promptly "remembered" how to make pots and "discovered" that their clay was suitable, after all. They had merely been creating a local shortage in order to have an excuse to visit an ally.

Often the specialization is less individualized than this. Kaobawä's group, for example, exports hand-spun cotton yarn to one ally but imports it from another. Moreover, the exported yarn frequently comes back in the form of hammocks, the importer of the yarn merely contributing its labor. Sometimes trade in a particular item is seasonal; Kaobawä's group may import cotton from an ally at one time of the year but export it at another. Most of the trade, however, is in items that are readily made or grown by any group, underscoring the fact that the trade is primarily a stimulus to visiting. Food does not enter the trading system, although hospitality dictates that it must be given to friendly groups. Occasionally a village will run short of plantains, perhaps because a long hot spell has damaged the crop, and its members may visit an ally to borrow enough food for a week or so. Such hospitality is usually reciprocated, but it is not considered a part of the trading network.

Alliances may stabilize at any one of three levels: sporadic trading, mutual feasting, or the exchange of women. They are cumulative levels; allies that exchange women also feast and trade together, and allies that feast also trade but do not exchange women. At the lower end of the scale of alliance solidarity lie those villages with which a group is at war, and at the upper end are usually those villages from whom one's group has recently separated—although sometimes the scale is reversed, and a village's mortal enemy is the group from which it has recently split. By way of example, Kaobawä's group trades sporadically with the Makorima-teri, the Daiyari-teri, the Widokaiya-teri, the Mahekodo-teri, and the Iyäwei-teri, villages that are unrelated to his. These are fairly weak alliances and even involve some limited fighting like prearranged chest-pounding duels. The group has closer ties with the Reyaboböwei-teri and the Mömariböwei-teri, with whom it feasts regularly. The alliance with the Reyaboböwei-teri has reached the stage of exchanging women, although more have come into Kaobawä's group than have left it. At the lower end of the scale, Kaobawä's group is at war with the Iwahikoroba-teri, the Möwaraoba-teri, and a segment of the Patanowä-teri. The first two of these groups, not historically related to Kaobawä's group, have a common history with two of his staunchest allies, the Reyaboböwei-teri and the Mömariböwei-teri, from whom they fissioned in the recent past. The Patanowä-teri are related to Kaobawä and his followers (this was discussed in chapter 2). Nevertheless, Kaobawä and his group are bitter enemies of one faction of the Patanowä-teri, and at present the groups are raiding each other.

There is no rigid geographical correlation between village settlement patterns and the degree of alliance solidarity, but usually immediate neighbors are at least on trading terms and not actively at war. When a war does break out between neighbors, one of them abandons its site and moves to a new location. The nature of the ties between neighboring villages—they may be ties of blood, marriage exchange, reciprocal feasting, or casual trading—depends on many factors, particularly village size, the current state of warfare with more distant groups, and the precise historical ties between neighbors. Whatever the ties, however, each neighbor strives to remain sovereign and independent.

The Yanomamö do not overtly concede that trade is a mechanism for bringing people together repeatedly in order to establish an amicable basis for a more stable alliance. Nor do they acknowledge the relationship between the trading and feasting cycles and village interdependency. In this regard, they are like the Trobriand Islanders of Melanesia in displaying a "functional ignorance" of the adaptive aspects of their trading institutions. Both the Yanomamö and the Trobrianders treat the mechanisms by which people from different groups are induced to visit each other as ends in themselves, not related to the establishment of either economic or political interdependency.

For a Yanomamö, the feast's significance lies in the marvelous quantities of food, the excitement of the dance, and the satisfaction of having others admire and covet the fine decorations he wears—and, if he is so inclined, in the opportunity for a clandestine sexual liaison. The enchantment of the dance issues from the dancer's awareness that, for a brief moment, he is a glorious peacock who commands the admiration of his fellows and that it is his responsibility and his desire to make a spectacular display of his dance steps and gaudy accoutrements. In this brief, ego-building moment, each man, guest or host, has the chance to display himself, spinning and prancing about the village periphery, chest puffed out, while all watch, admire, and cheer wildly. The dancer does not say, "We are feasting you so that if we are in trouble you will help us."

For the hosts, the feast serves as a display of their affluence and a challenge for the guests to reciprocate with an equally grandiose feast at a later date. (The competitive aspects of feasting in primitive societies have been dealt with at length by Marcel Mauss in his essay *The Gift*, now an anthropological classic.) Indeed, some villages provide so much food that the participants compete in drinking enormous quantities of banana soup or peach palm gruel, which they vomit up and then return for more (photo 31). The plaza rapidly becomes dotted with large pools of vomit, and one must be careful where he walks—and careful not to walk in front of a celebrant who is about to regurgitate. Each good feast calls forth another, and the allies become better acquainted as they reciprocate feasts in the dry season and over the years.

31. *A visitor vomiting peach palm gruel at a ceremonial drinking bout
in the hosts' village.*

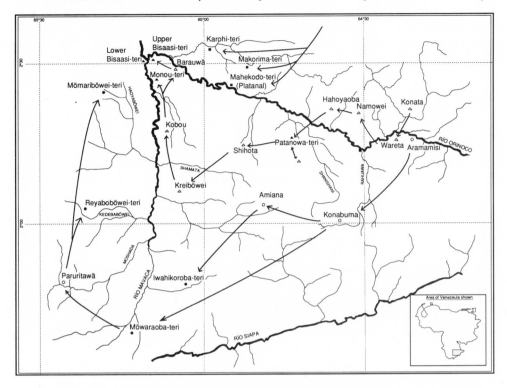

Historical Movements of Some Yanomamö Groups
Movements of the Bisaasi-teri (triangles) over approximately 125 years, beginning at the
ancient site of Konata. Some neighboring villages of other population blocs are also shown
to their north (squares) and south (circles). Solid symbols indicate contemporary villages.

Historical Background to a Particular Feast

All the features of intervillage politics that I have just discussed were in evidence at the feast I am going to describe. But first some historical background is necessary, including the recapitulation of a few events related earlier, in the context of the history of Kaobawä's village. The significance of what happened at the feast will then become clear, for the prior relationship between Kaobawä's group and the guests at the feast had a great deal to do with the outcome.

In 1950, Kaobawä's group, then living at a site called Kreiböwei-täka, was almost friendless, beleaguered by its enemies, and somewhat isolated. It began to cultivate an alliance with the Iwähikoroba-teri, a Shamatari village a day or two's travel to the southeast. The Iwähikoroba-teri were on friendly terms with another Shamatari group, the Möwaraoba-teri, from whom they had separated many years before. (The present locations and movements of these and other groups mentioned in this chapter are shown on the map entitled "Historical Movements of Some Yanomamö Groups.") Kaobawä's group, however, was at war with this village; some members of his group had treacherously killed a friendly Möwaraoba-teri visitor in the 1940s, touching off a series of raids between the groups. This is the killing described in the introduction.

Anxious to pursue an alliance, Kaobawä's group accepted an invitation from the Iwähikoroba-teri to attend a feast at their garden, called Amiana-täka. Until then, the two groups had only been on trading terms.

The Iwähikoroba-teri, however, had made a secret arrangement with their friends the Möwaraoba-teri to ambush the visitors. The Möwaraoba-teri and a few men from still other villages that they were allied to were hidden in the jungle outside the village when Kaobawä's group arrived.

The men of Kaobawä's group danced, both singly and en masse, and then were invited into the homes of their hosts, the normal procedure at feasts. Their wives and daughters, who had been watching from the village entrances, joined the men. The panting, highly decorated visiting warriors were now supposed to recline in their hosts' hammocks, motionless, and assume a highly ritualized pose, holding their hands over their mouths as they stared blankly up at the roof. Their hosts would then parade around the village, stopping in front of each reclining visitor and ritually intimidating him by pointing their drawn bows and feigning an attack with axes, clubs, and other weapons. The reclining men were expected to ignore these ritualized aggressive acts and exhibit stoic unconcern.

But the hosts were not pretending this time. They fell upon Kaobawä's men with axes and staves and killed about a dozen before the visitors could break through the palisade and escape. Kaobawä's father was among the victims. Once outside the village, they were ambushed by the Möwaraoba-teri, who killed a few more and wounded many others with their arrows. A number of women and girls were captured, although some were later retaken in revenge raids.

It was probably the hosts' greed for women that permitted any adult males to survive. The informants who told me this story solemnly and sadly spoke of how the Iwähikoroba-teri began chasing the women while the men were still vulnerable. A few of the Iwähikoroba-teri and the Möwaraoba-teri refused to participate in the slaughter and even helped some of Kaobawä's group to escape.

Many years later, these people were befriended by Kaobawä's people, who remembered their altruism.

The survivors fled to Kobou, a site the group had been clearing for a new garden. Here they removed the arrow points and nursed their wounds, before reluctantly returning to Kreiböwei, their only producing garden. Kobou was still too new to support them. But the Kreiböwei location was well known to their erstwhile allies, and they would have to abandon it soon, before the enemy could attack the badly weakened group again and abduct more women.

Within a week or so of the deadly feast, the Mahekodo-teri, an ally of Kaobawä's group, learned about the massacre and offered aid. The Mahekodo-teri headman himself came to the village and invited the entire group to his village to take refuge. They accepted the offer, and in January of 1951, after conducting one revenge raid on the enemy, they moved to Mahekodo-teri. The date is accurately known, since James P. Barker, the Protestant missionary who had escorted me to Bisaasi-teri on my first field trip, was then living with the Mahekodo-teri and witnessed the tragic arrival of the refugees, many of whom were still recovering from their wounds.

The Mahekodo-teri had been allied with Kaobawä's group a generation earlier, but after the group moved away from the Orinoco the relationship had dwindled to sporadic trading. Now, however, true to Yanomamö political behavior, the Mahekodo-teri, obviously in a strong bargaining position, offered their protection with gain in mind: they demanded and received a number of their guests' women. The members of Kaobawä's group suspected further trouble from their new protectors, and they worked assiduously at establishing their new garden. But they had to stay with the Mahekodo-teri until the garden could totally support them—almost a year. During this time, they would spend weeks away from their hosts' village while they worked on the new garden, carrying their food along with them. They would return to stock up on food, rest for a few weeks, and leave again.

Some time later, after the Mahekodo-teri village had split into three factions, Kaobawä learned from one of the factions that they had indeed been plotting an attack. The only thing that had prevented it was the outbreak of a new war between the Mahekodo-teri and another village—and they had needed the military assistance of Kaobawä and his group.

For a few years after the separation from the Mahekodo-teri, Kaobawä's group was occasionally invited to feast with them. Because they still suspected the Mahekodo-teri of plotting against them, only the men would attend the feasts, to reduce the chance of another massacre. The women and children would hide in the jungle while the men were away. Gradually the alliance cooled off again, and the two groups remained detached from each other but at peace.

By 1960, Kaobawä's group had regained some of its military strength, as boys grew into young men, and it formed an alliance with a third Shamatari group, one related to the two that had conducted the massacre of 1950. This group, the Paruritawä-teri, was at war with the Iwähikoroba-teri but on feasting terms with the Möwaraoba-teri. Kaobawä's group persuaded its new allies to invite the Möwaraoba-teri to a feast, at which a massacre similar to that of 1950 would be staged, but with the roles reversed. Kaobawä's group would lie in ambush outside the village while the Paruritawä-teri attacked the guests from within.

The Möwaraoba-teri, then an uncontacted group, were being ravaged by a malaria epidemic at the time, and only a handful of them came to the feast—the others were too sick to travel. With the aid of their newly found allies, Kaobawä's group was able to kill three of the five men and abduct four women. The other two men escaped to tell of the treachery. This revenge feast was considered only partially successful, and Kaobawä's group was not satisfied with the outcome. The Paruritawä-teri had to abandon their site to avoid revenge raids, splitting into two groups in the process, the Mömariböwei-teri and the Reyaboböwei-teri, both of which remained friendly to Kaobawä's group.

In early 1965, several months after I began my fieldwork, Kaobawä and his supporters went to visit the Reyaboböwei-teri, hoping to arrange another treacherous feast for the Möwaraoba-teri. They left a few men behind to protect the women and children, and were gone almost two weeks. All during this time, those who had remained behind flocked to my mud hut at dawn and stayed there the whole day, not even permitting me to leave and every hour or so asking where my shotgun was. I soon learned that they were afraid the Widokaiya-teri, whose village was to the north (not shown on the map), were going to raid them and abduct the women, since the Widokaiya-teri knew about the feast plot and about the men being away. My hut lay on the path the raiders were most likely to take, and the few men still in the village stood guard beside my door each night to intercept the raiders if they attacked.

So I was guarding the women and children by day with my shotgun, and the men were doing the same at night with their own weapons. It was a classic illustration of the almost complete lack of trust between Yanomamö allies. What we were protecting the women against was a raid by one of their friends and allies, not an enemy.

The men had been gone about ten days when six visitors from another allied village passed through Upper Bisaasi-teri hoping to trade. It was obvious to the visitors that the men were away and that the women were largely defenseless. They carried that news up the Orinoco River to their own allies, one of which was the Mahekodo-teri.

Then one evening a Salesian missionary, Padre Luis Cocco, arrived at my hut from his Ocamo mission (not shown on the map), about three hours by boat north of Kaobawä's village. He had traveled up the Orinoco after dark—a dangerous undertaking at that time of year, when the river was low and many rocks and logs were exposed—because he had just learned from the mission at Mahekodo-teri, via shortwave radio, that a large party of men had set out from there for Bisaasi-teri, intent on capturing women. Again my hut was full of women and children at dawn the next day, and the raiders were probably en route. I was in a difficult situation. If I said anything about the report that Mahekodo-teri raiders were on the way, it would be sufficient cause for war between Kaobawä's group and the Mahekodo-teri—a most unfortunate outcome if the story proved false. But if it was true, I did not dare remain silent. The raiders would probably kill the defenders to capture the women.

Fortunately, I did not have to make a decision. Kaobawä and the others returned early in the afternoon, and I was able to stay neutral. The treacherous feast had not come off as planned. The intended victims had accepted the invitation but were warned about the plot just before they arrived. One of the Reyaboböwei-teri who had close kinsmen among them had had misgivings and had told them.

Late in the afternoon, it was learned that many men from Mahekodo-teri were, in fact, in the vicinity of the village, allegedly on a camping trip. They had only a few women with them. Kaobawä, of course, was suspicious about their story, but to demonstrate his friendship he invited them to be his guests at a feast. Since he and his men had been away for nearly two weeks, they had an abundance of food in their gardens, and they could easily afford to entertain the Mahekodo-teri and their traveling companions, the Boreta-teri. Altogether, the guests would number about a hundred after the men sent for their women and children.

And this sets the stage for the feast, in a context that makes it more intelligible—the specific historical relationships between the participants and the nature of their mutual mistrust.

Kaobawä's Feast for the Mahekodo-teri and Their Friends

Perhaps because of his suspicions about the Mahekodo-teri and the Boreta-teri, Kaobawä also invited a group called the Karohi-teri to the feast. (This is Rerebawä's village.) They were a small but dependable ally who had themselves separated from the Mahekodo-teri many years ago. That established a better balance of power at the feast should trouble arise—the combination of the Boreta-teri and the Mahekodo-teri was strong enough to worry any host. Several of the Mahekodo-teri had well-deserved reputations as killers, and they were prone to escalate an innocuous fight to a more lethal level if they saw any advantage in it. With the aid of the Karohi-teri, Kaobawä's group felt more equally matched.

The feast started on a sour note. It is the Yanomamö custom for the visitors to arrive only after receiving a formal invitation from their hosts, which is delivered by messenger on the day of the feast. The Mahekodo-teri and the Boreta-teri, however, arrogantly showed up nearly a week early and set up a large temporary camp a short distance from the village. Since they were guests, they could legitimately demand to be fed. So Kaobawä and his fellow villagers took their one hundred or so visitors to their gardens and supplied them with enough plantains to last a week. Kaobawä was a little disturbed by their impoliteness in arriving early and uninvited, but he took the situation philosophically. After all, the Mahekodo-teri had fed his group for the better part of a year.

Meanwhile, Kaobawä and several other men cut an enormous quantity of plantains, which were hung in his house to ripen for a week before being boiled into *date*, a thick, sweet soup resembling banana pudding. This would be for the visitors to eat at the feast. He and a few of the older men also assembled a hunting party of young men, several of them Kaobawä's brothers, whose responsibility it was to find a large supply of meat to give to the visitors on the day after the feast. (Meat is never eaten in the village during a feast.) Most of the hunters were reluctant, since their feet were still sore from the long trip to Reyabobówei-teri, and a few managed to escape recruitment by claiming to be sick. This hunt—the *heniyomou*—along with the hanging of the plantains in the headman's house, formally initiated the feast preparations, and the excitement that usually attends a feast began to build.

That evening, the young men and women of the village danced and sang, an event called *amoamo*, to ensure the hunters luck. The Yanomamö *amoamo* on other occasions, but they invariably do so on the day the plantains are hung in advance of a feast. Every evening during the week that the men were away on their *heniyomou*, the young women and girls sang and danced to ensure their success.

The hunters left at dawn the following morning, carrying a large supply of roasted and green plantains for their food. They had picked a site some fifteen miles up the Mavaca River, where game was known to abound, and they traveled in canoes. They were looking for monkeys, armadillos, wild turkeys, wild pigs, caimans, tapirs, and paruri birds, the kinds of meat deemed suitable for ritual occasions. They were not permitted to eat any of this game, which was earmarked for the guests, but they could consume anything else they captured, such as amotas, agoutis, small birds, a species of small wild turkey, insects, or fish.

The hunters had miscalculated the amount of garden food they needed, and one of them returned after four days to fetch more plantains. He also gave Kaobawä a report on the hunt's success, and that created a small sensation in the village. The men had already killed many *basho*, a particularly large and desirable monkey, and they had come upon a quantity of turtle eggs at a sandbar and were eating as many as they could. When they returned, they cached the rest of the eggs in my hut so they would not have to share them with the visitors.

The visitors were making gluttons of themselves, and the hosts started to grumble about the large number of plantains they were eating. They ate the week's supply they had been given in about half that time, and they were allowed to harvest a second crop. This was not the usual way for guests to behave, and it soon became apparent that their gluttony was a form of deliberate intimidation. Still, Kaobawä and his followers continued to supply the visitors with all the food they needed, keeping their complaints to themselves. They did not want it known that they were worried about running short of food. Indeed, they were determined to put on so lavish a feast that it would be difficult for the guests to reciprocate.

The hunters returned and presented their smoked catch to Kaobawä. It was brought to his house and placed on the ground wrapped in leaf bundles. Kaobawä ignored it for a while, and then he rose from his hammock and slowly began to open one of the packages while everybody watched—especially the hunters, who were proud of the catch: seventeen *basho* monkeys, seven wild turkeys, and three large armadillos (photo 32).

The hosts were eager for the feast day to come, for then the visitors would have to leave for home, ending the drain on the gardens. (I have seen several instances of Yanomamö groups getting rid of visitors who have joined them semipermanently by holding a feast in their honor; after the ceremonial food is presented, the visitors are obliged to leave.) So the feast was scheduled for the day following the return of the hunters, even though the Karohi-teri allies had not yet arrived.

Kaobawä and his group were so anxious to rid themselves of their ravenous guests that they decided to hold a separate feast for the Karohi-teri after the other groups left. It would involve a considerable amount of extra work, but they were willing to undertake it if they could get rid of their present visitors. The guests had been eating their hosts' produce for a week, and their continued intimidating presence was making the hosts angrier and angrier.

On the morning of the feast, three large pieces of bark were cut from a *masiri* tree and brought to the village. The bark was made into troughs to hold the boiled ripe-plantain soup. All day long, Kaobawä's younger brothers, who had also been on the hunt, labored at cooking enormous quantities of ripe plantains and pouring boiling containers of soup into the troughs. The plantains that had been hung up to ripen were now *äbähäwä*—soft, a golden yellow, and blotched with black spots. To prepare the soup, the young men cut the bunches of plantains down from the roof, split each fruit with a thumb, threw the two halves of the flesh into a cooking pot, and tossed the skins onto a pile. They worked on the soup from early morning until late afternoon.

Next they started on the cooked green plantains, or *dehiyaö* food, that would be eaten in alternate bites with the meat. *Rasha* fruits or cassava bread could have been used instead of the plantains. Yanomamö etiquette requires that meat be accompanied by some such food; it is an insult to offer someone meat without simultaneously offering one of these other foods. Peeling green plantains is harder than peeling ripe ones, because they are tough and brittle. The Yanomamö solve this problem as they do many others, by using their teeth. The plantain is bitten in several places along its length to crack the peel, which

32. *Kaobawä unpacking a load of smoked meat, part of the catch his hunters have brought home for the feast.*

is then removed with the fingernails and a series of additional deft bites. On this occasion, the two young men peeled with their thumbs enough ripe plantains to make about ninety-five gallons of soup, and with their teeth enough green ones to fill a dozen large pack baskets.

In the morning, Kaobawä had gone to the center of the village clearing, where all could see him, and begun to pull weeds. The clearing, which serves as the dancing plaza, has to look presentable. Since a Yanomamö headman cannot directly order his followers to execute such a task, he usually initiates it himself and hopes that others will follow. By and by, a number of older men did join Kaobawä, as well as a few women, and when a sufficient number were at work, he quietly retired to his hammock to oversee the food preparation and calculate the distribution of the meat.

Excitement in the village was steadily growing, and by noon there was a constant din of laughter and chatter, punctuated now and then by a shrill scream from a young man overcome with the thrill of the feast and the impending opportunity to prance and parade in front of everyone. Occasionally the visitors, from their camp nearby, would reply to the shouts, setting off a brief screaming contest, which gradually died off as all resumed their preparations for the dance—painting themselves elaborately and donning their prize feathers.

Shortly after noon, a rumor circulated through the village that the visitors had been raiding the gardens at night and stealing additional plantains. A number of people, particularly the older men, were visibly upset by this, and their open complaints reached the visitors, giving rise to another rumor that there would be a chest-pounding duel to set matters straight. The guests had already worn their welcome thin, and the hosts were becoming increasingly impatient with them.

The men of the host group had now finished their preparations for the feast. They had painted themselves in red and black and put on their most colorful feathers. They had cleaned the debris from their houses, had hauled away all the weeds from the village clearing, and had brought in quantities of food for their guests. It was time for their *ebene*. They separated into small groups and began blowing the brownish-green powder up each other's nostrils through their three-foot-long hollow tubes.

While the men were taking their drug, the women decorated themselves with feathers and red pigment, and the visitors, too, were busy at the same tasks. A few women were still finishing baskets that they planned to present to the hosts, and Kaobawä's younger brothers were continuing with the monotonous cooking of what seemed like an endless number of plantains. But by midafternoon, the excitement of the feast was at fever proportions.

It was time for Kaobawä to send one of his men, highly decorated, to the visitors' camp to *teshimou*—to give a formal chant and invite them to send a delegate into the village to accept the first basket of vegetables and meat. The delegate was always someone important. Shortly after Kaobawä's chanter returned, an old man from the visiting group entered the village and walked unceremoniously across the clearing while the host group cheered. He was not the delegate. He was too old a man to join the dancing and too respected to wait behind with the women and children while the younger men put on their dance display, so he had been sent on ahead. His appearance was a sign that the delegate was about to arrive, to accept the invitation to a feast at Kaobawä's house.

An additional group present for the feast was the Lower Bisaasi-teri, as they, too, were on friendly terms with the Mahekodo-teri and had benefited from the latter's hospitality after the treacherous feast in 1950. (Besides, it was an opportunity for them to eat prodigiously of someone else's food.) Before Kaobawä's group had separated from the Lower Bisaasi-teri, the composite village had had a single headman, named Kumamawä, who was a brother of Kaobawä's father. After the groups split, the older man led the Lower Bisaasi-teri faction, and Kaobawä the Upper. Today, when the two groups had temporarily coalesced for the feast, Kumamawä was granted the honor of chanting with the visitors' delegate. He turned out to be Asiawä, the son of the Mahekodo-teri headman.

Ten minutes after the old visitor had come into the village, Asiawä entered the clearing, resplendent and haughty, touching off an explosion of wild cheering that marked the opening of the dance. He was spectacular in a bright new loincloth, long red parrot feathers that streamed from his armbands, and a black monkey-tail headband covered with white buzzard down. He marched dramatically to the center of the clearing as Kaobawä's followers cheered. He struck the visitor's pose—motionless, head high, weapons held upright next to his face—and held it for two or three minutes so that his hosts could admire him. This gesture signified that he had come in peace and was announcing his benevolent intentions by standing where all could see him. Anyone who bore him malice was supposed to shoot him then or not at all. I have a number of informants' accounts of visitors being shot down while standing in the clearing to announce their presence. Whenever I accompanied a Yanomamö to a strange village for the first time, I, too, had to participate in this rite, and it always made me feel uneasy.

Asiawä then marched to Kaobawä's house and was met by Kumamawä. The two men immediately began to chant. This constituted Asiawä's formal acceptance of the feast invitation on behalf of his entire group. The pair chanted for five minutes or so, bouncing up and down from the knees, at times face to face, at times side to side, but always lively and loud. Suddenly they stopped. Asiawä squatted, his back to the sun, and Kumamawä retired to his hammock. The cheering died down.

Asiawä remained squatting for several minutes, and then one of Kaobawä's younger brothers brought out a half gourdful of plantain soup and set it on the ground. Asiawä ignored it politely for a time, staring off into the distance and now holding his weapons horizontally next to his mouth. Presently he put the weapons down, picked up the container of soup, drained it in one draft, and set it down again. At that, another of Kaobawä's brothers brought him a large pack basket filled with boiled green plantains and smoked armadillo meat. Asiawä stood up, and the strap of the basket was placed over his head and adjusted carefully across the shoulders so as not to crumple his headdress. Trying to look dramatic, he staggered rapidly out of the village under his heavy burden of food, while the hosts again cheered wildly. This food was for the visitors to eat while they finished decorating themselves, each receiving a small portion.

In about half an hour, the visitors had completed their decorating and had assembled just outside the entrance to the village. The men, all finely decorated, were in front, and the women, girls, and young boys, also decorated but each carrying a load of family possessions, stood behind them.

At a signal from Asiawä's father, the headman, the first two dancers burst into the village, separated, and danced around the periphery of the clearing in opposite directions. Kaobawä's group welcomed them with shouts and shrill screams. The rest of the visiting dancers then entered two at a time, pranced wildly around the periphery to show off their decorations and weapons, and returned to the group waiting outside the shabono.

Each dancer had unique decorations or a unique dance step to exhibit. He might burst into the village screaming a memorized phrase, wheel and spin, stop in his tracks, dance in place, throw his weapons down, pick them up, aim them at the line of hosts with a fierce expression on his face, prance ahead a few steps, and then repeat the whole performance as he continued around the clearing. The hosts, each standing in front of his own house brandishing his weapons, would cheer wildly.

When everyone had had an individual turn, all the dancers came back together. In single file, they danced noisily around the periphery several times, clacking their arrows against their bows, and gathered in a tightly knit group at the center of the clearing (photo 33). There they stood motionless (except for the heaving of their chests), holding their weapons upright, in a final display of their decorations.

The hosts now emerged from their houses and approached the center of the village. Each man invited one or more of the visitors into his house, leading the visitor off by the arm. As the visitor left, his family, which was watching from the village entrance, unceremoniously joined him at the host's house, bringing their "luggage" along. Within a few minutes, the dance plaza was deserted and the visitors were resting comfortably in their hosts' hammocks.

Even in hammocks, Yanomamö dancers can put on a silent display of their finery, as they lie with legs crossed, one arm behind the head and the other hand across the mouth, staring at the ceiling and waiting for their ripe-plantain soup. It is almost as if they are strutting from a reclining position.

After the guests had been served one round of soup from the bark troughs, it was the hosts' turn to assemble outside the entrance and come in to dance around the clearing. They, too, had the opportunity to display their decorations, after which they returned to their houses to see to their guests.

The first of the three bark troughs of soup was emptied in the course of serving numerous gourdsful to the hundred visitors. The guests now assembled around the second trough to continue eating (photo 34). Before it was empty, they moved on as a group to the third trough and repeated their ceremonial consumption. Then they returned to their hammocks to rest and regain their appetites. Approximately two hours had passed from the time the first dancers entered the village until the guests retired from the third trough of soup. They had not yet eaten all ninety-five gallons, but they would manage to do so by morning.

At some feasts, the ashes of the dead are mixed with the boiled ripe-plantain soup and eaten by friends and relatives of the deceased. Also, feasts sometimes serve as the prelude to a raid involving two or more villages; the sponsor of the raid entertains his allies at a feast the day before the raiding party departs. Neither of these events occurred at this feast.

Shortly after dark, the marathon chanting (*waiyamou*) began, and it con-

33. *Visitors displaying themselves at the center of the village, after each has danced separately. They will now be invited to recline in the houses of their individual hosts.*

34. *After a polite period of reclining in their hosts' hammocks, the visitors go to the large troughs of plantain soup and begin drinking it. The soup trough can also be used as a crude canoe for crossing larger streams (chapter 1).*

tinued until dawn. A man would chant softly, bidding for a man from the other group to come forth and chant with him. A second man would join in, also softly, responding melodically to the first one's chanted phrases. The first man would move slowly toward the second, gradually coming face to face with him, and then he would go into his routine, a highly ritualized, partially memorized monologue that sometimes crescendos into loud staccato screams. The second man, unable to predict what the first is going to say, must respond to each utterance with some twist or nuance of it. It might be a rhyming line or a clever counterpoint, or perhaps a scrambled version, with the words reversed or the order of the syllables changed. It is something like a fast game of Ping-Pong, with the melodic, staccato phrases as the ball. After some fifteen or twenty minutes, the man who has been leading the chant stops, and his partner takes the lead as they continue in the same fashion. When the first pair of chanters has finished, the last one to chant starts bidding for a new partner from the other group, and so it continues. It is during these chants that the men reveal to each other what they would like to get the next day, when trading occurs; they often express their wants in metaphorical terms, such as "jaguar toenails" for "a dog."

Early the next morning, the hosts and the visitors conducted their trade, and the visitors were given their going-home food—large baskets of boiled green plantains with pieces of smoked meat on top. During the trading, the visitors made requests through their headman, and Kaobawä responded by asking one of his men to produce the item. It would be thrown at the feet of the man who wanted it. He would ignore it for a time and then give it a cursory examination before throwing it back on the ground. His peers would examine it in greater detail, extolling its virtues, while the giver apologized for its defects. Or, if the item was of poor quality, the opposite would occur: the giver would cite its not-so-obvious merits, and the recipient would draw attention to its conspicuous shortcomings. In every trade, the hosts always feel they have been overgenerous, and the guests complain afterward that they have not received enough.

The trade was conducted efficiently but with considerable arguing. The hosts had hidden their choicest items and vigorously denied having some things, and the guests had done likewise—sinking their prize bows in a river beforehand, for example, and bringing along an inferior one in case someone asked for a bow. As this was the first time in some years that the two groups had feasted together, there were no old debts to be repaid. Instead, the visitors asked for items *no mraiha*—to be repaid later—and the hosts did the same.

By eight in the morning—very early by feast standards—the going-home food had been distributed and the trading concluded. Had the visitors been polite, they would have packed up and left. But they were not polite, and said they had decided to stay and watch the second, smaller feast that Kaobawä was going to put on for the Karohi-teri. This capped the series of insults that the visitors had heaped on Kaobawä's group. The visitors were warned that if they stayed, the hosts would regard it as intimidation and would challenge them to a chest-pounding duel. The visitors said nothing.

It was obvious now that the visitors were looking for trouble and that Kaobawä's group had to react or be subject to further intimidation. Hence, the challenge to pound chests. Kaobawä had decided that enough was enough, and he could no longer afford to overlook the brazen and continuing insults. At this point, much to the relief of Kaobawä's group, the visitors broke camp and departed. The hosts assumed that it was because of the threatened challenge to a chest-pounding duel, and they were pleased at having intimidated their guests into leaving. The men gloated about it the rest of the day.

The Karohi-teri had arrived sometime during the morning, and the feast for them was held that same day, but without the assistance of the Lower Bisaasi-teri, who had left shortly after the previous day's feast.

The Fighting After the Feast

The feast for the Karohi-teri was essentially the same as the one for the Mahekodo-teri and the Boreta-teri. When the dancing was over and darkness fell, the chanting began again, even though the men in Kaobawä's group were quite hoarse from the previous evening's chanting.

The first pair of chanters had not even completed their rhythmic presentation when the jungle around the village erupted in hoots and shouts, causing all the men to jump from their hammocks and grab their weapons. As soon as they were armed, they proceeded to yell back at their unseen intimidators and to make a great racket by rattling the shafts of their arrows together or against their bows and by pounding the heads of their axes on pieces of firewood or on the ground.

It was the Boreta-teri and the Mahekodo-teri, who had returned to accept the chest-pounding challenge. They entered the village, each man brandishing his ax, club, or bow and arrows, and circled it once, feigning attacks on certain men among the hosts. Then they gathered in the center of the clearing. The hosts surrounded them excitedly, dancing about with their weapons poised and pulling out of the crowd opponents against whom they held a particular grudge. Heated arguments about the food thefts and the gluttony ensued, and both hosts and guests waved their weapons threateningly in each other's faces. Within minutes, the large crowd had divided and the chest pounding began.

The Karohi-teri aided Kaobawä and his followers, and their numbers were swelled further when the Lower Bisaasi-teri heard the commotion and rushed back. There were about sixty adult men on each side, and the fighting took place in two arenas simultaneously.

A man from each side steps into the center of the milling, belligerent crowd of weapon-wielding partisans, urged on by his comrades. One of the men steps forward, spreads his legs apart, bares his chest, holds his arms behind his back, and dares the other to hit him (photo 35). The opponent sizes him up, adjusts the victim's chest or arms so as to give himself the greatest advantage, and steps back to deliver a blow with his closed fist. He painstakingly measures off an arm's-length distance from the victim's chest and makes several dry runs before delivering the blow. He winds up like a baseball pitcher, but keeping both feet on the ground, and delivers a tremendous wallop with his fist to the victim's left pectoral muscle, putting all his weight into the blow. The victim's knees often buckle, and he staggers around for a few moments, shaking his head to clear the stars but remaining silent. The blow invariably raises a "frog"—a painful red lump—on the pectoral muscle.

After each blow, the comrades of the deliverer cheer, bounce up and down from their knees, and clack their weapons noisily over their heads. The victim's supporters frantically urge their champion to stand fast and take another blow. If the blow has knocked the recipient to the ground, the deliverer throws his arms over his head, rolls his eyes back, and prances victoriously around his victim, growling and screaming, his feet almost a blur from his excited dance—like a ruffed grouse doing a mating dance.

The recipient may stand and take as many as four blows before demanding to hit back. Then he is permitted to strike his opponent as many times as the latter struck him, provided that the opponent can take that many. If the opponent cannot, he has to retire, much to the dismay of his comrades and the delirious joy of the other side. No fighter is allowed to retire after delivering a blow

35. *Chest-pounding duel at the feast.*

until he lets his opponent return it. If he attempts to do so, his adversary will plunge into the crowd and roughly haul him back, sometimes aided by the man's own supporters. Only after having received his just dues can a fighter retire. If he has delivered three blows, he has to receive three or be considered a poor sport; only if he is injured can he retire after receiving less than three. Then one of his comrades replaces him and demands to hit the victorious opponent. But the injured recipient's remaining blows are canceled, and the man who delivered the victorious blow ends up receiving more blows than he delivers. Thus, good fighters are at a disadvantage, since they receive more punishment than they deliver. Their reward is status: they earn the reputation of being *waiteri*—fierce.

Some of the younger men in Kaobawä's group were reluctant to participate in the fighting because they were afraid of injury, and they lurked on the periphery hoping not to be seen. This put a strain on the others, who had to take extra turns. At one point, Kaobawä's men, sore from the punishment they had taken and worried that they were losing, wanted to escalate the contest to an ax duel. Kaobawä was adamantly opposed to that, knowing it would lead to bloodshed. He managed to force the reluctant younger men into the fighting, as well as a few older ones who had been standing back urging others on, and that reduced the strain on those who wanted to escalate the fighting (photo 36). A few of the younger men retired after a single blow, however, privately admitting later that they had pretended to be injured to get out of the fighting. Fatalities, though uncommon, can occur in chest-pounding duels.

The fighting continued for nearly three hours, as tempers grew hotter and hotter. Kaobawä and the headman from the other group stood by with their weapons, attempting to keep the fighting under control but not participating in it. Some of the fighters went through several turns of three or four blows each, their pectoral muscles swollen and red from the large number of blows they had received. The outcome had still not been decided, although Kaobawä's group seemed to be getting the worst of it. Now his side wanted to escalate the fighting to side slapping, partly because the men's chests were getting too sore for them to continue and partly because their opponents seemed to have the edge in the chest pounding.

A side-slapping duel is nearly identical to chest pounding, except that the blow is delivered with the open hand across the opponent's flanks, between the rib cage and the pelvis bone, often from a squatting position (photo 37). It is a little more severe than chest pounding—casualties are more frequent—

36. *The fight nearly escalated to clubs and axes. Kaobawä prevented this by compelling the reluctant men to take turns at chest pounding.*

37. *Side slapping can be modified to a form in which the men strike each other from a squatting position.*

and tempers grow hotter when a group's champion, gasping for wind, falls to the ground in a faint. (Several years after this fight, an argument developed between the Karohi-teri and some of their neighbors that precipitated a chest-pounding duel. It escalated to side slapping, and then to side slapping with stones held in the fist. Two young men died of their injuries, presumably ruptured kidneys.)

The side slapping lasted only fifteen minutes or so before one of Kaobawä's best men was knocked unconscious, enraging the others. The fighting continued just a few minutes after that, but during those few minutes Kaobawä's men were rapidly changing the points of their arrows to war tips of curare and lanceolate bamboo. Recognizing that the situation was getting serious, the women and children began to cry, and huddled in the farthest corners of their houses, near the exits. One by one the men withdrew to their houses, nocked their war arrows, drew their bows, and aimed them at their visiting opponents. The visitors pulled back into a protective circle around the few women and children who were with them and also fitted arrows to their bows.

The air was electric with suspense. The village grew silent as the lines were drawn and the two groups nervously aimed their arrows. People in both groups tore bunches of leaves from the *shabono* roof, ignited them, and waved them about to illuminate the tense scene. Others were using pieces of burning firewood for the same purpose.

Then Kaobawä, Asiawä, and a few other leaders from both sides stepped into the no-man's-land separating the two groups and began to argue violently, waving their axes and clubs. Suddenly several of the men from the visiting group surged toward Kaobawä and his supporters, swinging their axes and clubs wildly and forcing them back to the line of bowmen, whose bowstrings were now drawn taut. But Kaobawä and his men regained their footing, charged their adversaries, and repelled them, driving them back with their own clubs and bowstaves.

Women and children from both groups were fleeing from the village, screaming and crying. For a brief moment, I was sure that the Bisaasi-teri warriors were going to release their arrows point-blank at Kaobawä's attackers. But when he and his men turned the attackers back, the crisis was over. The leaders of the visiting group slowly and carefully rejoined their men and backed out of the village, weapons still drawn, their way illuminated by the waving firebrands.

Kaobawä's group maintained a vigil throughout the night, searched the forest around the village the next morning, but took no further action. Needless to say, the Mahekodo-teri never invited them to a reciprocal feast. Later in the year, the relationship got even worse, because of a club fight in yet another village, and for a while both groups were threatening to shoot each other on sight. Then a temporary rapprochement developed, when a group of raiders from Kaobawä's group, en route to attack the village of Patanowä-teri, met up with a group of hunters from the Mahekodo-teri. The men traded with each other and departed on nonhostile terms, although the raiders abandoned their raid, for fear of being ambushed afterward by the Mahekodo-teri, and returned home. The groups remained on trading terms, but the relationship was strained and potentially hostile.

Of the six feasts I witnessed during my first eighteen months with the Yanomamö, two of them ended in fighting. Even so, the feasts are exciting, for both hosts and guests, and contribute to mutual solidarity. Under normal circumstances, allies who are accustomed to feasting with each other do not fight. Nevertheless, even the best allies occasionally agree beforehand to end a feast with a chest-pounding duel—to demonstrate that they are friends but are willing to fight for their sovereignty if necessary.

Clearly, any feast, at least in Kaobawä's area, has the potential for ending in violence because of the Yanomamö's canons of behavior and their obligation to display ferocity—and because of long-remembered incidents from the past. Still, the feast and its antecedent, the trading relationship, serve to reduce the probability of neighbors fighting at a higher level of violence. Imagine what Yanomamö political relationships might be like *without* the trading and the feasts.

Chapter Six

Yanomamö Täbä Waiteri:
Yanomamö Are Fierce

In Kaobawä's area, people frequently say, "*Yanomamö täbä waiteri.*" This can mean, depending on the specific context, "Human beings are fierce," "We are fierce," or "Yanomamö [distinct from *nabäs*] are fierce." I am frequently, and, in my view, incorrectly, accused of diminishing the image of the Yanomamö by describing those I know in the very terms they use. This chapter illustrates what they mean by the word *waiteri*.

When feasts and alliances fail to establish amicable relationships between sovereign Yanomamö villages, two groups may still coexist for a time without any overt hostility. But it is an unstable situation, especially if the villages are fairly close to each other. Hostility is likely to develop between them eventually, often stemming from individual conflicts. Suspicions grow, leading to accusations of sorcery. A death in one village will be attributed to the malevolent *hekura* sent by the shamans of the other. Once this happens, raiding between the villages begins.

The raid, or *wayu huu*, is the ultimate form of Yanomamö warfare. But it is a mistake to think of the raiding between villages in modern terms of war as a lethal conflict between two independent entities. Yanomamö villages change in composition so rapidly that it may be more meaningful to think of their wars as contests between groups of *kinsmen*—kinsmen who may have lived as a group in several different villages and who sometimes are waging war on the very village from which they have recently separated by fissioning. I will return to this issue later, when I describe some specific wars.

Yanomamö wars, and tribal warfare in general, must be put into the context of *conflicts of interest*. Such a context, with the Yanomamö, encompasses a myriad of antecedent conflicts. These usually start between individuals, over scores of relatively trivial matters, and they escalate as more individuals and kinsmen become involved. Only after the conflict has reached the stage of communities fighting each other can we call it a war.

And not all lethal fighting between Yanomamö groups can be considered as war, although the values associated with war—bellicosity, ferocity, and violence—undoubtedly encourage all kinds of fighting.

Levels of Violence

Among the Yanomamö, war is, in fact, the last in a graded series of aggressive encounters. Indeed, some of their other forms of fighting, such as the formal chest-pounding duel, may even be considered the antithesis of war, for they provide an alternative to killing. The duels are formal and are regulated by stringent rules about the proper ways to deliver and receive blows. Such rules keep much of the Yanomamö fighting innocuous, so that the concerned parties do not have to resort to more drastic means to resolve grievances. The three most innocuous forms of violence—chest pounding, side slapping, and club fights—permit the contestants to express their hostilities in such a way that they can remain on relatively peaceful terms with each other afterward. The Yanomamö culture calls forth aggressive behavior, but at the same time it provides a framework within which the aggressiveness can be controlled.

The most innocuous form of fighting is the chest-pounding duel, which was described in the last chapter. These duels usually take place between the members of different villages and are precipitated by minor affronts like malicious gossip, accusations of cowardice, and disputes over food or trading.

If such a duel escalates, it usually turns into a side-slapping contest, also described in chapter 5. Occasionally the combatants will ask to use machetes or axes, but this is rare. Even when machetes are used, the object of the contest remains the same—to injure the opponent seriously enough that he withdraws but not so seriously as to draw blood or kill him. In a machete fight, the opponents strike each other on the chest or flank only with the flat of the blade, but, as you can imagine, it hurts.

In some areas, the Yanomamö have a more devastating variation of the chest-pounding duel. The opponents hold rocks in their clenched fists when they strike their adversaries, often concealing the rocks so that the adversary does not know they are "cheating." But they do try to keep the stone from touching the opponent's flesh. Even without the stones, they can deliver blows with such force that a participant may cough up blood for days afterward, and occasionally a fatality results.

Club fights represent the next level of violence (photo 38). These can take place both within villages and between them. Most of the club fights result from arguments over women, but a few develop out of other disputes, over thefts of food, for example.

Dikawa, a young man about twenty years old, came home one day and found hanging over his hearth a bunch of bananas that his father, about fifty-five, had put there to ripen. Dikawä ate a number of the bananas without his father's permission. When his father discovered the theft, he ripped a pole out of the house and began clubbing Dikawä. It was one of those unpleasant situations in which the son is a little too big to be punished physically by a father who is a little too old to handle him. Dikawä armed himself with a club, too, and attacked his father, precipitating a melee that soon involved most of the men in the village, each taking the side of either father or son.

In some fights, individuals seem to join in just to keep the sides even. But in most fights kinship relationships are important. A detailed genealogical analysis of one ax fight I witnessed clearly indicated that the closest kinsmen sided with each other. Most of those on the same side were related as half siblings, while their relatedness to their opponents was more like second or third cousins. If a group of fighters is badly outnumbered, they may be joined by remoter kin and friends prompted by a sense of fairness, no matter what the issue. The willingness of the more remote kin to take sides in a fight, however, is very much a function of what the risks are—if someone could get killed, they tend not to take the side of someone who is only a second cousin.

The net result of the father-and-son fight over the bananas was a number of lacerated skulls, bashed fingers, and sore shoulders. The contestants had been trying to hit each other only on the top of the head, but when the fight got out of hand, they began to swing wildly, and many blows landed on shoulders or arms. The episode probably taught Dikawä not to eat his father's bananas and to start planting his own. His father probably learned that it is not a good idea to spank a twenty-year-old son if you are fifty-five.

The clubs used in the fights are usually eight to ten feet long. They are flexible, heavy, and deliver a tremendous wallop. In their general shape and dimensions, they resemble pool cues, although they are nearly twice as long. The club is held by the thin end, which often is sharpened into a long point in case the fighting escalates to spear thrusting. In the latter, the club is reversed and used as a pike. Most club fights are duels, usually over an accusation that one man has been trysting with another's wife. The enraged husband challenges his opponent to strike him on the head with a club. He holds his own club upright, leans against it, and exposes his head for the opponent to strike. After he has sustained a blow, he can deliver one in return. But as soon as blood starts to flow, almost everybody in the village rips a pole out of a house frame and joins in the fighting, in support of one or the other contestant.

Needless to say, the tops of most men's heads are covered with deep, ugly scars, of which their bearers are immensely proud. Some men, in fact, keep their heads cleanly shaved on top to display their scars, rubbing on red pigment to make them more conspicuous. From above, the skull of an accomplished club fighter of forty years looks like a topographical road map of the Sierra Madre mountains, for it is crisscrossed by as many as twenty large scars (photo 39). Other men keep their heads shaved for decorative reasons only, irrespective of the number of scars, and some do not shave their heads at all.

Club fighting is more common in large villages, primarily because there are more opportunities for clandestine sexual liaisons. The larger the village, the more frequent the club fighting. And as the fighting increases, so, too, does the probability that the village will fission into two separate groups. Most of the village fissioning I have investigated originated out of a specific club fight over a woman, a fight that was but one incident in a whole series of similar squabbles. (Other factors that affect the frequency of conflicts are a village's lineage structure and kinship composition, as discussed in chapter 4.)

The village of Patanowä-teri, which split during the last month of my first field trip, provides a good example. A young man had appropriated the wife of another because she was allegedly being mistreated by her husband. That led to a brutal club fight involving almost every man in the village. The fight escalated to jabbing with the sharpened ends of the clubs, and the husband of the woman in question was speared by his rival and badly wounded. The headman of the village, a "brother" (parallel cousin) of Kaobawä, had been attempting to keep the fighting restricted to clubs. But the spearing of the husband sent the headman into a rage, and he speared the rival, running his sharpened club completely through the young man's body and wounding him mortally. The wife was given back to her legitimate husband, who punished her by cutting off both her ears with a machete.

The kinsmen of the dead man were ordered to leave the village before there was further bloodshed. The aggrieved faction joined the Monou-teri and the Bisaasi-teri because the latter groups were then at war with the Patanowä-teri, and the expellees knew that this would give them an opportunity to raid their old village in revenge. The Monou-teri and the two Bisaasi-teri groups

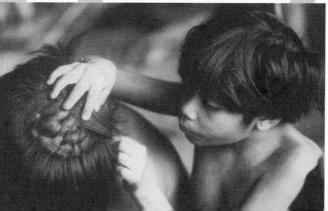

38. A nocturnal club fight over an accusation of infidelity.

39. Older men who have been in many club fights have enormous scars, of which they are very proud.

accepted the new arrivals because they were kinsman and would help to pros-ecute the war against the Patanowä-teri. The hosts, of course, took several women from the refugees as the price of their protection.

The Yanomamö do not commonly fight with spears. A rare form of fighting, however, does involve the use of these weapons. It is a formal contest, in the sense that it is prearranged and the participants have agreed to refrain from using bows and arrows. Fights like these take place when the members of two villages are not angry enough with each other to shoot to kill but are too angry to be satisfied by chest pounding or club fighting.

Raids and Nomohori

The raid is the next level in the Yanomamö scale of violence; it is warfare proper. The objective of a raid is to kill some of the enemy and flee without being discovered. If, however, the victims of the raid come after their assailants and kill one of them, the raid is not considered a success, no matter how many people the attackers may have killed.

Rerebawä told me of one such raid he had gone on, several years before I knew him, during which the raiders killed the headman of the village they attacked, abducted the headman's wife and her son, a boy of about ten, and killed another man who was running to find help. The raiders were chased, but they kept ahead of their pursuers for a while. Then the pursuers caught up with them, after dark on the second day, and attacked while they slept, killing one man in his hammock. This awoke the others, and in the ensuing skirmish the raiders killed two more of the enemy. Still, according to Rerebawä, the raid was not a good one because one of their own men was killed. (The son of the slain headman was later shot by a man who now lives in Monou-teri. The man got sick of seeing the boy constantly being tormented by the other children, so he shot the boy as he was bathing in the stream. Also, the boy reminded him of his enemies.)

Although few raids are initiated with the sole intention of capturing women, that is always a desired side benefit. But a few wars *are* started with the intention of abducting women. One village in Brazil that I visited in 1967 had a critical shortage of women. Some missionaries who lived in the village learned later of the treacherous means by which the group alleviated its problem and gave me this account. A raiding party organized by the group's headman went to a distant village and told the people there that they had received machetes and cooking pots from foreigners who prayed to a spirit for such items. The raiders volunteered to teach these people how to pray to the same spirit. When the men knelt down and bowed their heads, the raiders attacked and killed them with machetes, took their women, and fled.

Treachery of this kind, called *nomohori*—dastardly trick—is the ultimate form of Yanomamö violence. Kaobawä's group had suffered a treacherous massacre in 1950, as described in the introduction and in chapter 5, although in that case the treachery was in revenge for an earlier killing. Still, the assailants did attempt to abduct women after the objectives of their treachery were accomplished. In fact, had it not been for their greed to capture women, the massacre would have been even more successful.

Generally, however, the desire to abduct women does not lead to the initiation of hostilities between groups that have had no previous history of mutual raiding. But the situation is changing, especially in the villages where the Salesian missions operate along the Upper Orinoco, as shotguns become more common. In 1990, a party of mission Yanomamö from Mavaca, armed with shotguns, joined forces with a splinter group of Patanowä-teri and treacherously attacked a remote village that was becoming friendly with the Patanowä-teri. They killed two men with their shotguns and abducted seven women.

New wars are more likely to develop when one group levels charges of sorcery against another. Once raiding has begun, however, the raiders all hope to acquire women if the circumstances are such that they can flee without being discovered. For instance, if they catch a man and his wife at some distance from the village they are attacking, they will probably kill the husband and take the woman. But if the raiders are near the village, they may flee without dragging the woman along, as the husband's body will be discovered quickly, pursuit will be immediate, and a reluctant captive will hinder their flight. When a woman is captured, she is raped by all the men in the raiding party and, later, by men in the village who did not go on the raid. She is then given to one of the men as a wife.

Most wars are prolonged by motives of revenge stemming from earlier hostilities. The initial causes of such hostilities are usually sorcery, killings, or club fights over women in which someone has been badly injured or killed. Occasionally the theft of food from a village's garden precipitates fighting and, if it leads to a death, escalates to raiding. That was the immediate cause of the first raids between Kaobawä's group and the Patanowä-teri. They had split from each other after a series of club fights over women. Each group made a new garden, but both returned periodically to the old one to collect peach palm fruit from trees that were still producing. Someone in one group stole the peach palm fruit of a man in the other, resulting in another food theft in retaliation, a club fight, and then raiding. But it should be pointed out that the raiding came only after a long history of disputes between the groups; the food theft was merely the catalyst. And intimidation, not hunger, is often the reason for stealing food.

The Yanomamö themselves regard fights over women as the primary causes of the killings that lead to their wars. In 1967, on a return visit to a remote village I had gone to during my first field trip, the headman, Säsäwä, kept begging me to give him my knife, a military knife. He wanted to know all about the knife, its origin, its history, how often it had been exchanged in trades. When I told him that it was used by the people of my group when they went on "raids" against their enemies, his interest shifted to our military exploits.

"Who did you raid?" he asked.

"Germany-teri."

"Did you go on the raid?"

"No, but my father did."

"How many of the enemy did he kill?"

"None."

"Did any of your kinsmen get killed by the enemy?"

"No."

"You probably raided because of women theft, didn't you?"

"No."

This answer puzzled him. He conferred for a moment with the others, seeming to doubt my answer.

"Was it because of witchcraft?" he then asked.

"No," I replied again.

"Ah! Someone stole cultivated food from the other," he exclaimed, confidently citing the only other kind of incident that he deemed serious enough to provoke a war.

Säsäwä was killed the following year by raiders from Platanal (Mahekodo-teri), one of the Salesian mission villages. A son of the headman of that village blew off his head with a shotgun he had obtained from the missionaries—one of the first shotguns acquired by the Yanomamö of this area.

Perhaps the best way to illustrate the nature of Yanomamö warfare, its causes, and the techniques of a raid is through the recent military activities of the Monou-teri, a small group that split away from Kaobawä's in the mid-1950s.

A David-and-Goliath War

The headman of the Monou-teri village, Matowä, was a particularly aggressive man. According to both Rerebawä and Kaobawä, he was the only fierce man in the entire village, the true *waiteri* of the group. I met him only once, shortly before he was killed, and did not know him well.

Matowä had a long record of seducing other men's wives. That had led to regular feuding in the village and a number of club fights. Of his numerous affairs, two in particular illustrate what a range of consequences there can be. The first affair was with an abducted Shamatari girl who was married to his youngest brother. When Matowä seduced her, the brother was enraged, but he was afraid to vent his anger on Matowä, the real culprit. Instead, he shot the wife with an arrow. He had intended only to wound her, but the arrow struck a vital spot and she died.

In the second incident, a man named Manasinawä (some fifty-five years old by the time I learned of the incident) joined Matowä's group with his wife and young daughter. He had fled from his own village in order to join one that was raiding it, since he wanted revenge against it for a wrong he had suffered. Matowä, who already had several wives, decided he also wanted to add Manasinawä's wife to his household. This resulted in the club fight that led to the final separation of Kaobawä's group from the Monou-teri. Manasinawä's wife took her daughter and fled to yet another village, whose members refused to give them back. Kaobawä then organized a raid to recover them, and the two were taken by force by his warriors. Nobody was killed in the raid, and Manasinawä, his wife, and the daughter remained with Kaobawä's group. Manasinawä eventually gave the daughter to Kaobawä. She is his second wife, Koamashima (pictured in photo 8, in chapter 1).

At the time, Matowä's and Kaobawä's groups were both still at war with the Patanowä-teri, from whom they had separated some fifteen years earlier. After the separation from Kaobawä's group, however, Matowä's group attempted to make peace with the Patanowä-teri. The group was vulnerable and could ill afford to continue the hostilities. Matowä's group also made an alliance with the two Shamatari villages that had aided in staging the treacherous feast

discussed in the previous chapter. For about five years, relations between Matowä's group and the Patanowä-teri were relatively amicable, but as the former's
alliances with the Shamatari grew stronger, the relationship with the Patanowä-
teri cooled.

The Patanowä-teri now became embroiled in new wars with several villages
on the Orinoco and turned to Kaobawä's group for aid, hoping to patch up
their old grievances and establish peaceful relations. The first day of my fieldwork,
in fact, marked the initiation of peace. Kaobawä's group and the Patanowä-teri
were having a feast together in Bisaasi-teri.

Matowä's group, the Monou-teri, were not participating in the feast, but
a number of their men came to it. They discovered seven Patanowä-teri women
outside the main village and could not resist the temptation to take them by
force back to Monou-teri. Later in the day, when the Patanowä-teri men realized
that the women were missing, they searched around and found the tracks of
the Monou-teri men at the site of the abduction, along with abundant signs of
a struggle. The next morning, they went off to Monou-teri armed with clubs.
They were bound to get the women back, but they did not care to start another
shooting war with the Monou-teri. In a heated struggle, they retrieved five of
the women but had to pull back without the remaining two, unless they were
willing to shoot to kill. The Monou-teri were determined to keep those two
women at all costs.

The significance of the incident is that Matowä knew the Patanowä-teri
would not chance getting into a shooting war with him, since they already had
more enemies than they could comfortably cope with. It had been an excellent
opportunity for the Monou-teri to abduct their women, with relatively little
risk of being shot in retaliation.

But Matowä was furious that the Patanowä-teri had recovered so many
of the women, and he threatened to ambush the group when they left Bisaasi-
teri after the feast. In view of that, the Patanowä-teri cut short their stay and
left for home even before the feast was over.

However, Matowä was not satisfied with that, and he decided to raid the
Patanowä-teri. In January of 1966, he and a party of men from Monou-teri
raided the Patanowä-teri village. They caught one man, named Bosibrei, climbing
a *rasha* tree, a prickly palm that must be climbed slowly, by means of a movable
stick frame that protects the climber from the needle-sharp thorns on the trunk
(see photo 21, in chapter 2). Bosibrei was almost at the top when the raiders

spotted him—he made an excellent target silhouetted against the sky. They shot and killed him with one volley of arrows as he was reaching for the palm fruits. Ironically, one of Matowä's "brothers"—a participant in this raid—was married to one of Bosibrei's daughters.

In advance of the raid, the Monou-teri had been clearing a new garden site across the Mavaca River, where they planned to take refuge when the inevitable revenge raids from the Patanowä-teri began. They had hoped to complete the garden before the raids became intense, since the river would provide a natural obstacle. The Patanowä-teri, however, were infuriated by the killing and raided the Monou-teri immediately, in the first week of February. Two of the raiders were Matowä's parallel cousins, men he would call "brothers."

The raiders caught Matowä outside the new garden searching for honey. He had two of his wives with him and one child. He was looking up into a tree when the raiders shot a volley of arrows, at least five of which struck him in the abdomen. He managed to nock one of his own arrows and shoot back, cursing defiantly, although he probably was mortally wounded. Then Bishewä, one of the raiders, shot a final arrow that pierced Matowä's neck below the ear. He fell to the ground and died.

The raiders did not attempt to abduct the women. They were too close to the Monou-teri *shabono*, and they had to cross the Mavaca to escape. The women ran to the village and reported what had happened. Instead of giving chase, however, as they ought to have done—in the opinion of Kaobawä and others in Bisaasi-teri—the Monou-teri fled into the jungle and hid until dark, afraid that the raiders might return. Their awesome leader, Matowä, was dead, and they were demoralized.

The man who had fired the fatal arrow into Matowä's neck was a son of the man the Monou-teri had shot in their raid. Two of the men whose arrows hit Matowä were, in the Yanomamö kinship classification system, his brothers (members of the same lineage), three were brothers-in-law (including the one who shot the fatal arrow), and one was a man who had been adopted into the Patanowä-teri village as a child, after he and his mother were abducted from a distant Shamatari village.

The Monou-teri burned Matowä's corpse the next day. They held a mortuary ceremony the same week and invited their allies, the members of the two Shamatari villages and the two groups of Bisaasi-teri, to participate. Gourds of his ashes were given to certain men (who could not themselves drink the ashes but would be responsible for avenging the death) in several of the allied villages, an act calculated to reaffirm solidarity and friendship. Matowä's widows were given to his two oldest surviving brothers.

Kaobawä, classified as a brother to Matowä, assumed the responsibility of organizing a revenge raid. Matowä's own brothers did not step forward to do so, and for a while the Monou-teri had no leadership at all. Finally Orusiwä, the oldest and most competent member of the village, emerged as the de facto leader—somebody had to take the leadership. He was related to the slain headman as a brother-in-law, and their respective descent groups dominated village politics. So the leadership in Monou-teri shifted from one lineage to another, equally large one.

Kaobawä delayed the revenge raid until April, to give the Monou-teri time to expand their new garden. The date also coincided with the beginning of the rains, which would put off the prospect of a retaliation raid until the next dry season and give the Monou-teri additional time to work on their new garden.

The Monou-teri were afraid now to return to their old producing garden. They divided their time between the newly cleared site, where they were cutting and burning timber, and Kaobawä's village, where they occasionally stayed for a rest. (The illustration in chapter 2, "Macro Movements of Several Villages," shows some of the Monou-teri's moves.) They returned to the old site only to collect plantains, which they carried to the new site. Kaobawä's group built a new *shabono* and fortified it with a palisade, in anticipation of the war to come. His group, the Upper Bisaasi-teri, had been maintaining two small *shabonos* a few yards apart (known as *he borarawä*), but now they coalesced into a single group and moved into the new *shabono*. The visiting Monou-teri helped with the work on the new structure.

Meanwhile, the Patanowä-teri, knowing that they would be raided by the Monou-teri and their allies, were also clearing a new garden and preparing to move. The site was near a garden that Kaobawä's group had abandoned many years before, and the peach palm trees were still producing. The Patanowä-teri were in rather desperate straits. Some old enemies, several groups on the Orinoco, were raiding them regularly, having learned that they were again at war with the Monou-teri and the Bisaasi-teri. A few additional villages also began raids on them to settle old grudges. This kind of ganging up on a weak adversary is quite characteristic of Yanomamö politics and warfare—and is a solemn reminder to large villages to think twice about fissioning into smaller and more vulnerable ones.

The Patanowä-teri now began to move from one location to another, hoping to confuse their enemies. In the dry season, they divided their time between their main producing garden, the village of the Ashidowä-teri, their only ally, and the new garden. But each raiding group simply passed on word to others as to where they had found the Patanowä-teri, and all knew that they were at one place or the other. Raids were frequent and took a heavy toll. At least eight Patanowä-teri were killed by raiders that first year, and a number of others were wounded. Some of the dead were women and children, in retaliation for the Patanowä-teri's having sent a heavy volley of arrows into an enemy village and killing a woman. Women are not normally a target of raiders' arrows.

The Patanowä-teri were raided at least twenty-five times during my initial period of fieldwork. They retaliated as frequently as possible, but they could not return tit for tat against every enemy for every raid. They did manage to drive one of their biggest enemies, the Hasuböwä-teri, away from their garden and forced them to flee across the Orinoco. They concentrated their raids on this group until they had killed most of its *waiteris*. They were so successful, in fact, that the Hasuböwä-teri finally withdrew from the war, nearly as demoralized as the Monou-teri were. Several of my informants said it was because all their "fierce ones" were dead, and they had nobody capable of prosecuting the war against a village as ferocious as the Patanowä-teri. The informants considered them to be harmless and impotent now.

After the Hasuböwä-teri withdrew, the Patanowä-teri turned their attention to the Monou-teri. Every time the latter returned to their main site, they found numerous tracks around the village, always coming from the direction of Patanowä-teri. The Monou-teri therefore moved in with Kaobawä's group for protection, afraid to return to the old site until the jungle was inundated by the rains. Kaobawä's group was somewhat resentful and made no bones about reminding the Monou-teri how much of their food they were eating. When the complaining became intense, the Monou-teri moved into the village of the Lower Bisaasi-teri and lived off their produce until the latter also began to complain. Then they traveled to the Mömariböwei-teri and lived with them for a while, returning to Kaobawä's village when those allies wearied of them. Whenever the hosts—the Lower Bisaasi-teri, say—wanted to get rid of the Monou-teri, they would hold a feast in their honor. After the presentation of the going-home food, the Monou-teri had no alternative but to leave—it would have been an insult to remain any longer. In between moves, they returned to their old producing site to collect plantains and carry them to the new garden, where they subsisted on the food they brought with them.

Soon tiring of their treatment as pariahs, the Monou-teri began to regain their courage. Much of the treatment was because they had failed to chase Matowä's slayers, had displayed cowardice rather than ferocity. The men of the Bisaasi-teri groups were especially offended by this and were not timid about showing it. The Monou-teri were also a burden, since they rarely helped the Bisaasi-teri in their gardens and ate a good deal of their food. Besides, Matowä had had many close relatives among the Bisaasi-teri, and they felt that his death should be avenged—but by his even closer relatives in Monou-teri.

The raid Kaobawä organized to avenge Matowä's death took place late in April, as planned. His Shamatari allies, the Mömariböwei-teri and the Reyaboböwei-teri, were invited to participate, but they failed to send a contingent. The raid was even put off for a few days because some of the Bisaasi-teri suspected that these allies were waiting for the raiders to leave so that they could descend on the unprotected women and make off with captives. Finally a few did arrive. But the Bisaasi-teri still feared treachery on the part of their Shamatari friends, so at the last minute the men of Lower Bisaasi-teri decided to stay at home to guard all the women. As I have said, Yanomamö allies never completely trust each other.

Now the *wayu itou*—the warrior lineup—could get under way.

In the afternoon, a *no owä*—an effigy of the enemy—was set up in the village, and the men who were to go on the raid conducted a mock attack on the effigy, a grass dummy that was supposed to represent a Patanowä-teri man. Sometimes a painted log is used as the effigy, but this time it was a grass dummy. The men painted themselves black and crept slowly around the village with bows and arrows ready, searching for the "tracks" of the enemy. They converged at one point, then spread out, crept toward the dummy, and, at Kaobawä's signal, let fly with a volley of arrows. The Yanomamö are good archers. None of the arrows missed its mark, and the dummy, looking like a pincushion, toppled ominously to the ground with a dozen or more bamboo-tipped arrows protruding from it. Then the raiders screamed and ran out of the village, simulating their flight from the enemy. They drifted back, one at a time or in small groups, and retired to their hammocks to wait for darkness.

Shortly after dark, the village became unusually quiet. Suddenly the stillness was pierced by an animallike noise, half scream and half growl, as the first raider marched slowly out to the center of the village, clacking his arrows against his bow and growling his own fierce noise, usually in mimic of a carnivore's—a wasp's or a buzzard's. At this signal, not fully knowing what to expect and a little nervous, I crept from my hammock and went toward the center of the village with my tape recorder. The other raiders joined the first man, coming one at a time at short intervals, each clacking his arrows and growling a hideous noise. I turned my flashlight on for a few seconds, but decided that was probably a bad idea—or even a dangerous one. I saw Kaobawä standing by to make sure that the line was straight and faced in the direction of the enemy village; he would push or pull the individual warriors until they formed a perfectly straight line. He joined the line after the last warrior had taken his place.

The procession to the lineup, in which about fifty men participated, took around twenty minutes. When the last man was in line, the murmuring among the women and children died down, and all was quiet again. Absolutely quiet. I squatted there, unable to see much of what was going on, growing more nervous by the moment, half suspecting that the warriors were sneaking up to murder me for tape-recording what was undoubtedly a sacred rite.

The silence was shattered when a single man began to sing, in a deep baritone voice, "I am meat hungry! I am meat hungry! Like the carrion-eating buzzard, I hunger for flesh." It was Torokoiwä, one of Matowä's brothers. When he completed the last line, the other raiders repeated the song, ending in an ear-piercing, high-pitched scream that raised goose bumps all over my arms and scalp. A second chorus, again led by Torokoiwä, was followed by the collective scream. This stanza referred to the meat hunger characteristic of a particular species of carnivorous wasp. They screamed again, sounding distinctly more enraged. On the third chorus, they referred again to the buzzard's meat hunger, and a few men interjected such descriptions of their ferocity as "I'm so fierce that when I shoot the enemy my arrow will strike him with such force that blood will splash all over the possessions in his household."

Then the line of warriors broke, and the men gathered into a tight formation, weapons held above their heads. They shouted three times, beginning modestly and increasing the volume until it climaxed at the end of the third shout: "Whaaaa! *Whaaaa!* WHAAAA!" They listened as the jungle echoed back the last shout, the echo representing the spirit of the enemy. They noted the direction from which the echo came. On hearing it, they pranced about frantically, hissing and groaning, waving their weapons, until Kaobawä calmed them down. The shout was repeated two more times. At the end of the third shout of the third series, the formation broke, and the men ran back to their houses, each making a noise—"Bubububububububu"—as he ran.

When they reached their hammocks, they simulated vomiting, ejecting from their bodies the "rotten flesh" of the enemy they had symbolically devoured during the *wayu itou* lineup. The symbolic association of killing enemies with eating human flesh reminded me of the contradictions in their myths about Jaguar—their seeming fear that men were dangerously close to becoming cannibals or "were-jaguars." Perhaps in a time of war this was an acceptable transformation.

Now they retired for the night. Many of them wept and sang melancholy songs, mourning the loss of their friend and kinsman Matowä and tenderly referring to him by endearing kinship terms. At dawn, the women went to the gardens and gathered large quantities of plantains. These they carried to the edge of the village, wrapped them in vine hammocks, and deposited the bundles there for the men to collect as they marched past in single file on their way to war.

The men painted themselves black again. Some even put on the bright red loincloths I had traded to them, for the warrior lineup is another spectacle in which the younger men can show off for the girls; the loincloths were left behind when they departed. They tinkered with their bows, checked to see if the bowstrings had any weak spots, sharpened their best arrow points, and waited nervously and impatiently for Kaobawä to signal for the lineup to begin again.

The *wayu itou* was repeated, each man marching to the center of the village and taking his place in line (photo 40). This time, however, they did not sing the war song. They only did the shout, the same as on the previous night, waited for the echo to return, and then marched dramatically out of the village, full of rage and determination. Their mothers, wives, and sisters shouted last-minute bits of advice, like "Don't get yourself shot up. You be careful, now." And then the women wept, fearing for the safety of their sons, husbands, and brothers. The men picked up their supplies of food where the women had stacked them and left for Patanowä-teri.

Kaobawä had been complaining all year of severe pains in his lower back, abdomen, and urinary tract, and walking caused him considerable distress. Still, he had insisted on leading the raid, suspecting that the others would turn back if he did not. Sure enough, the raiders had not been gone five hours when the first one, a boastful young man, came back, complaining that he had a sore foot

40. *Raiders lining up at dawn prior to departing for a raid on their enemy. They paint their faces as well as their legs and chests black with masticated charcoal.*

and could not keep up. The next day a few more returned, complaining of malaria or pains in the stomach. They had enjoyed participating in the drama of the *wayu itou*, for that impressed the women, but once pressed into duty, they were afraid.

Raiders travel slowly on the first day away from their village, carrying their heavy burdens of food. They try to pace themselves so that they arrive in the enemy's territory just as the food runs out. Also, they try to camp the night before the raid at a point that will permit them to reach the enemy village at dawn—far enough away that enemy hunters will not happen on them but close enough that they can reach the village in an hour or so. They have fires only when they are camping at a considerable distance from the enemy's territory. As they approach their destination, they exercise greater caution. The final night is spent shivering in the darkness, since they dare not make a fire. Most of the raiders I have talked to put great emphasis on this. Sleeping in the jungle without a fire is not only uncomfortable but dangerous, because of the risk of jaguar attacks and the fear that evil spirits will molest them. On the last evening, the raiding party's fierce ones often have trouble with the younger men. Most of them are afraid, cold, and worried about every sort of hazard, and all of them complain of sore feet and bellyaches, trying to find a justification for fleeing before they encounter their enemy.

The raiders always have some strategy in mind for their attack on what they hope is an unwary enemy. They usually split into two or more groups before the attack and arrange to meet later at a predetermined place somewhere between the enemy's village and their own. These smaller groups should contain at least four men—six is better—so that they can retreat in a pattern. While two men flee, the other two lie in ambush to shoot any pursuers who may be following. Then they reverse positions.

If there are any novices in the raiding party, the older men conduct mock raids to show them what to do. A grass dummy or a soft log is frequently employed for this, as it was in the *wayu itou* ceremony. The youngest men are positioned somewhere in the middle of the single file of raiders, so that they will not be the first ones exposed if the raiders themselves are ambushed. These young men are also permitted to retreat first.

Matowä had a twelve-year-old son when he was killed, and this boy, Matarawä, was recruited into the raiding party to give him a chance to avenge his father's death. As this was his first raid, the older men made sure he was exposed to a minimum of danger. Several years later, in about 1979, Matarawä was killed by a group of Daiyari-teri men, in revenge for the deaths of two of their people in a chest-pounding duel with Kaobawä's group a few weeks earlier. This led to another war, one of the last that Kaobawä orchestrated. He and his allies inflicted heavy casualties on the Daiyari-teri and drove them out of the area and far to the east. There they rejoined the larger villages from which they had earlier fissioned.

The separate groups of raiders approach the village at dawn and conceal themselves near the paths to the village's source of drinking water. They wait for the enemy to come to them. Many victims of raids are shot while fetching water or while urinating just outside the *shabono*.

When there is an active war going on, the enemy is wary and acts defensively at all times. People leave the village only in large groups accompanied by armed men. Raiders will not attack such a group, but can only retreat or shoot a volley of arrows blindly into the village, hoping to strike someone. They retreat after releasing their arrows, hoping that gossip from other villages will eventually let them know if the arrows hit their mark. Rarely, a single raider will attempt to enter a village during the night and kill someone while he sleeps. One of Matowä's younger brothers is alleged to have done this once, but few men are brave enough to try it. Most of the time, the raiders manage to ambush at least one person, kill him, and retreat before they are discovered. That is considered a desirable outcome of a raid.

The women in Kaobawä's village were nervous, frightened, and irritable while the men were away, and constantly on the lookout for raiders from other villages. It is always a time to be on the alert, since allies occasionally turn on their friends when they know the women are poorly guarded. After a few days, the women were so frustrated and anxious that fights began to break out among them. One woman got angry because another woman, her sister and cowife, had left her small baby in the first woman's care. When the mother returned, the angry woman picked up a piece of firewood and bashed her on the side of the head, knocking her unconscious and causing her ear to bleed profusely.

The raiders had been gone almost a week when Kaobawä and Shararaiwä, his youngest brother, staggered into the village, nearly dead from exhaustion. Kaobawä's pain had gotten so bad that he had turned back just before the raiders reached the Patanowä-teri village. He could barely walk by then and would have been unable to elude any pursuers had the enemy given chase after the raid. Shararaiwä had accompanied him, for fear he might run into a group of Patanowä-teri hunters or his condition worsen. Shortly after they started back, Shararaiwä had stepped on a snake and been bitten. The rains had started, and the snakes were beginning to seek higher ground, making walking a hazard. Shararaiwä's leg began to swell immediately, and he could not walk. Kaobawä, who could barely walk himself, had to carry him on his back. In two days, they managed to reach the Orinoco, where Kaobawä intended to make a bark canoe and float the rest of the way back. But they happened on a dugout canoe that someone had concealed, borrowed it, and reached the village about dark. It had been three days since Shararaiwä was bitten, but he survived. Kaobawä was completely exhausted from the ordeal.

That night, an advance party of the raiders returned and chanted briefly with Kaobawä. They reported that they had reached Patanowä-teri, shot and killed one man, and fled. The Patanowä-teri had launched a pursuit, which got ahead of them at one point and ambushed them. The pursuers had wounded Konoreiwä of the Monou-teri, shooting a bamboo-tipped arrow completely through his chest just above the heart. His companions had to pull the cane shaft out from the front and, with their teeth, pull the protruding *rahaka* point out from the back.

The next morning, the main body of raiders returned, carrying Konoreiwä in a pole-and-vine litter. He was very weak and constantly coughing up mouthfuls of blood. The others put him in his hammock and tended his fire. They asked me to treat his wound, and I gave him several shots of penicillin.

He lay in the hammock for a week, not eating or drinking in all that time—the Yanomamö have a taboo against anyone's taking water when he has been wounded by a bamboo-tipped arrow. Konoreiwä was slowly wasting away and becoming dangerously dehydrated. Finally I could stand it no longer and made up a batch of heavily sugared lemonade and salt. I called for the men to gather around, ceremoniously crushed an aspirin into the lemonade, and explained that this was very powerful medicine. So powerful that it had to be diluted with a large amount of water. I then ordered Konoreiwä to drink some, which he was glad to do, seeing that the others were not going to interfere. But he was so weak that he could not sit up, so I spoon-fed him. A knowing glance passed between us as he gulped down the first spoonful of that sweet liquid. He eventually recovered.

The two men who had shot the fatal arrows into the Patanowä-teri were both brothers of the slain Matowä. They were killers of men now, *unokai*, and had to purify themselves by going through the *unokaimou* ceremony.

They were given space in Kaobawä's *shabono* for their hammocks. This area was sealed off from the adjoining houses by palm leaves, and the men's food was brought to them for the week they were confined here. They had to use a pair of sticks to scratch their bodies and could not touch their food with their fingers, but used the sticks as eating utensils. I was struck by the similarity between the *unokaimou* ritual purification and the first-menses ceremony for pubescent girls.

At the end of the confinement, the vine hammocks the men had slept in while on the raid, along with the scratching sticks, were taken out of the village and tied to a certain kind of tree. The hammocks were placed about six feet above the ground and about a foot apart. Then the men resumed their normal activities, but began to let their hair grow. Informants later told me that the men had to wait until the hammocks rotted and fell off the tree before they could resume a completely normal life.

Kaobawä felt that the raid had satisfied his obligation to avenge Matowä's death. The Monou-teri, however, wanted to continue prosecuting the war against the Patanowä-teri. It was at this point that Hontonawä, the man who wanted to take over Kaobawä's position as leader, began to emerge as a prominent man in the village. Encouraged by the esteem the Monou-teri expressed for him, he stepped forward and volunteered to lead raiding parties. Still, he was not enthusiastic enough for the Monou-teri. On one raid he led, he elected to turn around and go home when the Patanowä-teri were not found at their main garden. The Monou-teri wanted the party to keep looking for them, but Hontonawä refused to go any farther. When he turned back, so did the entire party.

The Monou-teri and the Bisaasi-teri raided the Patanowä-teri six times while I lived with them, and each time the preparations for the raid closely followed the description I have given. The Monou-teri did not return to their producing garden except when the jungle was inundated, the only time they could be sure of living there without being attacked. The remainder of the year, they had to take refuge in various allied villages.

The Monou-teri also raided the Patanowä-teri without the aid of their allies. One of those raids came near the end of the rainy season, and I was living with them at the time.

A special ceremony took place on the day before the raid. The gourds containing the ashes of the slain Matowä were put on the ground in front of his oldest brother's house. Everyone in the village gathered around the ashes and wept, loudly and fervently. Matowä's bamboo quiver was brought out, smashed, the arrow points taken out, and the quiver burned. All the time this was going on, the mourners were in a frenzied state, pulling at their hair, striking themselves, screaming and wailing. One of Matowä's brothers took a snuff tube and blew some *ebene* drug into the gourds containing the ashes (photo 41). Then the tube was cut into two pieces. One of Matowä's arrow points was used to mark the place at which the tube was cut.

I was never able to determine whether the arrow points taken from the quiver were Matowä's own or were the points removed from his body. There were ten of them, but my informants were too touchy about it for me to ask them much. I received affirmative nods to both questions. I suspect that they were his arrow points, and that the ones that killed him were burned with his corpse. In any case, the ten bamboo points were now distributed among the raiders, who fondled them lovingly, examined them, and wept profusely. Each man brought his point along on the raid. The severed snuff tube and the gourds of ashes were tenderly wrapped in leaves and put back in the thatch of the brother's house.

That night I became emotionally close to the Yanomamö in an entirely new way. The tenderness and sadness I had witnessed earlier in the day moved me deeply. I remained in my hammock and gave up working on my genealogies. As darkness fell, Matowä's brothers began to weep softly in their hammocks. I lay back and listened, not bothering to tape-record it, or photograph it, or write notes about it. One man asked me why I was not making a nuisance of myself as usual, and I told him that my innermost being (*buhii*) was cold—that is, I was sad. A deep, silent, understanding gaze passed between us, the kind that penetrates to the soul. After a while, he whispered something that was quietly passed around the village. As each person heard it, he or she glanced over at me, making me feel like an intimate part of the group. The children, who, as usual, had gathered around my hammock, were told by their elders to go home and stop bothering me. In their terms, I was *hushuo*—in a state of emotional disequilibrium—and had finally begun to act like a human being. Those whose hammocks were close to mine reached over to touch me tenderly and softly stroke my arm. I wept.

The next day, the raiders lined up, shouted in the direction of the Patanowä-teri, heard the echo come back, and left the village to collect their provisions and hammocks. I allowed them to talk me into taking the raiding party up the Mavaca in my canoe. There, they could find high ground and reach the Patanowä-teri without having to cross the numerous swamps that lay between the two villages. The raiding party contained only ten men, the smallest

41. *Matowä's brothers assembled around his remains, blowing* ebene *into the gourd containing his ashes.*

a war party can get and still be effective. As we rode up the river, the younger men began to complain. One had sore feet; two or three others claimed to have malaria and said we would have to turn back because I had forgotten to bring my malaria pills, as I had promised. Hukoshikuwä, one of Matowä's brothers, silenced the complaints with angry reprimands about the men's cowardice (photo 42).

I let them out at the mouth of Shamata kä u, the stream they were going to follow. They unloaded their enormous supply of plantains and politely waited for me to leave. I sat among them and chatted, thinking that they were doing essential tasks as they fiddled with their arrows and retied their provisions. Finally one of them hinted that I ought to be leaving; it was a long trip, and I might not get home before dark. It was then that I realized they were dallying out of politeness. They all thanked me for bringing them upstream—one of the few times a Yanomamö ever expressed gratitude to me—and I got in my canoe.

Hukoshikuwä came down to untie the rope and shoved the canoe off the bank. He watched silently as it got caught up in the current and drifted away. He looked frightened, reluctant, and anxious. After I got the motor started and was under way, I looked back to see him turn, pick up his plantains and weapons, and disappear into the jungle after the others, who had already disappeared.

So even he was not enthusiastic about the raid, despite his lecture to the younger men about their reluctance and cowardice. He was older, however, and had to display the courage that all adult Yanomamö men are supposed to show. In short, although Hukoshikuwä probably had little desire to participate in the raiding, he was obliged to do so by the pressures of the system. He could ill afford to remain neutral, for his very own kinsmen—even Kaobawä—had implied by word and action that they were disgusted with him for not having avenged the death of his brother. Some of his kinsmen in other villages had openly accused him of cowardice for not having chased the raiders who shot Matowä. His erstwhile allies, when they complained about having to feed him and his relatives, were blunt and discourteous. The Shamatari allies had even demanded a number of women from Hukoshikuwä's group, in payment for girls the allies had given his group much earlier, when the Monou-teri were high in the alliance pecking order. If Hukoshikuwä failed to put on a show of military determination and vindictiveness, it would not be long before his friends in allied villages would be taking even greater liberties and demanding even

42. *Hukoshikuwä waiting for me to leave so he could lead his warriors into the jungle to find their enemy, the Patanowä-teri.*

more women. The system worked against him and demanded that he be fierce, whether he wanted to be or not. Since his group was small, it had to protect its sovereignty all the more rigorously, or be absorbed by a greedy ally whose protection would be tendered at the price of women.

Hukoshikuwä and his party did not locate the Patanowä-teri on this raid, although they searched for more than a week. They had known it would be difficult in the rainy season, largely because of the many detours they would have to make around impassable swamps. It was with this in mind that they had brought a larger-than-usual supply of plantains.

The war was still going on, but on a less ambitious scale, when I returned to the Monou-teri a year later. They had managed to kill two Patanowä-teri men and abduct two women. The Patanowä-teri at this stage had killed only one Monou-teri, their headman.

Ten years later, they and the Bisaasi-teri were still trying to avenge Matowä's death and were actively raiding the Patanowä-teri. But by then they had acquired shotguns. At least two Patanowä-teri were killed with the shotguns, including the headman, Kumaiewä. Kumaiewä's head was blown apart from the blast of a gun fired by a man who then lived at the Salesian mission at Mavaca. It was one of the first shotguns to be acquired from this mission.

The Patanowä-teri group fissioned, losing a significant part of its size advantage. The Monou-teri completed their move to the new garden and lived there for several years, but eventually they coalesced with the Bisaasi-teri, ending their days as a separate sovereign entity. They fused with the people from whom they had originally fissioned and, as of 1992, were still living among them.

I do not know for sure, but I suspect that some of Matowä's ashes are still carefully stored away somewhere in the village—twenty-six years after his death.

The Human Costs of War and Violence

In chapter 2, I discussed differences in the extent of violence, warfare, and abductions in different areas of Yanomamöland. I have only recently started field research in similar areas, and there is much yet to learn.

Most of my work up to 1990 was conducted in Kaobawä's area. There, warfare, violence, and the abduction of women have been extremely important as far back in their history as I have been able to trace it with informants who were very old—perhaps in their seventies or eighties—in 1964, when I began my work.

In 1988, I was invited by Daniel Koshland, the editor of the prestigious journal *Science*, to contribute the lead article for one of their issues. In the article, I summarized some of what I knew about warfare and violence among the Yanomamö, based on my nearly twenty-five years of field observations.

I focused only on men who were alive at the time and who lived in one of the many villages I had studied between 1964 and 1987. I concentrated on about a dozen villages whose total population in 1987 was nearly 1,400. I knew who each of the living men had killed up to that date, where the deaths had occurred, what weapons had been used, the genealogies of all the men and their victims for four or five generations back—among other things.

Many highly prominent men who had killed numerous enemies—Matowä, for one—were not even considered in this analysis. One Shamatari man I had known well, Möawä, was also not considered, because he was dead by 1987; he alone had killed or participated in the killing of twenty-one people, the record for one man's victims so far in my research.

Among the more significant results of this analysis were these findings, which put the nature and the extent of violence among Kaobawä's people into a regional perspective.

(1) Approximately 40 percent of the adult males had participated in the killing of another Yanomamö. The majority of them (60 percent) had killed only one person, but some were repeatedly successful as warriors and had participated in the killing of up to sixteen.

(2) Approximately 30 percent of all the deaths among adult males were due to violence.

(3) Approximately two-thirds of the people aged forty or older had lost through violence at least one of these close biological relatives: a parent, a sibling, or a child. Most of them (57 percent) had lost two or more such close relatives. That helps to explain why large numbers of the people are motivated by revenge, and why kinsmen keep gourds containing the ashes of slain heroes for many years.

The most unusual and impressive finding, one that was subsequently discussed and heatedly debated in the press and in academic journals, was the correlation between military success and reproductive success. *Unokais*—men who have killed—were more successful at obtaining wives and, as a consequence, had more offspring than men the same age who were not *unokais*. The *unokais*

had, on average, more than two and a half times as many wives as non-*unokais*
did, and more than three times as many children.

The most plausible explanation for the correlation seems to be that the
unokais are socially rewarded and have greater prestige than other men, and
therefore are more often able to obtain extra wives, by whom they have more
than the average number of children. Thus, cultural success, in this cultural-
historical circumstance, leads to biological success, a thesis first suggested by
my lifelong colleague and friend William Irons.

Many cultural anthropologists find these facts disturbing, especially those
anthropologists who try to look at the Yanomamö as representing more than
just one isolated example. It is particularly disturbing to them when we know
that, by comparative ethnographic standards, the Yanomamö mortality rate due
to violence is much *lower* than that reported for other tribal groups for which
this statistic is known but the associated reproductive facts are not. Some seem
to be concerned that it might have been a general pattern in our history as a
species. It is a concern that, to me, resembles the Yanomamö fear that if we
do not cook our food well, we might all become feral, like the jaguar, or like
cannibals.

If cultural success always leads to biological success, then one ought to
be able to make this prediction: if being a pacific religious leader (a cultural
success) consistently leads to greater marital and reproductive success, then
more men would choose to be religious functionaries, such as priests, shamans,
or others. I would predict *exactly* that when one's neighbors are nice guys,
pursuing altruistic goals like being a good religious leader or a good shaman
and subscribing to such rules as "Thou shalt not covet thy neighbor's X, Y,
or Z" is easy. But when one's neighbors covet your X, Y, and Z and will take
them from you if you turn the other cheek, being an altruistic religious leader
or shaman isn't a very smart strategy. That is probably why we have more
soldiers than we do priests.

The more appropriate evolutionary question has to do with the likelihood
that, throughout history, people have based their political relationships with
other groups on predatory versus religious or altruistic strategies and on the
cost-benefit advantages of pursuing one strategy or the other. We have the
evolved capacity to adopt either. Turning the other cheek on neighbors who
are led by men like Matowä might not be the best strategy if your own—and
your group's—survival is of any concern. Men who do the things he did are
generally called warriors or soldiers and, historically, those among them who

survive seem to have been generously rewarded in the status, wealth, or power that their societies deem valuable.

We ourselves elect such men to Congress or to the presidency, and we give them medals and other honors. Among the Yanomamö, whose brand of government does not include legislative or executive structures or the awarding of medals, such men get more wives and have more children. Important aspects of our biologies are similar, but our cultures are different. Yet we both reward our warriors with the tokens that are appropriate to our cultural circumstances.

Chapter Seven

Acculturation and the Future

In the Americas, acculturation—the process of change that occurs when two cultures impinge on each other—has gone pretty much in one direction. Ever since the time of Columbus, native tribal societies have been "contacted" (as anthropologists say) by representatives of the European cultural tradition—explorers, missionaries, homesteaders, prospectors, and so on. These early contacts have set in motion changes that have drastically altered the tribal societies, and have often caused their extinction as cultural entities. Compare the cultural face of the Americas in 1492 to what exists—and does not exist—today. Perhaps 95 percent of the distinctive cultures that existed in 1492 have vanished completely, languages and all. Most of those that remain are shadows of what they were, and even these are disappearing rapidly.

Only a handful of native American societies have survived the five hundred years in anything resembling their earlier cultural and ecological circumstances. Those few that have survived owe it to their fortuitous isolation in one of the remotest outposts of the hemisphere, the Amazon Basin, which was almost inaccessible until the advent of outboard motors and aircraft. While there are probably a dozen or so uncontacted tribes in various unexplored pockets of the Amazon, most of them are very small groups that are basically refugees from elsewhere. The Yanomamö are the major exception.

They are the last large, relatively unacculturated Native American tribe left, and possibly the last such people in the world. When they become acculturated, an epoch in human history that has lasted tens of thousands of years will end. A species of human social existence very like that of our ancient past will disappear. I think that it is important to try to understand as much as we can about this kind of human existence while we still can. That is my position as a scientist. I also think that we should do everything possible to prevent the eradication of this last intact aboriginal culture. That is my moral and ethical position.

Gradual or Catastrophic Change?

When just a few Yanomamö villages were first entering into sustained contact with outsiders—becoming acculturated—their experiences were both humorous and anthropologically instructive.

I took Rerebawä on his first visit to Caracas, in the late 1960s, in a military airplane. He was white as a sheet during the flight, he was terrified that we would bump into the next layer of the Yanomamö cosmos. Like most of his fellow villagers, the only outsiders he knew about were the neighboring Ye'kwana Indians. He had heard just the name "Caraca-teri," whose people were thought to be the only non-Yanomamös and non-Ye'kwanas in the cosmos.

When we landed at the Venezuelan air force base in Maracay and I invited him to get into a car, a vehicle he had never seen or heard about, he walked up to it, scratched his head, and finally dived in through an open window. It was not at all obvious to him that cars had doors that opened. I have mentioned earlier that he thought auto headlights at night were *bore* spirits, the supernatural beings with glowing eyes that prowl the jungle.

He was astonished at the high-heeled shoes worn by the Caraca-teriyoma, remarking that they would never be able to walk on the Yanomamö trails. Nevertheless, he wanted to snatch a few of them—they were so unprotected, and there were so many of them—to take home as extra wives. Vending machines that immediately disgorged icy cold cans of delicious sweet soda pop for a coin thrilled him. He tasted my beer, described it as "very sweet," but didn't like it and asked for orange soda.

The sheer size of Caracas overwhelmed him; it wasn't the extra-large thatched structure with a central plaza that he had imagined. He mistrusted suspended staircases and crawled up them on his belly, afraid they would collapse any minute under their own weight, and surely would with his weight added. And the look on his face when we got into an elevator, the door closed, it opened again, and we were somewhere else!

He was puzzled that there were no gardens and wondered where all the food came from and why nobody made fires in the houses at night. In fact, he had asked me about the fires before we left the jungle. I had thought it was an odd question but hadn't paid it much attention. When we reached Caracas, I discovered that one of the few things he had brought along was a container of wood ashes, to mix with the dried bundle of tobacco leaves he had also brought.

When we got back to Bisaasi-teri, his friends asked him if Caracas was as large as I had said it was. He looked at me and blushed, knowing that he could do no more than what I had repeatedly done when the Yanomamö asked me the same kind of question. He moved to one side, bent his knees, pointed to the horizon, and with his finger slowly drew an immense arc all across the sky to the opposite horizon, saying, as his finger moved, "It stretches from way over there to w a y   o v e r   t h e r e." The others clicked their tongues in amazement. It was bigger than they had thought—possibly as big as the Patanowä-teri's *shabono*.

Some of the early signs of change were more portentous. I once asked Rerebawä why a certain Yanomamö from one of the Salesian mission villages had raided so far away and had killed a man with a shotgun—a man from a village that his own had never had any contact with. Rerebawä said, "If you give a fierce Yanomamö man a shotgun, he will want to use it to kill with, simply because he has it." Incidents like this are increasingly common as more and more of the Venezuelan Yanomamö acquire shotguns from the missionaries and other sources. And the situation is far worse in Brazil, where shotguns are much cheaper and are traded to the Yanomamö there almost as freely as I would trade machetes to them in Venezuela.

I can no longer describe the changes in humorous or even in neutral terms. My observations and much of the data I have collected in my most recent field research have alarmed me. In this chapter, I will discuss the developing problems and frankly suggest what ought to be done about them, in the best interests of the Yanomamö themselves. That will annoy some "good" people, the Salesian Catholic missionaries in particular.

Anthropologists who head off in this direction are usually called applied anthropologists: they apply the information they are gathering to alter a cultural situation. This is not traditional anthropology, which describes cultures as they are, relates them to broader theories, and takes no role in promoting or engineering changes. Traditional scientific anthropologists like me have simply been letting others do it. Well, the ones currently doing it in Yanomamöland are doing it all wrong.

Most of the applied anthropologists working with the Yanomamö believe that only "politically correct" data—data useful to their cause—should be collected and publicized, and that any other kind of data is "bad." An example of what they regard as "bad" is much of what you have been reading here—descriptions of warfare, abductions, club fights, intrigues, chicanery, and competitiveness among real people, and a general argument that these variables are important in shaping the actions of individuals. Such data are "bad," these anthropologists seem to believe, because they make the Yanomamö culture look bad, and it becomes difficult to cultivate sympathy for them among politicians and the public at large.

I take the peculiar position that *all* facts about the Yanomamö are relevant to their future. It is condescending to believe that intelligent people will not feel sympathy for or want to help the Yanomamö just because they have turned out to have the same social, emotional, and political defects as we do. I would go further: I would describe that attitude as academic racism. It insinuates that the only people worthy of our assistance are those who approach the purest form of the mythical noble savage, that naive image of primitive man held so dear by morally correct anthropologists. For my part, I think the Yanomamö warrant our sympathy and our help just as they are. It would indeed be an unjust world if foreign aid and disaster relief were distributed on the basis of the recipients' approximation to a hypothetical moral and ethical standard that the givers of the aid come nowhere close to achieving.

In our rapidly changing world, it is increasingly difficult and inadvisable for anthropologists to remain neutral. We are all becoming advocates of the rights of the peoples we have lived among, sometimes quietly and at other times very publicly. The stakes are the survival of a whole people—the Yanomamö in this case, now a symbol of beleaguered tribal societies everywhere.

Acculturation is too benign and antiseptic a word to describe what is happening to the Yanomamö society and people in Venezuela and Brazil today. If acculturation means the slow and steady erosion of independent and sovereign native lifeways and their absorption into larger cultural, political, and economic spheres, we need a new term to characterize the jolting and catastrophic set of events that is transforming the Yanomamö and threatening their biological and cultural survival. Perhaps *catastrophic change* comes the closest.

Variations in Degree and Kind of Contact

The degree of change among the Yanomamö groups that I have witnessed in almost thirty years varies radically from one place to another and, increasingly, from one country to another. In Venezuela, growing numbers of villages, like Kaobawä's, are in direct contact with missionaries. Some, again like Kaobawä's, have been in direct contact with missionaries for as much as thirty-five years.

Other villages—a few—have not yet been contacted by outsiders, at least not directly, and still live a life very much like that described here.

Most of the changes occurring among the Venezuelan Yanomamö are the result of the expanding activities of the Salesian missions. This is a Catholic order that maintains three mission posts along the Orinoco River, Mavaca, Platanal, and Ocamo. Mavaca is at the confluence of the Mavaca River and the Orinoco, where Upper and Lower Bisaasi-teri are located. Platanal is at the Yanomamö village of Mahekodo-teri. The third, Ocamo, is to the north, at the junction of the Ocamo River and the Orinoco. A satellite to the Mavaca mission, Mavakita, is on the Mavaca River just downstream from the mouth of the Shamata River. (All these sites except Ocamo fall within the area shown on the map in chapter 5.)

The missions extend their influence outward from these posts, mainly following the navigable rivers but also reaching inland in some places. The Yanomamö villages close to the mission posts are becoming inexorably tied to and dependent on them. The missionaries have even started schools and economic cooperatives in some villages, and have trained some Yanomamö as teachers.

Mission contact with villages diminishes and becomes less regular as the distance from a post increases, especially if the village is not near a navigable river. To reach the more remote villages, the missionaries must either walk in or send groups of Yanomamö men they have trained. This is inconvenient and inefficient. Consequently, they have been urging inland groups to move out to a navigable river or near the mission post itself. In effect, the policy seems to be to reduce the small, widely separated, isolated villages to a few large and accessible ones. Many of the recent moves in the area of Kaobawä's village suggest that the policy is working. More and more villages are moving close to the missions, and factions of large villages are splitting away to do so.

The sphere of mission influence has expanded dramatically in the past fifteen years and is pervasive around the Ocamo, Mavaca, and Platanal posts. No Yanomamö village on or near a navigable river or stream between or near these three posts can any longer be considered unacculturated.

Three degrees of culture contact and change are associated with the mission activities: (1) highly missionized Yanomamö who live at the three mission posts and have close daily contact with the missionaries and the growing number of other non-Yanomamö now living at the missions; (2) moderately missionized Yanomamö, who live within easy motorized boat distance of the posts and are regularly visited by the missionaries; (3) minimally missionized Yanomamö, who live at some distance from the missions and are visited sporadically and irregularly.

The pattern is similar in areas where Protestant missions operate among the Venezuelan Yanomamö, except that the distances between their missions are so great that they are unlikely ever to develop a wide sphere of influence. The same pattern has developed in Brazil, and the spheres of influence of mission posts in the two countries almost meet. For example, people from a few of the villages in the Mavaca headwaters that I have been studying for years occasionally visit both the Mavaca mission and a Protestant mission, Abruwä-teri, in Brazil, several days' walk to their south.

In Venezuela, only a few areas of any size remain isolated from outsiders—missionaries and others. Or, if they have been contacted, the contacts have been very recent, very brief, and often once only. The eastern half of the Siapa Basin and the region immediately to the north of it in the Orinoco Basin is one such area. In 1990 and 1991, thanks to several helicopters made available by the Venezuelan government, I initiated work here and was able to visit a number of villages that had no outsider had ever visited before.

That is not as romantic as it sounds, since these Yanomamö already were aware that there was a larger world, peopled by subhuman foreigners, or *nabäs*. It was not like the first-contact experiences I had in the 1960s and '70s, which I have spoken of earlier. And I had known about some of these groups for years, because they figured prominently in the history of groups I was studying. Many of their people, living and dead, were in my genealogies, and I knew something about their migration patterns and even about a few of their political leaders. Not surprisingly, many of them had heard about me, too, through their contacts with other villages.

I had met a few individuals from some of these villages, mostly women who had been abducted and were living elsewhere. A number of older women in Kaobawä's village were from places called Konabuma-teri, Akawaiyoba-teri, Rahakaböwei-teri, and Bohorowabihiwei-teri—abandoned sites and existing villages that I am only now visiting. Many of the older people in the several Shamatari villages I had studied were born in this remote Siapa Basin area, in old sites I have recently been in or have flown over and located with my GPS instruments. (I had also flown over the area twice in the late 1960s and '70s and had located several villages from the air.) And I met a few men from these groups who had married into villages in which I was working.

Many of the men of these remote villages had seen outsiders before my visits of 1990 and 1991, usually at the Brazilian missions they occasionally visited to obtain steel tools—sometimes a walk of five or six days. In 1972, a Venezuelan border commission team had flown to an island in the Siapa River and traveled down the river, briefly stopping at several villages along the way, and in 1974 one of my former graduate students who was working in the upper Orinoco, in the northern part of this area, briefly visited some of the isolated groups immediately to the south.

These sporadic contacts aside, the area is one of the last major redoubts of the traditional Yanomamö culture and of relatively unacculturated villages. It is possible that an area in the Parima mountains to the northeast contains comparable clusters of isolated villages.

Thus, the Yanomamö villages in Venezuela fall roughly into four degrees of contact; the three levels associated with mission activities and a fourth level of almost no direct contact. That makes it difficult to generalize about culture change, except to say that accelerating contacts with the outside world have created serious health problems for all, differing in severity based on the level of contact.

It should surprise no one that I find many groups vastly changed since I began my work in the 1960s. It is nothing short of astonishing that even a few still exist in isolation.

The picture was similar in Brazil until very recently. All that changed in 1987, however. Tragically, there are probably no Yanomamö groups left anywhere in Brazil that are comparable in their degree of isolation and lack of contact to the remote villages on the Venezuelan side of the border.

The 1987 Brazilian Gold Rush and Its Aftermath

What is happening to most of the Brazilian Yanomamö today is a tragedy of enormous proportions. It was brought on primarily by a gold rush on the Brazilian side of the border that simmered for several years and then exploded in 1987.

The diseases introduced by the Brazilian gold miners—the *garimpeiros*—could easily spread to the remote Venezuelan villages near the border. I was in one of them in 1991 when five Brazilian *garimpeiros*, lost, hungry, and sick, staggered in. My Venezuelan coresearcher, Dr. Charles Brewer, and I had them sent out by helicopter and handed over to the Venezuelan authorities, who jailed them for a few days and returned them to Brazil. *Garimpeiros* had not been in this village before, but the people said they had been in other villages just to the east.

The Brazilian gold rush of 1987 has been the single most devastating event in recent Yanomamö history. All the other forces of change pale in importance. It began near a place called Mucajai, a remote mission site on the Mucajai River in Brazil's Roraima Territory (I had briefly visited there in 1967), spread rapidly, and peaked in 1989. A detailed account of it, up to around the beginning of 1991, has been published by a Brazilian action group, the Committee for the Creation of a Yanomamö Park, or CCPY, which advocates the creation of a native reserve to protect the Brazilian Yanomamö and their traditional lands. The book is entitled *Urihi* and is available in English.

Ironically, I first learned about the gold rush in my backyard in Santa Barbara a few weeks after it began. My houseguest was a Consolata priest named John Saffirio, who had been living among the Brazilian Yanomamö for many years. I had met John in 1975, when I was on the faculty at Pennsylvania State University. He had just entered the graduate program in anthropology at the University of Pittsburgh, knew of my work, and wanted some advice on his doctoral thesis. I helped him design his field research and, later, the computer programs for analyzing it, and he was awarded his Ph.D. in 1985. We have been good friends ever since.

On that day in September 1987, John was about to return to his mission in Brazil and made a last-minute phone call to his bishop from my home. He was white and trembling when he finished the call. The bishop had told him that the Brazilian government had closed his Catrimani mission and that he could not go back. It seems that John and others at the mission had dutifully been reporting the presence of illegal gold miners in Yanomamö territory and filing official reports that forced the authorities into removing the miners, as Brazilian law stipulated. With the gold fever heating up, the miners were claiming that if they couldn't be there, then neither should the missionaries and other outsiders. The government buckled under the pressure and ordered the missionaries, anthropologists, and others sympathetic to the Yanomamö to leave. Now the miners invaded in force—soon reaching the number of approximately 40,000.

It was not long before the first ugly incident occurred. A group of miners clashed with a group of Yanomamö near Mucajai, gunning down four of them and desecrating their dead bodies. One miner was killed by a Yanomamö with a recently acquired gun.

In a short time, more than a hundred airstrips deep in Yanomamöland were cleared to support the mining operations. Scores of mining camps popped up almost overnight, some elaborate enough to have brothels, general stores, and bars. The equipment was destructive to the land. Hydraulic pumps sucked the river bottoms of their gold-bearing ore, passed it through troughs into which toxic mercury compounds were added to extract the gold, and sent the poisoned residue flowing freely back into the rivers. The miners occasionally raped Yanomamö women and shot their men and children. The diary of a Brazilian gold miner, excerpts from which appeared in Venezuelan newspapers in 1990, recites one hideous incident after another that he and his *socios*, or partners, participated in or witnessed as they moved from camp to camp over a large area of Yanomamöland. Most of the officials in Brazilian President José Sarney's government turned a blind eye to the tragedy and tried to accommodate the slightest demand of the mining interests.

Eventually President Sarney, along with many other Brazilian officials, realized that the government's public declarations about the measures it was taking to protect the Yanomamö were being received with considerable skepticism all around the world. Brazil had made such promises before, and then, when a native Amazonian people got in the way of progress, it had simply been exterminated. Brazil's post-1966 record on dealing with native Indians was abominable. In 1967, a Brazilian air force pilot casually told me of having dropped bombs on uncontacted native villages in the Amazon Basin that were suspected of being hostile toward Brazilian homesteaders. Other researchers in Brazil's Amazon Basin have told me of hearing similar stories from other pilots. In the 1960s, members of Brazil's official Indian Protection Service were "protecting" whole tribes of Amazon Indians by shooting them and poisoning their food, in order to file claims to their land.

The international outcry grew. Too many people knew about the Yanomamö, were enchanted by them, and were seriously concerned for their future. Many who had read my writings about them began writing letters of complaint to Brazilian officials. Dozens of other publications by knowledgeable anthropologists contributed to their international visibility.

In early 1990, a new Brazilian president took office, Ferdinand Collor de Mello. Within weeks of his inauguration, he visited the Yanomamö region and, in the presence of a large press corps, dramatically assured the world that he was going to right the tragedy. For a first step, he ordered the destruction of the illegal airstrips.

The number of miners in Yanomamöland fell significantly in Collor de Mello's early months in office. International optimism rose cautiously. Then the government began to delay implementing crucial programs and seemed to back away from its highly publicized intentions to stop the destruction and to legally assure the Yanomamö of a continuous tract of land. (The predecessor government had instituted a program to demarcate some nineteen small, discontinuous "islands" in the jungle, leaving the rest of the land open for development—a division that would have ensured the demise of the Brazilian Yanomamö as a culture.)

Only fourteen of the airstrips were dynamited, and many of them were back in operation shortly afterward. As 1990 wore on, miners again began to enter the region illegally, and by early 1991 there were reported to be thousands of them in Brazilian Yanomamöland. High-ranking members of the Collor government, especially military officers, effectively prevented the removal of the miners by delaying the demarcation of their lands and by refusing to establish the necessary regulations. Programs announced in the capital of Brasília were ignored or defiantly resisted by local politicians and police, many of whom were receiving monetary compensation from the mining interests. Some of the police were even charging landing fees at the illegal airstrips. International alarm about Collor's ability to control the situation was growing, and now it was being expressed in harsh economic terms.

Prominent U.S. lawmakers have been indicating their concern for all the Native Americans of Latin America, for the Yanomamö in particular—and for native peoples everywhere. In 1991, Senator Alan Cranston of California introduced a bill that would peg U.S. aid to Caribbean and Latin American countries to their respect for the human rights of native peoples. Similar legislation pegging aid to the conditions of native peoples in all countries is also being developed. And in mid-June of 1991, eight U.S. senators wrote to President George Bush urging him to keep the plight of the Yanomamö in mind in his upcoming dealings with Collor de Mello. (The eight were Cranston, De Concini, Gore, Harkin, Kennedy, Moynihan, Wellstone, and Wirth.)

Collor visited Washington that month and professed to be irritated at learning from U.S. lawmakers and environmentalists that up to 8,000 miners had reinvaded the Yanomamö area. This was on the eve of Brazil's presentation to an international funding group, which included the United States, of an appeal for a $1.5 billion aid package for conservation in the rain forest—a subsidy that hinged on how well his government was fulfilling its previous commitments on conservation and native rights. On his return to Brazil, Collor immediately fired the president of FUNAI, the so-called Indian Protection Agency (long dominated by ex-military officers and others unsympathetic to Indian rights) and announced a number of plans that would benefit the environment and native rights.

The illegal invasion of the Brazilian *garimpeiros* left colossal problems in its aftermath. As many as 1,100 Brazilian Yanomamö may already have died and hundreds are suffering from new sicknesses introduced by the miners (venereal diseases, hepatitis, tuberculosis, flu, new strains of malaria) or from traditional maladies like local malaria strains that became epidemic following the miners' influx. Major aspects of the traditional culture have been changed forever, particularly those sensitive to traumatic alterations in the culture's demographic underpinnings, like the marriage, kinship, and descent systems.

The largely uncontacted Yanomamö villages in the adjacent areas of Venezuela where I am currently working are also in jeopardy now, because of their proximity to the Brazilian border. In a few villages that I visited in 1990 and 1991, I found suspiciously low numbers of children in some age categories, most likely the result of recent epidemics. Although most of the contacts the Venezuelan Yanomamö have with outsiders are with mission posts in Venezuela, there is occasional contact between the accessible villages and the remote ones. Ironically, these remote villages, which have a few indirect contacts with the Brazilian miners, may be the channel for exposing all the Venezuelan Yanomamö to sicknesses brought in from the mining areas of Brazil. To my immense relief, my latest data from those villages indicate that most of them are still demographically intact and have not recently been hit by any major epidemics.

A stark contrast to the Brazilian policies is the attitude of the Venezuelan government. Under the leadership of President Carlos Andres Pérez, it has been developing exemplary policies for the Yanomamö and their neighbors and for the tropical forests within which they dwell. President Pérez took an admirable initial step in June of 1991 when he introduced legislation defining a very large area of his country's tropical forest of Amazonas—32,000 square miles—as part special biosphere reserve and part national park, presumably closed to mining and other development. It officially became law on August 1, 1991.

Specific rules to carry out the law have yet to be established. A commission appointed by the president will write them, and as of now the composition of that important commission is not publicly known. It is an issue that demands serious attention, since Catholic church figures can be expected to seek to ensure that the policies do not interfere with the evangelizing work of their missions or with the now obvious strategy of reducing the most remote villages to living at or near one of their mission posts. The church will be represented on the commission, because of legal bonds between it and the government. So, also, will a few selected Yanomamö "leaders," most of whom, as we shall see, are creatures of the missions.

The Pérez government has also shown a sincere concern for Yanomamö health problems, both through government programs and through the president's quiet support of private Venezuelan-based organizations. One of these is the Fundacíon para las Familias Campesinas e Indígenas (FUNDAFACI), which sponsors research on health problems among the Yanomamö and develops programs to remedy them. Another nonprofit organization, called American Friends of Venezuelan Indians (AFVI), was inaugurated in Washington, D.C., in July 1991. This group, of which I am a member, could also be an important force in the health crisis, especially by securing private funding for various programs. AFVI's board of directors consists of an equal number of Venezuelan and U.S. citizens, and as plans now stand it will collaborate with FUNDAFACI and government agencies.

In mid-November of 1991, the constant stream of depressing news about the Brazilian Yanomamö took a dramatic turn for the better. President Collor de Mello signed legislation setting aside a continuous tract of land embracing some 36,000 square miles and containing virtually all of the Brazilian Yanomamö. It guaranteed them exclusive rights to their traditional lands. The president signed the law against powerful opposition from high-ranking military officials, the governors of the states of Roraima and Amazonas, and mining and economic-development groups.

In a futile last-ditch move, the Brazilian military tried to exclude from the tract a strip of land approximately twelve miles wide along the entire border with Venezuela and turn it into a security zone. Their argument was that if the Venezuelan and the Brazilian Yanomamö held contiguous lands on both sides of the border, they would join in declaring themselves a separate state, abetted by Communist-inspired agitators. The collapse of Communist governments in Europe and the dissolution of the Soviet Union served to discredit *that* notion. According to the Brazilian military, even anthropologists advocating native rights were agents of the Communist plot to promote a revolution and foment exotic ideologies among the natives. Do they mean the belief that the natives have legal rights in Brazil and human rights in the larger world community?

Collor's signing of the legislation fulfilled a goal of millions of people all over the world, an effort coordinated by CCPY, the Brazilian-based action group that has been advocating Yanomamö land rights for many years. It is likely that the actions of the Venezuelan government under the aegis of Carlos Andres Pérez were a crucial catalyst and model for the Brazilian government to emulate.

What is truly inspiring is that the collective and frequently expressed concerns of a highly informed international public clearly played an important role in the Brazilian decision. In a word, the efforts of individuals *can* make a difference. Perhaps the international reaction can repeat itself if Pérez's commission ignores the causes of the deteriorating health conditions among the Venezuelan Yanomamö.

While the landmark decision of the Brazilian government is a cause for optimism, the extent to which that optimism is justified will be known only when the legislation is translated into action at the local level. The past history of the Brazilian government as regards native rights and conservation leads me to believe that the optimism should be guarded for the moment. It would be unwise to relax our vigilance just yet.

What happens to the Brazilian Yanomamö in the years immediately ahead is crucial to their biological and cultural survival. Central to that are the legal assurance and the scrupulous legal enforcement of their land rights as guaranteed by the new legislation. As a start, it appeared that as of early 1992, nearly all the miners had been removed from the Yanomamö lands in Brazil.

But there are still Brazilian miners in Venezuelan Yanomamö territory, some of whom fled there to escape expulsion from Brazilian Yanomamö areas. This has complicated the normally amicable relations between Venezuela and Brazil and has the potential for developing into a military confrontation, with devastating consequences for the Yanomamö on both sides of the border. It has long been known that Brazilian miners have regularly crossed the border into Venezuela to mine for gold there. As of this writing, there are three or four Brazilian mining camps, complete with airstrips, in the headwaters of the Orinoco, in Venezuelan Yanomamö territory. The Venezuelan authorities have exercised patience about these incursions so far, but that could change if the Brazilian government does not take firmer action about getting the *garimpeiros* to withdraw. Many Venezuelans suspect that aggressive elements in the Brazilian government are deliberately encouraging the border crossings, in order to provoke a military incident and justify a Brazilian invasion of Venezuelan territory.

In late January of 1992, a large number of Brazilian gold miners were captured in Venezuela and imprisoned, and the Venezuelan national guard shot down a renegade *garimpeiro* aircraft inside Venezuela, killing at least two of the miners in the plane. Some Brazilian government officials protested angrily that the Venezuelans had fired on an "innocent civilian Brazilian aircraft" and called the incident a morally reprehensible crime. The bodies of the dead *garimpeiros* were exhumed from their shallow graves and taken to the Ocamo mission post in early February, to be sent to the territorial capital of Puerto Ayacucho for autopsies. There were many Brazilian and Venezuelan military officials in Ocamo on February 2, with the bodies of the *garimpeiros*, when I passed through en route to Caracas from a remote Yanomamö village.

Two days later, on February 4, a dissident officer group initiated a coup d'état and tried to assassinate President Pérez, a rebellion that was quickly suppressed. I watched and listened to the shooting from my hotel room, which was not far from the center of the action, La Carlota airport in Caracas. It is not beyond imagination that the Venezuelan government's preoccupation with the aftereffects of the coup will embolden the *garimpeiros* to launch more incursions into Venezuelan Yanomamöland.

Change in Kaobawä's Village

I have said that broad generalizations about culture change among the Yanomamö are impossible. I will therefore comment on changes that have occurred in the vicinity of Kaobawä's village, hoping to illustrate the general issues by focusing on specific instances.

I was unable to return to the Yanomamö between 1976 and 1984, when many important changes were occurring. This is not the place to elaborate on the story behind this ten-year hiatus, except to say that it stemmed from the actions of a handful of Venezuelan anthropologists who had opposed my research almost from the outset. None of them, to my knowledge, has ever conducted what I consider any meaningful field research among the Yanomamö, and therefore it cannot be that my presence is interfering with their activities. I think they resent me because my years of fieldwork make their casual visits to the missions look pretty skimpy as serious anthropological research. They seem adamantly opposed to having a foreign anthropologist, especially an American, profit professionally from studying the Yanomamö. Now that the Yanomamö have become an international cause, some of these Venezuelan anthropologists eagerly anticipate the occasional visits of mission-trained "Yanomamö leaders" to Caracas.

When I resumed my field studies in 1985, I was stunned by what I saw. It was like trying to make sense of a movie plot when you have seen only the first and last few frames and have to reconstruct what took place in between.

Kaobawä, by then an aging but dignified man, was still the respected leader of what remained of his once powerful village of Bisaasi-teri.

The Protestant missionaries had withdrawn from the area some years back because of intense pressure from the Salesians. This part of Venezuela, a federal territory, is governed by different laws than the states are. Many years earlier, the Venezuelan government had signed over to the Salesian missions a large measure of secular authority, and their bishop in Puerto Ayacucho, the territorial capital, has as much civil authority in many matters as the territorial governor does. Although Venezuelan law guarantees freedom of religion, the Protestant missionaries have always had to contend with the opposition of the powerful Catholic church.

Different views of Catholics and Protestants can have some amusing ramifications among native peoples. The Ye'kwana Indians, northern neighbors of the Yanomamö, have both Catholic and Protestant missionaries among them. A Ye'kwana man had just delivered a boatload of manioc flour to the Ocamo mission one day when I overheard a Catholic priest casually ask him, "Tell me, Juan, are you a Catholic or a Protestant?" Without hesitating, Juan replied, "I'm a Catholic, padre. I smoke cigarettes, I drink rum, and I have two wives." On another occasion, I had guided a new Salesian priest into the area, and we were at the mission talking to another priest when a local man, a peasant, knocked at the door and asked for a written document pertaining to the recent death and burial of one of his children. The priest got up, went to his ledger, looked up the man's name, and asked, "Tell me, José, was the child who died by your wife or by your concubine?" I glanced into the ledger and saw that most of the men were listed as having a wife and, in some cases, two or three "concubines." I wasn't sure whether I was witnessing good ecclesiastical ethnography or official church endorsement of rural polygamy.

The Salesian missionaries viewed Kaobawä with a kind of paternalism. To them, he was a former leader who was too fixed in his ways, too old to change, and incapable of dealing with the new world they were helping to create.

Younger men were emerging as leaders, their prominence determined by new, nontraditional factors. They could speak Spanish, would do personal favors for the missionaries, and were willing to give up their freedoms and their traditions and enter a market economy, exchanging their labor or products for material items from the outside world. (Also, some of them were polygynous long before they reached the traditional time for that.) These young men were given exciting opportunities to travel to the territorial capital, to Caracas, and occasionally abroad. They would meet with political leaders, anthropologists, directors of various government programs, and so on, acquiring the exotic skills they needed to deal with the outside world. In Kaobawä's area, these young leaders invariably come from one of the three missions and have been carefully groomed for their roles. By granting them privileges, the missionaries have gained a commanding advantage in determining the direction of native leadership. Traditional leaders, even those as respected as Kaobawä, are now almost totally disregarded in the process of selecting new leaders because, it is said, they do not understand the changing world or they consider it irrelevant to their traditional standards.

The older leaders did not foresee what would happen to the leadership patterns when the younger men began to learn Spanish and to spend a lot of time with the missionaries. At first, the young men were viewed merely as youngsters who were smart enough to get the foreigners to give everyone fishhooks or machetes. To a large extent, that is how these young men initially behaved: like a kind of Robin Hood, taking from the rich missionaries and giving to the poor members of their communities.

Now the stakes are higher: to acquire nearly exclusive political power in an arena unfamiliar to leaders like Kaobawä. Unfortunately, the motives of some of the young contenders no longer appear to be the well-being of the community.

One particularly ambitious man named "César" Dimanawä was appointed as *commisario* of the Mavaca area in 1985. This is a salaried position that carries considerable authority under Venezuelan law—a kind of justice of the peace and policeman. Dimanawä was not reluctant to use his authority to harass those who were his enemies. I once had to dissuade him from calling in the Venezuelan national guard from Puerto Ayacucho to arrest and jail Kaobawä and others in his village. The provocation was the claim by a visitor from a distant, highly acculturated village on the Padamo River that someone in Kaobawä's village had stolen money from him. "César" Dimanawä's rather draconian move may have been motivated by the fact that Kaobawä's group wanted him punished for allegedly leading a gang rape, a year earlier, on a young girl married to Kaobawä's brother's son.

One of the most dramatic changes I noted in 1985 was the acceleration of village fissioning. Some families were even living in their own separate nuclear-family houses. Besides these scattered houses, there were twelve villages at Mavaca where there had formerly been two traditional *shabonos*. The villages were spread along the banks of the Orinoco, mostly downstream from the mission. Kaobawä's group, with 111 people, was still the largest Mavaca community, and the most conservative.

For example, nobody in his group owned a motorized dugout canoe. They did not want to become dependent on the SUYAO, the Shabonos Unidos del los Yanomamö del Alto Orinoco (United Yanomamö Villages of the Upper Orinoco), a cooperative sponsored by the missionaries. For the first several years of its existence, it was operated out of mission facilities. To get involved in SUYAO would have meant the communal manufacturing of such goods as baskets, bows, and arrows and the commercial production of manioc flour. Such products had to be sold through the cooperative, for community credit, and eventually the community could earn a motor, which would be owned by the whole village, regardless of who had done the productive work. Kaobawä's group preferred to work as individuals, if they had to work, which the missionaries interpreted as collective laziness.

I wanted to buy Kaobawä's group a boat and a motor in 1987, but the missionaries urged me not to. They felt it would detract from their attempts to get the Yanomamö to recognize the value of engaging in productive work to earn a desired item. We compromised. They allowed me to deposit $500 in the village account, and the members of the village would have to work to earn the balance they needed to buy a communal motor. Much to the dismay of the missionaries, the group whittled away the $500 credit on purchases of communal gasoline; they used the gas to take long hunting trips or visit distant allies in borrowed boats.

Later on, my co-researcher, Ray Hames, and I gave a small outboard motor to a man in Kaobawä's village as payment for some work he did for us in 1985, 1986, and 1987. This motor became, in effect, the village motor.

There appear to be two reasons for the fissioning of the larger villages into increasingly smaller subgroups, both at the mission sites and in adjacent regions where the missionaries now travel regularly.

One reason is that warfare is diminishing and is less and less of a worry to the Yanomamö who live at the mission posts. They also have little trouble getting shotguns and ammunition, and that reduces the probability of being raided by enemies with bows and arrows.

Shotguns originally were available only from the missionaries or their employees at the mission, but in recent years many have been traded in from Brazil, via a long network that includes several isolated, intermediate villages in the headwaters of the Mavaca and in the Siapa Basin. Still more recently, some shotguns have come from the SUYAO cooperatives, which began stocking them in about 1989. In addition, two Venezuelan national guard posts were established in the area, during the Brazilian gold rush, to guard the border, and one of them, at the Platanal mission, has become another source of shotguns. Construction of a third military base, at Ocamo, was begun in 1991.

The Brazilian gold rush has had the indirect effect of leading the Venezuelan government to station military personnel among the Yanomamö, and that will only increase their health and other problems. There is little security justification for locating the military contingents at the missions, which are some distance from the border. The military presence simply provides another avenue for introducing disease.

The shotguns give those living at the missions a great sense of security against attack, and so do their outboard motors and canoes, as a means of pursuing raiders. The security reason for living in large *shabonos* is thus disappearing.

Unfortunately, the shotguns are not used only for defense or for hunting. Now that they have an arms advantage, raiders from the mission villages are attacking more remote villages, on the pretext of revenge. Often the groups have had no historical relationship. Yet significant numbers of people in the remote villages are being killed.

Certainly the missionaries have not provided shotguns and ammunition with the deliberate aim of encouraging warfare; the Salesians and all missionaries have stated their opposition to that. Indeed, the Yanomamö assiduously conceal their fighting from the missionaries, insisting that they use the guns only for hunting.

On the other hand, some missionaries refuse to believe that guns or ammunition originating from their missions could be used in Yanomamö warfare, and they often dismiss such reports as rumor. In the late 1960s, I began collecting genealogical data on a group of villages immediately to the east of the Ocamo mission, then directed by Padre Luis Cocco. He had provided a number of shotguns to the Yanomamö at the mission. As my work progressed, I discovered that a number of men in remote villages had recently been killed, with shotguns, by raiders from the mission. I immediately brought that information to Padre Cocco's attention. At first, he angrily denied that it could have been anyone from his village and was upset with me for suggesting such a thing. I asked him to call in a young man and see if I was right. The young man replied; "*Sí, padre.*" To his credit, Padre Cocco immediately confiscated all the shotguns at the mission. But he later returned them, when the Yanomamö promised not to use them against other Yanomamö. You can guess what happened.

In 1967, while working in Brazil near the Mucajai mission, I discovered that Yanomamö from the Protestant mission there, armed with shotguns, had recently attacked and killed a group of men from a remote village. The missionaries conceded that they knew about this unfortunate incident. Of the seven or so shotguns used they said, at least one or two had come from a Brazilian trader who had brought in supplies. They couldn't be sure which guns had been used in the killings, though, and were not going to ask. One of the women added, "If we ask and find out that *our* guns were used, we would have to confiscate them. The Yanomamö told us that if we did that, they would move away. You don't know how hard we have worked to establish our mission here. My husband carried our kerosene refrigerator on his back all the way from the top of that mountain over there, where the cargo plane dropped it off."

In 1990, a remote village called Hiomöta-teri was treacherously attacked by supposedly friendly neighbors who had just formed an alliance with some Salesian mission Yanomamö who had shotguns. The attackers shot and killed two men and abducted seven women, on the excuse that the isolated village had not delivered some dogs, as promised. Several of these women are now living in Mavaca. Later in the year, two more Hiomöta-teri youths were shot and killed, in broad daylight, while visiting a village near the satellite mission at Mavakita, whose director was trying to persuade them to move close to the post.

I was further angered and depressed to discover that a number of shotgun killings have occurred recently in the extremely remote villages I have just started working in. These villages are many days' walk from the groups raiding them but are reached more quickly when motorized canoes can be used for part of the trip. Particularly disturbing is the large number of shotgun killings of Venezuelan Yanomamö in isolated villages in the Siapa Basin by Brazilian Yanomamö who have obtained guns from such mission posts as Abruwä-teri. Such shotgun killings are well outside the patterns of traditional Yanomamö warfare.

A second reason for the fissioning into smaller communities or into single-family households has to do with the desire for material possessions—machetes, cooking pots, axes, clothing, flashlights—and what it takes to obtain them: hard work, for pay. The smaller residential units are walled on all sides to ensure the privacy of the occupants—totally different from the traditional open *sha-bonos*, where everything is visible and highly public. In these walled structures, the Yanomamö can conceal their possessions, so that they do not have to give them in trade to visitors from other villages who come begging for them. The Yanomamö are losing their cultural tradition of obligatory generosity to visitors as the result of a subtle process that is making market-economy consumers of them.

Initially, the missionaries provided items to anyone, for free or for a trivial price. Then they began to give them only to influential men, or members of their families, whose cooperation they wanted. For example, Kaobawä's rival, Hontonawä, was persuaded to fission from the group in 1968 by the offer of shotguns and outboard motors. A Catholic priest who had arrived in 1965 finally lured him to move across the river from the "Protestant" to the "Catholic" side, bringing some hundred people with him. Over the next few years, the children in Hontonawä's group learned Spanish at the mission, and now, as young men, they are emerging as leaders. And old Hontonawä, like Kaobawä, is no longer in charge and no longer enjoys the favors and material privileges that induced him to move.

The prominence initially accorded to Hioduwä, the headman at the Ocamo mission, followed a similar course. Padre Cocco had been replaced, around 1974, by younger missionaries with a different policy of cultivating leaders among the younger Yanomamö who spoke some Spanish. When I saw Hioduwä in 1985, for the first time in ten years, he almost wept. I was a reminder of the good old days, when Padre Cocco was in charge and Hioduwä was the undisputed leader of the village. He told me, in the most peculiar mixture of Spanish and Yanomamö that I have ever heard, how very sad and *pobrecito* he was because the new missionary did not respect him or give him expensive things, as had been the case under Padre Cocco's regime.

Gradually the people learned that they had to work to get items they wanted, often putting in days of labor on such jobs as hauling sand from the river, during the dry season, for making the cement blocks used in constructing new mission facilities. There is no such thing as a free machete today. To get one, a person must produce other items or engage in labor of an equal value. In addition, the number of items the Mavaca and other missionized Yanomamö now see as "necessary" has increased to include some very expensive things, like shotguns, ammunition, boats, motors, gasoline, spare parts, tools, radios, watches, kerosene lanterns, and powerful headlamps with rechargeable batteries. Understandably, those who have worked hard for these things are ever more reluctant to give them away to visitors in the old way. The owners can no longer replace them simply by asking for them from a missionary.

A far-reaching and related change is taking place at some of the mission posts, especially those at Mavaca and Ocamo. Large numbers of Yanomamö, sometimes whole communities, are moving to the missions in order to be closer to the source of the goods they want. The Salesians encourage this. In 1968, I counted approximately 225 Yanomamö at Mavaca, all related to each other and all from the same original village (save for a few abducted women). My 1987 census of the Mavaca group put the population at 485, distributed in twelve separate small villages and a few individual or extended-family houses. Much of the increase was due to the immigration of several whole groups and also to the immigration of a number of individuals from distant villages.

The process of "peasantization" is starting: the community is becoming less self-sufficient economically and is increasingly comprised of unrelated or distantly related people. As this happens, new social problems are appearing, including widespread instances of theft, among the Yanomamö themselves, but especially victimizing foreign visitors. The original inhabitants of some mission villages complain openly about the thefts, resenting the appearance of strange Yanomamö who camp there for several days, beg food, and when they are ready to leave steal everything they can get their hands on.

In 1990 and 1991, despite the efforts of my Yanomamö friends at the Ocamo mission to protect my possessions, two expensive solar panels, one expensive tape recorder, and a variety of other personal items were stolen while I was spending a few nights there. On one recent trip, I woke at three o'clock in the morning to find a young visiting Yanomamö trying to sneak out of my hut with my $3,000 computer. He probably thought it was a radio or a tape recorder, and when he discovered it wasn't, he would most likely have thrown it in the river—along with all the data in the hard drive. I always make back-up copies of my data, but I had stupidly been storing them in the computer case. Who would ever suspect that a Yanomamö would want a computer?

Reduction and Concentration of Villages

As I have said, the Salesian missionaries in Venezuela are encouraging Yanomamö villages to move to accessible sites on the navigable rivers or to a handful of large settlements, where the missionaries can more efficiently educate, transform, evangelize, and civilize them. Sometimes a whole group will move together, but sometimes only a fraction of the larger group will. In the mid-1970s, for example, the mission at Mavaca persuaded a portion of the Mishimishimaböwei-teri to fission and move far down the Mavaca River, where the missionaries could reach them by motorboat in a few hours. The new group became known as the Haoyaböwei-teri. The mission then established a satellite post there, Mavakita, which became the operations center for the continuing effort to "reduce" other remote villages. This began the process by which the isolated villages of the Mavaca headwaters were brought into sustained contact with the missions—villages whose only previous contact with the outside world had been my visits, about once a year and lasting a month or two. It was during the ten-year period I was unable to continue my fieldwork that the ambitious Salesians invaded this remote area.

When I returned to the Mavaca area in 1985, after this ten-year absence, I planned to go immediately to the headwaters of the Mavaca to resume my work with the Mishimishimaböwei-teri and their relatives, the Kedebaböwei-teri, still very large and isolated groups. The Mavaca missionaries informed me confidently that such a trip would not be necessary; they had persuaded both groups to make the long move down to the lower Mavaca and settle at the satellite post of Mavakita, reachable from Mavaca in three to five hours. In fact, they said, both groups were already en route to Mavakita, where they would join the Haoyaböwei-teri.

I went to Mavakita to begin my work. A few of the Kedebaböwei-teri did visit me there, and were excited at seeing me again after ten years. But they spent only a day or two and then returned to their distant village. None of the Mishimishimaböwei-teri showed up at all. I soon left Mavakita and went into the headwaters of the Mavaca, where I found the Mishimishimaböwei-teri near the site where they had been ten years earlier. They had numbered nearly 300 people in the period from 1968, when I first contacted them, to 1974, the last time I had visited them.

The Mishimishimaböwei-teri (down to 188 people in 1986, a reduction due mainly to fissions) and the Kedebaböwei-teri (164 people in 1987) later told me that they had given up waiting for me—and for the medicines and trade goods I always brought—and had been considering a move to Mavakita or another site on the lower Mavaca, in order to get these items from the missionaries. Neither group actually moved to Mavakita, although the Kedebaböwei-teri did move out to a navigable stretch of the Mavaca River in 1987 and are now being irregularly visited by the missionaries. When I visited them in 1990 at the new site, they complained about much sickness and about their disappointment that the missionaries were not bringing the medicines they had promised—one of the advantages that they had expected to gain from the move.

In January and February of 1992, just as I was completing the manuscript for this book, I made a brief trip to the Yanomamö and came back with some tragically instructive information about mortality among the Kedebaböwei-teri between 1987 and 1992.

In 1985, when I learned that the missionaries were urging them to move out to a navigable stretch of the Mavaca, I had been both annoyed and concerned. I was annoyed because it would unnecessarily subject the Kedebaböwei-teri to the acculturation policies of the missions. The Salesians could not possibly serve adequately another village so large, so remote, and so unacculturated, given the number of other villages they were trying to acculturate with the few personnel at their disposal. The move would only expose the Kedebaböwei-teri to desultory and damaging contact with the outside—enough contact to cause them health problems but not enough to ensure them reliable health services or the other benefits the missionaries promised. It was like putting a rotten apple in the middle of a basket of perfectly ripe ones, I thought.

I was concerned because the move would expose the Kedebaböwei-teri to an avalanche of new contacts with the outside world—not just with the missionaries, who would not visit them very often, but with their Yanomamö agents, young men with outboard motors, shotguns, and an irrepressible urge to lord it over these "primitive" people.

It had not surprised me to see that scenario unfolding in 1987, when I found the Kedebaböwei-teri camped along the Mavaca and living in *yanos*, the temporary three-cornered huts normally used while camping out in the forest. They had cleared and planted a huge garden prior to moving, but it was almost entirely cassava, a crop that normally takes up only a tenth of the Yanomamö's cultivated plots. A Salesian brother had convinced them to plant it so that they could sell to the mission the manioc flour they made from it, with machines he promised to give them.

I was angered to see that the brother had constructed a school at the new location, even before the Kedebaböwei-teri had built their *shabono*. The school was a large, open hut with a double-gabled roof and was equipped with tables and chairs, and with a makeshift storage area for the food with which the brother would entice the children to attend classes. The food consisted of oatmeal, rice, milk, sugar, and salt, all items that made the ordinarily caries-free Yanomamö teeth rot and fall out. It did not take long for fighting to erupt over the unguarded food. In early 1988, a young man named Maroko was beaten to death in a violent club fight over accusations of theft of the school food.

There had been 164 people in the village at the time of the move. Between 1987 and 1990, five deaths occurred at the new site, not extraordinary by aboriginal standards. Between 1990 and 1992, another ten deaths occurred, a higher mortality rate than normal, leading me to conclude that exposure was affecting their health. In January 1992, when I returned to the area briefly, the alarming news I heard was that a major epidemic had struck the Kedebaböwei-teri. Twenty-one people had died over the preceding week or so, all of them mature or older adults, most of them males, and among them the most prominent leaders in the village. Old Sibarariwä, the fabled headman I talked about earlier in this book, was one of them, as was the new headman, Örasiyaborewä. In a span of approximately one week, nearly 14 percent of a largely unacculturated Yanomamö village perished from sicknesses that they might never have been exposed to had they not moved out to a river site where they could be more easily acculturated by the missionaries.

These are not just mortality statistics to me. These are men and women I had known for twenty years, cherished friends I had visited and revisited, deaths that probably would not have occurred if the Kedebaböwei-teri had remained inland and outside the range of mission contact. The Mishimishi-maböwei-teri, their more remote southern counterparts, have elected to pursue the latter path and, as of this writing, have not suffered epidemics of this sort.

On the same trip, during a brief stop at the nearby village of Washäwä-teri, some six miles to the east of Kedebaböwei-teri, I heard constant rumors that "César" Dimanawä of the Mavakita mission and some shotgun-wielding followers were going to raid the village. A year earlier, in broad daylight, two young men of the village had been killed with shotguns fired by raiders from the missionized group. The helicopters that brought me and my research companions into the village apparently thwarted Dimanawä's plan. Knowing I was there and probably armed, he and his followers turned back. Knowing, also, that most of its male leaders were dead, he visited the anguished Kedebaböwei-teri instead. There were only a handful of them in the village—most had scattered into the jungle, a common practice when epidemics strike. Dimanawä seduced one of the poorly defended women and provoked a violent club fight. He escalated it into an ax fight, in which a number of the Kedebaböwei-teri men were seriously injured, and then he returned with his followers to his mission redoubt at Mavakita.

The most depressing and shocking aspect of the tragedy was that the missionaries at Mavaca, just a few hours by boat from Kedebaböwei-teri, had heard about the epidemic shortly after it broke out but had not even sent anyone to investigate or to tender aid. Yet it was they who had urged the Kedebaböwei-teri to move out to the fateful site—for God only knows what reasons.

One factor in the decision of the Mishimishimaböwei-teri not to settle at Mavakita, within easy striking distance of Mavaca, may have been the presence of the Bisaasi-teri at Mavaca. The Bisaasi-teri still wanted revenge for earlier killings, and the Mishimishimaböwei-teri probably felt safer at their isolated location in the Mavaca headwaters. They are still there. Because of past wars and the very real possibility of vengeance raids, they are apprehensive about moving closer to the Bisaasi-teri or to a navigable river where they can easily be reached.

Mortality Rates and Age/Sex Distributions

The missionaries also persuaded the Washäwä-teri, a large faction of the traditionally elusive Iwahikoroba-teri, to move close to the satellite mission at Mavakita, onto a navigable stretch of the Washäwä kä u, a tributary of the Mavaca. The move put them into semiregular contact with the outside world for the first time in their history. I initially had contacted them in 1971, the first time they had ever seen an outsider, and they moved to the new location just prior to my 1985 visit.

I made a census of the village then and again in 1987 and 1991. Between 1987 and 1991, they sustained a mortality rate of 15 percent, one of the highest rates among seventeen villages I was surveying. The first graph, "Four-Year Mortality Rates in Seventeen Yanomamö Villages," summarizes the mortality data for the seventeen villages between 1987 and 1991, based on how many deaths there had been in the villages during the four-year period. The percentages ranged from zero to nearly 25 percent.

When the villages were grouped into three categories reflecting their degree of contact with the missions, a disturbing pattern emerged, as shown in the second graph, "Mortality Rates by Degree of Contact." Those living at the

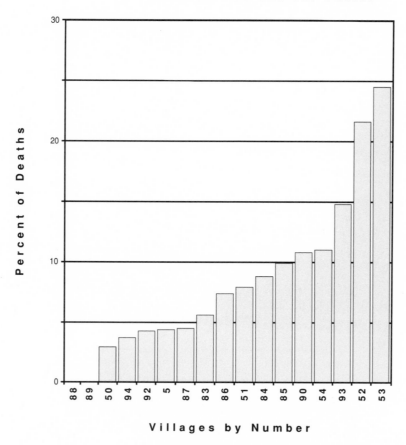

Four-Year Mortality Rates in Seventeen Yanomamö Villages, 1987–1991
The total population of the seventeen villages in 1987 was 1,407. In 1991, each village was
reinvestigated to determine how many deaths had occurred during the four-year period. The number
of deaths in each village is expressed as a percentage of the village's total population. The village
numbers are the identification numbers I have assigned to every Yanomamö village throughout the
entire area.

missions had a low four-year mortality rate (about 5 percent), as did those living in remote areas (about 6.5 percent). But those with intermediate contact, such as the Kedebaböwei-teri and the Washäwä-teri, suffered nearly a 20 percent mortality rate over the same period *not* counting the twenty-one deaths in 1992. The reason appears to be that they had enough irregular mission contact to be exposed to new sicknesses but were far enough away that mission medical

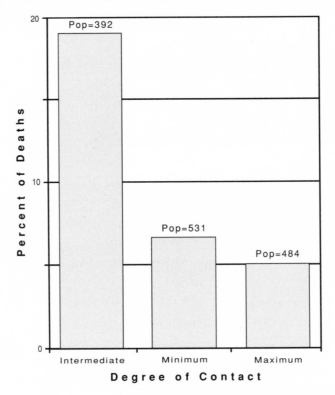

Mortality Rates by Degree of Contact, 1987–1991
The data from the first graph rearranged into three categories according to the degree of contact with
mission posts. Maximum contact describes villages whose members live at a mission post (Boca
Mavaca only). Minimum contact describes villages in remote areas that are sporadically visited by
missionaries (from Platanal and Boca Mavaca). Intermediate contact describes villages that are
easily reachable from the missions (Platanal and Boca Mavaca). The populations given are for 1987.

services reached them too late—if, indeed, as was the fate of the Kedebaböwei-teri in 1992, any help was sent at all.

The low mortality rate for mission villages is probably due in part to the fact that they have been in steady contact with outsiders for some thirty years and have lived through and bounced back from most of the "health shock" of the initial contact. Perhaps more important, they have immediate access to medical attention.

However, some of the mission villages, especially those immediately down-stream, had slightly higher death rates. This may have been due to water-borne contamination. A great deal of garbage and trash has been dumped into the Orinoco directly in front of the mission settlement at Mavaca. Much of the dumping was by employees of the Venezuelan malaria control station, which was located there for over twenty-five years but left in about 1988. I bathed at the site several times in 1986 and had to wear shoes to avoid injury from all the broken glass, tin cans, outboard motor parts, sheet-metal roofing, and other debris of civilization that littered the once-clean sandy bottom of this stretch of the Orinoco.

The data summarized in the two graphs are one way of showing the effects of disease on a population such as the Yanomamö. Another way is to examine age and sex distributions, that is, how many people of each sex there are in, say, the group ranging from the recently born to ten-year-olds. This is probably the most reliable method for detecting high mortality rates in villages for which there is no previous census.

Taking censuses and obtaining other such historical data about the Yano-mamö are difficult, because of their reluctance to talk about the recently deceased. Unless a deceased person has been married or has produced offspring, the researcher often does not even know that person existed. For example, if an eighteen-year-old unmarried female dies, her existence will probably not be uncovered as the wife or mother of someone, and informants are unlikely to volunteer any information about her, such as that a man had a young sister who died three years ago. Therefore, the first census of a village is bound to miss some recently deceased individuals, including those who may have died just a few weeks or months ago. Also, epidemics tend to kill the very young and the very old. Dead adults can be identified, since they will have had children and will be mentioned as the father or mother of someone. It is even possible to get a reasonable estimate of an adult's year of death, if he or she had a young child. A male parent could not have died too long before the birth of the child, and the mother would certainly have died after the child's birth. But these can never be entirely accurate—the Yanomamö simply do not have language to describe dates that are accurate enough for some kinds of demographic and epidemiological studies. It is almost impossible to get any reliable data at all on deceased children. The Yanomamö try to push these tragic memories out of their consciousness and, after a few years, forget about many of the deaths. While a specific mother may remember her deceased children, it is considered offensive to ask her about them. One must rely on other informants and work cautiously and discreetly, knowing that the informants will always forget some of the deaths.

Thus, in the absence of a previous census, the best way to identify an unusually high recent mortality rate is through age and sex distribution data. The Yanomamö population is typical of the primitive world in that it ordinarily has many children and fewer adults. A large part of the population of an average village or group of villages will be children under the age of eleven—usually between 30 percent and 40 percent of the total population. When a village or group of villages has a lower percentage of children, there is reason to believe that something drastic has happened to the children in the recent past. (This assumes, of course, that one's sample size is sufficiently large; there are wide fluctuations in the percentages in various age categories in villages that are very small.)

The next two graphs show age and sex distributions in two different clusters of Yanomamö villages that I recently visited and made complete censuses of. The first one, "Age/Sex Distribution in a 'Normal' Yanomamö Population," includes eight villages with a total population of 797. It shows a normal Yano-mamö age/sex distribution, in that a large percentage is children up to the age of ten—nearly 40 percent of the total population. Since tribal populations always have a relatively high rate of infant mortality, even in the absence of epidemics, the next age category is usually much smaller, as it is here: about 21 percent of the population is between eleven and twenty years old. A continuing high mortality rate, still in the absence of epidemics, makes each successive age category smaller, giving the diagram its pyramid shape. By comparison, the shape of the age/sex distribution in our own population looks something likethe Washington Monument—very slightly wider at the bottom than at the top. This is because advances in medicine have radically reduced mortality rates among infants and young children; almost all our children have a very high chance of surviving to a relatively old age. That is not true in the primitive world.

This graph is very similar in its overall characteristics to Yanomamö pop-ulations I have repeatedly documented under nonepidemic circumstances. The villages on which it is based are all in the remote Siapa Basin and have had no direct contact with either missionaries or gold miners, although some individuals from most of the villages have visited missions in Brazil, and probably gold miners, in some cases. While the villages are, as of 1992, still demographically intact, in that they do not exhibit characteristics that suggest recent and severe epidemics, they are nevertheless in considerable danger. The travelers to Brazil are at risk of being exposed to a new disease at the mission posts they visit and of bringing it back to their villages, where the disease can spread. Their

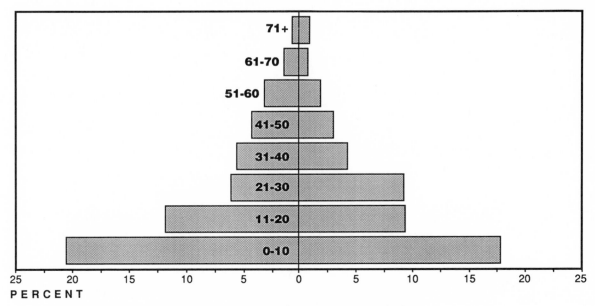

Age / Sex Distribution in a "Normal" Yanomamö Population

Age / sex distribution of 797 individuals in eight remote villages studied in 1991, showing a normal population distribution. (Males are on the left, females on the right.)

isolation makes it unlikely that missionized Yanomamö, especially those in Brazil, will visit them regularly and bring in diseases, since the Yanomamö visiting patterns are usually from trade-goods-poor villages to trade-goods-rich villages, rather than the reverse. Brazilian missionaries will probably not try to cross the border illegally to evangelize, and for the present the villages are too remote for the Venezuelan missions—unless airstrips are cleared or helicopters are available.

The next graph, "Age/Sex Distribution Showing Evidence of a Major Epidemic," tells a different and much less happy story. It also is based on censuses of eight villages taken in 1991 (I took censuses of four of them in 1987, as well). The total population of the eight villages was 474. The overall shape of the pyramid is different from that of the normal distribution; there is a smaller percentage of children, especially in the lowest age category. This strongly suggests that a large number of children had died recently, that an epidemic of some sort (perhaps more than one) had hit them. My previous census of four of these villages, showing exactly who died, confirms a higher-than-normal mortality rate over the four years, especially among children. In fact, these four villages are the same ones as those showing high mortality rates due to inter-mediate contact in the graph on page 268.

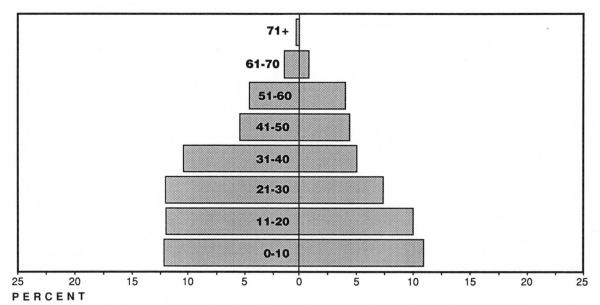

Age/Sex Distribution Showing Evidence of a Major Epidemic
Age/sex distribution of 474 individuals in eight villages with intermediate contacts studied in 1991.
These villages show evidence of a major recent epidemic that caused the deaths of many children.

To estimate how many children are missing from the graph—that is, have probably died—we can do a calculation based on the assumption that all the mortality caused by a hypothetical epidemic fell on children up to the age of ten. We want to know how many children there ought to be under normal circumstances. In order to make the population distribution look like the one in the normal distribution graph, we must have 38.6 percent of the population in the lowest age category, but in fact we have only 23 percent. In other words, the graph seems to be missing about 15.6 percent of its youngest age group. We must add another 10.4 percent of males and 5.2 percent of females. If we do that and recalculate the other age/sex distributions, the resulting diagram will look much like the other distribution—38.6 percent of the population will be below the age of eleven years and the percentages of the other ages and sexes will be reduced accordingly.

None of the eight villages in the graph showing evidence of an epidemic are in contact with Brazilian miners; they are all in the Shanishani or the Washäwä drainage area, and their only outside contact, which is sporadic, is with personnel (natives and non-natives) at the missions at Mavaca and Platanal, the latter now the base of a Venezuelan national guard contingent. It is their contact with the missions that best explains the mortality pattern.

Such a pattern is probably characteristic of what happens when isolated tribal peoples are exposed to contact with the outside world. Mortality is usually very high shortly after regular contact begins. That happened along the upper Mavaca in 1973, when regular visiting from the Mavaca mission began. The mortality rates probably remain fairly high if contact continues to be sporadic and is not accompanied by effective medical care. Chronic contact, and the more reliable medical services it usually brings, leads to declining and then stabilized mortality rates. While this pattern has probably been widespread and predictable wherever native peoples have come into initial contact with the outside world, it is not inevitable. As concerns the Yanomamö groups I have studied, I am convinced that much of the high mortality in villages with intermediate contact can be controlled or eliminated if effective health programs are put in place and if some of the ill-advised policies of the Salesian missions are radically modified. Representatives of our culture—including missionaries—who are going to have sporadic contacts with remote villages should be obliged to provide those villages with proper medical attention.

Education and Growing Awareness of the Outside World

The children at Bisaasi-teri, including those in Kaobawä's village, regularly attend school at the mission now and follow an academic year like that found all over Venezuela. They even have the equivalent of a school bus—a large dugout canoe that picks up the children at each of the twelve villages every morning and returns them in the afternoon.

The school calendar has fundamentally affected the traditional Yanomamö subsistence economy in this area. I was dumbfounded at the answer I got from one Bisaasi-teri man, in 1986, to this question: "When are you going on your next *waiyumö* [food-gathering trip of a week or more]?"

"*Vacación dähä yamakö waiyumö huu* [We will go gathering during the school vacation break]."

In the planning of other activities, like hunting trips or visits to neighboring villages, I also heard phrases like "the weekend," or "when school is out." I still find it difficult to hold a straight face when a Yanomamö refers to "the weekend," even at a mission post.

Fluency in Spanish is growing rapidly at the mission locations, as well as the ability to read and write in both Spanish and Yanomamö. (Despite the fact that the Yanomamö do not write their language, it is possible for linguists and anthropologists to convert the spoken language of the Yanomamö into a written form using linguistic conventions.)

Some individuals from the more remote villages have even been to the mission school at Mavaca and are remarkably literate. This caused me some embarrassment in 1985, when I returned after that ten-year absence. I was updating my census and demographic data in Haoyaböwei-teri, the small village that had fissioned from the Mishimishimaböwei-teri after 1976 and was now living near Mavakita. My informant, a young man named Ushubiriwä, some twenty-two years old, was at my side. (He hadn't even been pubescent the last time I had seen him, but now he had two wives. He worked at the mission for Brother Juan.) I opened the file in my portable computer that contained my earlier data on his group. He watched in fascination as I scanned through the file for his demographic and genealogical record and stopped when I came to it.

He stared at the screen. His face lit up and he hissed an expletive in disbelief. Then he grabbed me by the arm with one hand and mischievously jabbed me in the ribs with the opposite elbow. Grinning from ear to ear, his voice faking anger, he whispered, "You have my [dead] father's name in your machine."

He pointed to the screen, traced out each entry with his finger, and read, in whispers, all the lines under his name—father's name, mother's name, garden of birth, village of residence, and so on. Thankfully, his entry into the world of reading and writing was, at least for that moment, balanced by a reduced sensitivity to the cultural prohibition on openly using the name of a deceased person. In fact, he seemed pleased that he and I shared a mysterious skill. He mischievously asked me to show him the records of several other people whose dead parents' names we both knew. As I cautiously produced the records, he whispered, excitedly but very quietly, "You've got it right."

During that same field trip, Ushubiriwä and another young man accompanied me on a brief visit to a remote village. We camped along a small stream the first night, and as we settled into our hammocks the two began to converse. I wasn't paying much attention, but their voices got louder and more excited, and I began to hear snatches that seemed familiar but strangely out of context. Then it dawned on me why the conversation seemed so out of place: they were talking about the movie *Jaws*. They had both seen it at the mission and been fascinated by it. I felt somewhat offended when they asked me if I had seen it, as if I were a country bumpkin from the outback, and I tried to restore my dignity by saying, dishonestly, "No, but I read the book."

Not all the films the Yanomamö see are of this genre. In 1990, the national guardsmen at Platanal were showing them pornographic films, and some of the Yanomamö had apparently seen pornographic films before then. When I returned in 1985, after my long absence, several of the men angrily said that they did not want me to take any more photos in their village because I made "filthy" pictures of them. When I asked what they meant, they said that the missionaries had taken them to Caracas for an anthropology conference, and while there the Venezuelan anthropologists had invited them to see some of my films about the Yanomamö. The projectionist had stopped the film at the titles, so that those who could read were able to see my name, and then resumed the running of the film. Several of the men independently confirmed that one of the things they saw was close-up footage of men sticking their fingers into vaginas and licking the fingers. Someone had spliced pornographic footage into one of my films, apparently to discredit my ethnographic research in the eyes of the Yanomamö.

An awareness of the larger world and of global issues is also emerging at the mission villages. A particularly cosmopolitan Yanomamö, whom I had first known as an infant in a very remote village in 1968, asked me one day, in Spanish, "I understand your people have the atomic bomb. Is that true?"

The growing awareness of the larger world includes, of course, their increasing knowledge of events that affect them directly, such as the gold rush in Brazil. A few from the mission villages have gone to Brazil to meet Yanomamö there and discuss some of the issues. They know what gold is now, and how it can drive *nabäs* crazy trying to find it—and they are vaguely aware of the devastation the *nabäs* can inflict on them in pursuit of it.

A few of the mission Yanomamö in Venezuela are also intrigued by the prospect of visiting Caracas and places beyond, and they know that one of their tribesmen in Brazil, Davi Kobenawä Yanomamö, has taken many exciting trips to faraway places and has met important leaders on his travels.

Davi Kobenawä Yanomamö was educated by the New Tribes missionaries, a mostly American Protestant group, in a village on the Demini River in Brazil. There he learned Portuguese. His non-Yanomamö supporters in Brazil, intelligent and well-intentioned advocates of the Yanomamö cause, are promoting him as a spokesman for his people. Such a role exists largely because *our* culture must deal with other cultures through their leaders—it is the only way we know how to deal with them. Everything I know about Davi Kobenawä is positive, and I am confident that he is a sincere and honest man. When I read his proclamations, I am moved—but I am also sure that someone from our culture wrote them. They have too much the voice of Rousseau's idealism and sound very non-Yanomamö. My concern is that he is being put into a difficult position fraught with consequences for the future of the Yanomamö. For one thing, there is currently no such thing as a pan-Yanomamö awareness, and so he cannot possibly be speaking for the Venezuelan Yanomamö. When leaders like him emerge on the Venezuelan side of the border, one might assume that the two groups are recognizably different. And yet many groups of Venezuelan Yanomamö are more closely related to groups in Brazil than they are to groups next door to them in Venezuela, and vice versa.

There is also the danger that if outside parties can so easily create Yanomamö leaders, everyone who has a special interest will promote his own leader. For example, in 1990 the Brazilian mining interests introduced their own Yanomamö leader, a young man they called Marcelo Yanomami, who advocated their rights just as strongly as Davi Kobenawä advocates the policies of his mentors (fortunately, in my view, the latter are more consistent with the Yanomamö's future well-being). In an article in the Brazilian journal *Veja* in January 1990, Marcelo Yanomami, obviously reflecting his mentors' interests, argued that the Indian has the right to exploit the material riches in his territory in any manner he wishes—presumably meaning the right to turn them over to powerful Brazilian mining interests for a modest fee.

The problems could become very complex as the various religious groups put forth their own leaders, a process that is already under way at the Salesian missions. Yanomamö political self-awareness is just beginning to rise, at a few points of contact, and faces enormous problems. This is the first time I have witnessed the birth of such a phenomenon, and I am astonished at how manipulative and self-serving the various outside interests are in grooming their candidates. That is why deliberations of the commission appointed by President Pérez to establish the rules for the Venezuelan biosphere are crucial to the future of the Venezuelan Yanomamö.

The problems that the Yanomamö will face as political self-awareness emerges and leaders come forth will be complicated by the fact that not all the outside advisers are local missionaries, anthropologists, or others who know them. International concern for the future of the Yanomamö has grown rapidly because of the highly publicized impact of the 1987 gold rush in Brazil. That has set in motion some extraordinary activities over the past three or four years, many of which must be absolutely baffling to the Yanomamö—many are baffling even to me. A kind of competition is developing among many of the interest groups, including missionaries, survival groups, conservation activists, anthropologists, government agencies, and others, over which shall gain the exclusive privilege of representing the Yanomamö to the world at large. Each seems to want the sole credit for saving them from the ravages of civilization. Potential Yanomamö leaders can easily become pawns in this contest. Now that the Yanomamö are famous, they seem to be a commodity that interest groups are competing for. In 1990, the head of the Venezuelan Indian affairs office asked a friend of mine, "Why are so many people so interested in this tribe? What makes them so important?" This official has since learned that they are widely known, and she is busily trying to get in on the act.

A major stimulus for the competition is the high visibility of the Yanomamö as a symbol of the plight of all indigenous peoples, especially those in the Amazon, and of efforts to conserve the world's biodiversity and its tropical forests, especially those of the Amazon. Not surprisingly, many groups are attempting to relate their own programs to the highly publicized issues of Yanomamö survival. They know that the very word "Yanomamö" will bring them attention.

In 1989, for example, the English branch of the World Wildlife Fund sponsored a fund-raising tour in the United States that featured the rock star Sting and a children's chorus. They sang charming songs about wild birds, insects, and animals of the tropical forest, and the program, astonishingly, was entitled "Yanomamo." I say "astonishingly" because, so far as I have been able to determine, nothing about the tour had anything to do with the Yanomamö except the name. The promoters knew that that would attract attention and donations—earmarked for worthy conservation causes elsewhere, but not for the Yanomamö. One wonders if the members of the tour might have been under the impression that a Yanomamö was an endangered owl or a rare hummingbird. It is immensely to the benefit of the Yanomamö that so many groups are aware of their plight and identify strongly with efforts to help them. But it is to be hoped that contributions made on the strength of the Yanomamö name will actually get to the Yanomamö. Sting, to his credit, later spoke out for the rights of several Brazilian native groups, especially the Kayapo Indians.

Contending Influences and Misinformation

Yanomamö leaders—both the newly emerging ones and the traditional leaders—cannot make important decisions about who, from the outside world, is a friend and who is not, until they learn how to assess the conflicting information and misinformation that is being put into circulation among them.

Complex information about the outside world enters at mission posts, where some individuals are fairly sophisticated and know how to interpret it. But when the information is passed on to remote groups that are less familiar with that world, it becomes garbled, distorted, and seriously misinterpreted. Recall how Rerebawä described the size of Caracas with his vocal tones and a sweep of his arm, only to have his audience translate it as being as big as the Patanowä-teri *shabono*. Many Yanomamö at the missions, because they have some education, know that the *garimpeiros* utilize a substance called mercury to extract gold from soil and mud. They also know that the mercury residue in the rivers is toxic and can kill fish, animals, and humans. They have never actually seen this happen, but they can understand the process. They have seen DDT kill insects and small animals, like the house cats of the missionaries. However, when such information is passed on to remote villages, it becomes translated into very different concepts because these Yanomamö have no technical knowledge on which to base their interpretations. But they do understand harmful magic and charms, and they believe that their enemies poison them with a substance called *oka*, which causes them to sicken and die. To them, therefore, the mercury becomes something like *oka*, a magical and deadly substance that their enemies blow at them, and the *oka* comes from a foreign people or village called "Garibero," for *garimpeiro*.

A frightening personal experience will illustrate what I mean. In May of 1991, I was asked to escort a Venezuelan television team into a remote Yanomamö area and to assist the team in making a documentary film, for a Venezuelan audience, about the Yanomamö's health and cultural survival problems. My coworker was Charles Brewer-Carías, a Venezuelan colleague I have known for thirty years: we had previously collaborated in biomedical studies of the Yanomamö in the 1960s and '70s.

We spent the first three days in Hiomöta-teri shooting scenes of what a remote village looked like. Then we tried to move on to one or two less known groups but found their *shabonos* empty. We decided to spend the next few days in Dorita-teri, which was to be our example of a Yanomamö community that had intermediate outside contact but was in a remote area. Brewer and I had been there briefly several months earlier and had had an ecstatic reception; the people had begged me to come back and live with them, as I had several times in the past. The film *Yanomama: A Multidisciplinary Study*, which includes footage of Brewer and me with our biomedical co-researchers in 1968, had been shot among the Patanowä-teri, who subsequently fissioned, and the largest group became the village of Dorita-teri, where we were going now.

We were anticipating another warm welcome. The Venezuelan air force helicopter dropped us off, with no equipment, in an abandoned garden near the *shabono* and immediately left to refuel; the pilot promised to return in two or three hours with our equipment and the rest of the party. There were seven of us on the ground, four Venezuelan TV crew members, me, Brewer, and his research assistant, Javier Mesa.

As soon as the drone of the helicopter faded, I heard angry shouts from some dozen Dorita-teri men, all armed with bows and arrows, who had come out to intercept us.

I immediately knew that we were in serious trouble. They had no idea who the people with me were. They insulted and berated me, saying that I was their enemy and they did not want me back. They threatened to kill me. I asked them why they were so angry. They kept their distance, continuing to shout abusive insults and accusations. I asked if I could come into their *shabono* to talk with them. They disappeared into the *shabono* and consulted with others. Finally an angry shout came out: "Come into the *shabono*. Be quick about it. We will talk here." It transpired that the men had been sent out to shoot me and apparently desisted only when they discovered that there were seven of us.

I entered the *shabono* first, squeezing in through the low and narrow entry. My Venezuelan companions followed. I was the only one of us that the villagers seemed to recognize, and the only one who spoke Yanomamö. Their violent anger was directed at me. There were no women or children in sight—they had fled to the nearby garden, fearing that a violent confrontation was about to occur. Most of the adult men, some twenty or so, all clutching bows and arrows, were assembled in a semicircle around a man about fifty years old, clearly the *pata*, or big one. His name was Harokoiwä, and I had known him since he was a young man.

Harokoiwä was wearing a dirty baseball cap and an even dirtier T-shirt. He glared at me and angrily ordered me to come over to him. My companions remained some ten yards behind, except for Brewer, who stayed close to me, slightly behind and to my right. I reminded the men that Brewer had been there in 1968 working with me, and they acknowledged that they remembered him.

Harokoiwä began to rock rhythmically from side to side, violently denouncing me for killing their babies and causing epidemics among them, slapping his thighs for emphasis as he rocked. When he got through reciting his denunciations, he reached down, picked up his ax, thrust it menacingly into my face, and drew it back over his head, poised to crush my skull. I recall that it was a relatively new ax but had a nick in the blade. I don't know why that struck me as important. Then he was rocking forward and back, repeating his denunciations, but now saying he was going to kill me with the ax. He was measuring the distance and the swing he needed to do it in a single blow.

I kept moving closer, to make it hard for him to take a good swing, and he kept trying to stay at the best striking distance. Some of the men, inflamed by Harokoiwä's violence and his vitriolic accusations, surged toward me and Brewer, but we held our ground. One of them grabbed at Brewer's arm, but backed away when he noted its strength and our apparent fearlessness.

I thought of a comment Kaobawä had made to me two years earlier about showing fear before an enemy: "Never show fear to your enemy. Be strong and calm. The moment you reveal that you are afraid, you are in mortal danger. That is when your enemy will kill you."

Harokoiwä calmed down when I began to recite all the good things I had done for his group during the past twenty-seven years—all the medicines I had brought when I heard they were sick, and the time I and my medical companions walked in to their remote village and vaccinated them for measles, saving them from a devastating epidemic that was decimating all the groups around them. I asked him who had been telling him such lies. He said many people had told him, during a visit to the mission at Platanal, some three days' walk away, including one Alfredo, a man from the mission who was emerging as one of the new Yanomamö leaders there. Alfredo was a *policía*, he said (probably meaning that he was the Yanomamö *commisario*, replacing "César" Dimanawä). He said that Alfredo had advised them to keep me out of their village because I took photographs of them that caused their babies to die (I took ID photos for census purposes). All the mysterious deaths in their village since I began visiting them were due to my ID photographs, they thought, and they were going to kill me to avenge the deaths. Alfredo had also said that I sold photographs of them to foreigners in my country for vast amounts of *madohe*—trade goods—and thus was cheating them. I made "filthy" (pornographic) pictures of them. Besides all that, I put strange substances in their water that poisoned the fish and the people who drank it. And, Alfredo said, I would cause the game to disappear; the noise of my helicopter would frighten the game away forever, and they would go hungry.

Brewer and I promised that we would take up all these accusations with the "big" police in Caraca-teri, and perhaps would even ask them and Alfredo to participate in the discussion.

The accusation about the noise of the helicopter causing game to flee made it clear to me that Alfredo was being coached by someone. It was a common allegation of Brazilian and French anthropologists against the gold miners in Brazil, that the frequent illegal aircraft landings at the mining camps were causing a scarcity of game animals. (It was more likely that any game scarcity was due to the hunting of the shotgun-carrying miners.) It was apparent that someone who knew all about the *garimpeiros* was trying to make the Yanomamö believe that I was a *garimpeiro*, and it didn't take much thought to arrive at some logical possibilities. Just a few months earlier, the people of Kedebaböwei-teri, eager to have me return to their village and live with them, had told me that they were angry with the brother at the Mavaca mission. He had said that they should drive me out of their village if I showed up because both Brewer and I were prospecting for gold in their area—were *garimpeiros*.

After a long talk, we left the *shabono*. I was angry about the threats to kill me—which they might have done had I been alone. As we sat outside in the hot sun for an hour or so waiting for the helicopter, groups of men came out periodically, continuing to express their anger and hostility at my rumored malevolence, but softening their attitude each time. A group of older women came out, allegedly to fetch water, and they stopped to talk. I was touched by their sympathy—they addressed me in affectionate kinship terms and assured me that they did not believe the lies. Several groups came and went, and then the headman, Harokoiwä, came out. His violence had abated, but he was aloof and reserved. He asked me to come back into the *shabono*, explaining that the women were criticizing him for the way he had treated me and were calling me the "nephew" of one, the "brother" of another, and the "father" of his own wife. I told him I would think about it, adding that I never returned to villages whose people had threatened to kill me because of lies and rumors spread by my enemies. He must understand, I said, that lethal incidents could be provoked by false rumors and by accusations that one person was sending charms to kill others—as described in the introduction. Eventually the helicopter returned and we all left.

I have come close to being killed by a Yanomamö several times during my years of working among them. But those were quite different situations from this one. In those cases, I had known in advance that I was taking a big risk. Most of the men involved later became my friends, and we even joked, gingerly, about those long-ago incidents. I had come to believe that now, in the 1990s, any danger was past, for the Yanomamö have come to accept and respect me and to welcome me as a friend. I have always treated them fairly, have not taken sides in their quarrels or wars, have given them medicines and treated their sick, have brought them things I knew they wanted or needed, mostly at a time when they had no other way to get them.

In August of 1991, I flew over Dorita-teri in a helicopter en route to Ashidowä-teri, a village just to the south, where I landed to do some research. Two days later, Harokoiwä arrived with a large delegation of his men and marched straight across the *shabono* to where I was staying, next to the house of the Ashidowä-teri headman. The Dorita-teri had seen and heard the helicopter and guessed that I was in it. I was apprehensive that a new and more serious incident was about to unfold and was dumbfounded at the flagrant lack of courtesy toward the Ashidowä-teri and their headman—it was almost as if they were not there at all. Harokoiwä's village was a bellicose one; the Ashidowä-teri were clearly subordinate politically and were now peripheral refugees.

Harokoiwä announced loudly that he wanted to talk to me and launched into a dramatic, impassioned speech. He and his people had thought things over, he said, had reflected on my long-term friendship, and had decided that they had indeed been lied to, by Alfredo and some foreigners at the mission, naming one priest and one nun, as well as by two Yanomamö leaders at the Ocamo mission. It was these people who had said that I was bad, that I put mysterious poison in their water, chased away their game animals with my helicopter, and caused their babies to die by taking photographs of them. He had only been acting on these lies when he threatened to kill me. Now, after seeing that they were lies, he wanted me to come and live in his village and be friends again.

A week later, my research companions and I moved by helicopter to Dorita-teri and spent a pleasant week with Harokoiwä and his people, as I had many times in the past. I learned several new things during that week. One was that certain people at Platanal did not like me because I brought in my own trade goods—machetes, axes, fishhooks, and the like—without going through the Yanomamö or the priests at the mission, and I gave them away for free. While I was around to give things to the Dorita-teri, they did not have to go to the mission to get them and would not become caught up in the economic process of having to produce goods in order to obtain their machetes, pots, and fishhooks.

One other, and the saddest, thing I learned was that the Dorita-teri had suffered a 25 percent mortality rate since my census of them four years earlier, from an epidemic that had killed mostly children and older people. That is the highest mortality rate I documented in the seventeen villages I did censuses of in 1987 and again in 1991. The village's only contact with outsiders was with people from Platanal, not *garimpeiros*. Platanal is a mission community that now includes an increasing number of non-Yanomamö, including the national guard contingent.

Political, Moral, and Philosophical Dilemmas

Complex political, moral, and philosophical issues are involved in deciding whether agents of our kind of culture should encourage the Yanomamö to change or should try to prevent change. My comments here are based only on my knowledge of what is happening in Venezuela.

The ethical issue is this: Is it right to interfere with what could legitimately be viewed as the Yanomamö's increasing need for at least some features of Western culture? One of these is medical help. Who would argue that we should deliberately deny them access to reliable medical services—services to remedy problems created by their contacts with us? It is hardly possible to halt or reverse the processes that the contacts have set in motion, and the complex ethical question is whether we should even try to.

Politically, the question is: Who should be responsible for guiding the changes, if change it is to be, and what policies should guide them? My deepest fear is that one of the major—and arguably legitimate—participants in the process of change, the Salesian missions, will pay insufficient attention to the health issues, will, indeed, downplay or deny many of them, because the missions' presence as the focus of contact has in some measure helped to create the problems. The missions are increasingly opposed to my research, for example, perhaps because aspects of it focus on causes and rates of death, and reveal apparent patterns that missionaries have said they would not like me to make public, including the number of shooting deaths caused by shotguns obtained at their missions. On several recent field trips in villages at or near the missions, some informants have indicated that the missionaries were pressuring them not to give me any information about causes of death. The missionaries also are prone to point the finger of blame at others for unfortunate occurrences involving the missions. A major epidemic struck the villages in the upper Mavaca in 1973, right after the missionaries began visiting this remote area. I documented the tragedy in one of my academic publications, including the astonishing statement by one nun at Mavaca that epidemics were being *brought to* the mission by Yanomamö from the remote, uncontacted villages of the upper Mavaca.

The 1968 Measles Epidemic in Platanal

The missionaries' callous attitude toward lethal epidemics has not been confined to that 1973 incident or the 1992 Kedebaböwei-teri incident. In 1967, my medical associates and I determined, through blood samples we had been collecting, that the Yanomamö had no antibodies for measles. This indicated that they had never been exposed to this highly contagious disease, which hits tribal populations with a deadly impact. On our next field trip, in 1968, we brought in 2,000 doses of measles vaccine, with the intention of vaccinating the groups most likely to be exposed. But measles hit just about the time we reached the field, and we ended up spending most of our research time trying to vaccinate a "ring" around the epidemic, to prevent it from spreading. Nobody we vaccinated got the disease, but we were unable to reach many villages, and the death rates there were in the range of 20 percent to 30 percent (photo 43).

I passed through the mission at Platanal toward the end of this field trip, en route to the airstrip and home after several weeks at Patanowä-teri, a remote village to which I had returned after our vaccination efforts ended. None of the Platanal Yanomamö, whom we had not vaccinated, were at the mission. They went to visit the Patanowä-teri after we were done vaccinating. And I was dismayed to discover that a Brazilian employee of the mission was sick with the measles. I urged the priest, Padre Sanchez, and the Indian commission physician to remove the man immediately, for he would surely infect the Yanomamö when they returned—and they were now en route. The two promised to evacuate the sick man. I also told Padre Luis Cocco at Ocamo what

43. *A father and son recovering from measles during the 1968 epidemic.*

was happening and urged him to radio the Platanal mission to reinforce the gravity of the situation.

The missionaries did nothing, and the Yanomamö returned to Platanal. The subsequent mortality rate was about 25 percent. It was an epidemic that could have been prevented. And, tragically, the death toll might have been significantly lower if the priest and the doctor had remained in the village to help the sick and dying. Both of them had left the village in the middle of the epidemic.

In my view, responsibility for the future health programs and policies that will affect the Yanomamö should be given to secular medical anthorities rather than missionaries, whose mission is quite different.

There is one spark of hope glimmering among the Venezuelan Yanomamö, a group of dedicated young Venezuelan physicians whose organization is called Parima-Culebra. They answer to the Venezuelan Ministry of Health, but they are really volunteers, and receive no pay for their work. Parima and Culebra are two geographical features of Yanomamö territory. The Parima are the mountains separating Brazil from southernmost Venezuela, and Culebra is a valley pocketed in the high mountains on the northern edge of Yanomamöland. The organization offers newly graduated Venezuelan doctors one means of fulfilling their obligatory year of service. Needless to say, those who volunteer to serve the year in the harsh and unhealthy atmosphere of the Amazonas tropical forest are very special people, genuinely interested in native health problems and are respected by the Yanomamö. The two dedicated directors of the organization, Dr. Teodardo Marcano and Dr. Hector Padula, have both traveled with me to remote Yanomamö villages during my 1990–1992 research trips, as have several of their trainees.

These well-trained young specialists are concerned about health conditions among the Yanomamö and are determined to do something about them. The odds are oppressive, and their facilities and resources are both primitive and exceedingly limited. While the trainees working for Parima-Culebra change every year, the two directors maintain continuity in the program and slowly are building it into an ever more effective public health program. The organization is badly underfunded and could radically improve its programs with outside financial support. The directors are very much aware that, for instance, they need to develop a system for keeping good records on each village, so that they can identify changes in health patterns and redirect their efforts as necessary. The aim is to develop an effective program of preventative medicine.

One of several projects I have planned for the coming years is a collaboration with Parima-Culebra in setting up a reliable demographic data base, utilizing the information that I have been collecting for years. Such data are essential to a medical program like that of Parima-Culebra. Funds from the Yanomamö Survival Fund and AFVI will support these and similar efforts.

The basic medical dilemma is this: Should the Yanomamö who have not yet been directly contacted be left alone? Or should we go into these areas to provide medical services, on the assumption that it is probably too late to insulate them against the spread of epidemics? The first option could ultimately result in devastating epidemics and a predictable decimation of the population. The second option would increase outside contact and speed the rate of cultural change.

Is there a middle ground? The only one I can think of is a kind of compromise in which the remotest villages have the option of becoming involved in the process of cultural change or of remaining aloof from it—that is, not be compelled to join the forces of change. The villages already in chronic contact will continue as they are. All this might be a romantic fantasy on the part of we who do not want to see the tribal world disappear, but it would ensure that a free and independent Yanomamö life continued. It is highly likely, however, that, whatever the safeguards, all will someday suffer from introduced sicknesses and increasing mortality rates unless medical programs are developed to prevent this. And those require going into the remote areas. A potentially negative side of the coin is that those Yanomamö who will be left in charge of dealing with our kind of world—the groups now well on the road to being incorporated into that world—will also be left with the responsibility (and the privileges that go along with it) of deciding for all the Venezuelan Yanomamö what is good and bad for them. I have serious misgivings about how it will all turn out, and whether the decisions will be made solely with the best interests of the Yanomamö in mind.

Some might ask why I have not addressed the health issue sooner. The quick answer is that I was not aware of it for a long time. From the very beginning, my work took me farther and farther away from the missions, and I spent little time there. The remote villages I studied were always healthy and robust. Then, between 1975 and 1985, when I was prevented from returning to Venezuela, a great deal happened. But it took me some time afterward to marshal the data necessary to demonstrate the problems (photo 44). I have here presented enough of my recent findings to sketch a broad outline of what

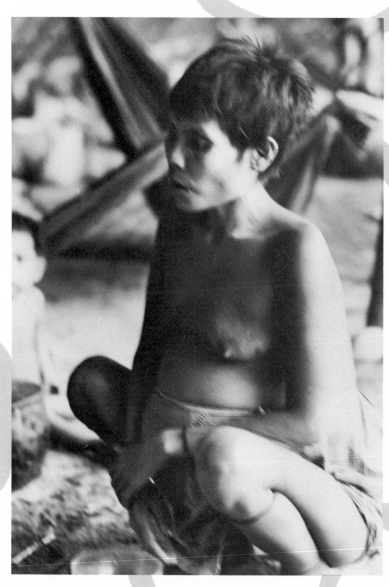

44. *A woman dying of hepatitis in 1987 in a village with sporadic mission contact. Hepatitis was not found among the Yanomamö during my early years of research, but it is now a major killer.*

is happening and will continue to happen in Venezuela unless major policy changes are initiated.

Those changes must entail the intervention of some degree of secular authority over the missions. They appear intent on winning a complete monopoly over the Yanomamö area in Venezuela, and they do not want investigators collecting scientific data that might reveal their shortcomings. They are behaving much like the Brazilian government did at the beginning of the illegal gold rush: remove anyone who might be documenting an unfolding tragedy—remove the messenger—and then the tragedy will not officially exist.

The Salesian bishop of Amazonas and the director of the missions have pressured my official Venezuelan sponsors in Caracas to cease supporting me in the kind of research I do. These include mustering the votes of their large Catholic constituency against those who favor policy changes. The struggle between state and church is very much alive in Venezuela. Its innocent victims may be the Yanomamö and their aboriginal neighbors, the Ye'kwana, the Piaroa, the Hoti, and others.

The Future of the Yanomamö— and of All Tribal Peoples?

Land and health are the two most significant factors in the cultural survival and welfare of native peoples like the Yanomamö. Venezuelan President Carlos Andres Pérez, in his 1991 decrees, has set into motion official action that will presumably guarantee the Yanomamö exclusive control over their habitat, including the right to prohibit economic development of their lands. Let us hope that the commission he names to implement this policy will treat the health problems with the utmost seriousness. Let us also hope that future presidents continue to advocate the protection of the area. If those things come to pass, then I am optimistic that the Venezuelan Yanomamö will be able to survive culturally and will be able to avoid the devastating epidemics that ravaged their Brazilian counterparts (photo 45).

The Brazilian government has acted to safeguard the Yanomamö lands on its side of the border. As of this writing, the extent of the epidemics' damages in Brazil is not yet clear, but well-informed sources say it has been great. There is, however, conflicting information about specific regions.

In 1991, the American Anthropological Association (AAA) set up a com-

45. *The only defense the Yanomamö have against diseases is supernatural. A prominent shaman tries to cure a critically sick visitor of malaria in 1974. The patient recovered after I provided antimalarial pills.*

mission to investigate the plight of the Brazilian Yanomamö, especially with regard to the health situation. A synopsis of the commission's report, published in the AAA's *Anthropology Newsletter* of September 1991, stated that the fertility rate of the Brazilian Yanomamö had dropped to zero, that the death rate was more than 10 percent per year, and that many villages were left with no children or old people. I am skeptical about what these statistics mean and how representative they are of all the villages. Surely there are villages where at least one child has been born and where there are some children and old people, even in areas that saw a big influx of miners. The full AAA report does not offer much additional information, but it does suggest that there is a considerable variation in mortality rates and health problems from region to region, those villages closest to the most intense mining operations predictably being the hardest hit. The statistical robustness of the report was, of course, seriously hampered by the political and logistical difficulties of getting into the area in which the devastation was most severe. The Brazilian government had expelled missionaries and others sympathetic to the Yanomamö plight in 1987, and it refused to allow observers in until after most of the damage was done. Unless detailed censuses of the villages were made prior to the gold rush, it will be extremely difficult to establish mortality rates with any degree of precision. It is patently obvious, however, that there is much suffering and sickness among the survivors, particularly malaria and respiratory infections.

At about the time that the AAA report was published, I received a letter from my friend and colleague John Saffirio, the Consolata priest I have spoken of before. He was trying to document the mortality rates caused by the *garimpeiros'* introduction of disease in the Catrimani River basin, a major focus of mining activities and a place where he had worked for many years. He had expected the rates to be extremely high, but he had been unable to show that this was the case, even though the area had suffered great cultural devastation. That was good news. Let us hope it portends that fewer Yanomamö have died than we feared.

However, cumulative reports from other Brazilian Yanomamö areas indicate that large numbers of people—perhaps as many as 1,100—have died of diseases introduced by the *garimpeiros* or of diseases already present but brought to epidemic proportions by the invasion of the miners. How close to the truth those estimates are must be documented by field investigations of the sort that John Saffirio is now conducting. Those will take many months—and the unflinching cooperation of the Brazilian government.

As I have said, the U.S. Congress is considering legislation to make foreign aid contingent on how the recipients treat native peoples like the Yanomamö. That could prove a powerful instrument in encouraging the Brazilian government to improve its policies toward the Amazon Basin natives. But I also believe that we need to know just what has happened there, and for that we need meticulous studies of many villages, in Brazil and in the vulnerable Venezuelan villages close to the border. I have recently begun to work there—not just for the purpose of documenting a past tragedy, but of determining if it is an ongoing tragedy, and if ways can be found to stop it.

My anthropological career has now run the full gamut. I started out as one more scientist, attempting to describe and analyze a different culture as best I could. In returning over and over again, I became intimately associated with such people as Kaobawä and Rerebawä. I became involved in their culture. Now I want to make sure that they and their children get a fair shake in the inevitable changes that are occurring (photo 46). I cannot do that except by becoming an advocate of their right to a decent future, one that does not consign them to the lowest rung of the socioeconomic ladder, to a life as bums and beggars in Puerto Ayacucho, or alcoholics and prostitutes in the ghettos of Caracas. The rest of my useful career will be devoted to them.

Two closely related issues are involved in that future. One is the preservation of the biodiversity of their bioregion—their traditional culture ecological zone. The other is the protection of the people who live there, those who have been the guardians of that bioregion. Whatever protects the one will benefit the other. That is why the efforts of both biodiversity advocates and native rights advocates are, in the last analysis, the same.

Students and others often ask me, "How can *I* help?" The simplest answer is to become actively involved in current efforts to protect the long-term welfare of the Yanomamö and their habitat. While a book like this is not a proper forum for spelling out an action plan, it is appropriate for an author to give people a starting point. Readers who want information about programs in support of the Yanomamö may write to me, in care of the Yanomamö Survival Fund, P.O. Box 30426, Santa Barbara, CA 93105.

The goals of the Yanomamö Survival Fund overlap with those of Conservation International, a prominent organization dedicated to advocating the cultural survival of native peoples like the Yanomamö, preserving the biodiversity of their region, and involving them whenever possible in planning for their

46. *Let us hope that the future for the Yanomamö holds room for the happiness expressed on this boy's face. The boy died in the late 1960s of a respiratory infection introduced by outsiders.*

future. The organizations are collaborating to, I hope, make an even bigger difference and a more promising future for the Yanomamö.

The future of the Yanomamö hangs in a delicate balance, and I will no doubt be writing updates on what is happening in this, the most critical period in their history. While most of the international attention has focused so far on the tragic events in Brazil, critical changes are rapidly taking form in Venezuela as well, and they, too, deserve our faithful attention. Many important things are in place that could lead to a more hopeful future for the Yanomamö there, but the present constellation of events, timing, and the concern of influential people could well be short-lived.

What you and I do now might make a big difference. The Yanomamö are the most highly visible native people in the world today. If we can't do something for them, with all the publicity their cause has received, what chance does some other, largely unknown, native group have—*anywhere?* If the Yanomamö go down, so also might many other native peoples, along with the biospheres they have been keeping intact. The Yanomamö are a symbol for all tribal peoples and their habitats, everywhere—perhaps the ultimate test case of whether ordinary concerned people can stay a destructive process whose course is inexorable if you and I do nothing about it.

Kaobawä's most beloved child, Ariwari, died just before I returned to his village in 1985. Ariwari was by then a young man with a new wife and an infant child. He had much to live for. He died of a disease brought to the Yanomamö by outsiders. Hepatitis.

Acknowledgments

The field research on which this book is based has been supported over many years by a number of public and private foundations. My initial research from 1964 to 1966, as a doctoral student at the University of Michigan, was sponsored by the National Institute of Mental Health. While I served on the faculty of the University of Michigan's department of human genetics, between 1966 and 1972, my field studies were supported by the department's long-term contract with the U.S. Atomic Energy Commission to monitor the possible genetic effects of atomic radiation on the descendants of survivors of Hiroshima and Nagasaki. That work included a comparison of the Japanese family and marriage system with those of other peoples, including tribal societies like the Yanomamö. The National Science Foundation eventually assumed the funding for this research, as part of the U.S. contribution to the International Biological Program. The many films Timothy Asch and I produced were funded by the National Science Foundation, as much of my fieldwork through 1987 has been. Between 1974 and 1978, the National Institute of Mental Health sponsored my field research and data analysis. Generous support for both field studies and data analysis also came from the Harry Frank Guggenheim Foundation several times between 1975 and 1989. Several of my more recent field studies, in 1990 and 1991, were made possible by funds from the Office of Research Development of the University of California, Santa Barbara, and by a grant from that school's academic senate.

I would like to thank the Trimble Navigation Company and the Magellan Systems Corporation for loaning me GPS instruments and other equipment during 1990 and 1991 and the Patagonia Corporation for supplying me and my coworkers with useful items of field clothing during this period.

I am also deeply indebted to the board of directors of the Fundación para las Familias Campesinas e Indígenas (FUNDAFACI), especially to that group's founder, Mrs. Cecilia Matos, for its unprecedented support during the six field trips I made in 1990 and 1991, support that included transport by both fixed-wing aircraft and helicopters, arranged through the Venezuelan air force. I especially thank the helicopter pilots and crews who skillfully flew me and my research colleagues into many remote areas, often landing in places where a helicopter could barely set down. I also want to thank Dr. Alfredo Riviere and Norma Riviere for their support of my most recent field trip, in January and February of 1992, during which I was collaborating with a medical team from the Johns Hopkins Medical School.

The cooperation of members of the Parima-Culebra medical group during several of my recent field trips, especially that of Dr. Teodardo Marcano and Dr. Hector Padula, is also gratefully acknowledged.

I am very much aware that the data analyses and interpretations I make in this book, especially those regarding the health effects of the Salesian mission policies, may provoke criticism from church officials directed at my Venezuelan sponsors, and I apologize to them in advance. It is necessary to know the sources and patterns of health problems if anything meaningful is to be done about them, and unfortunately this requires identification of the sources of the problems.

Charles Brewer-Carías, a lifelong Venezuelan friend and colleague, deserves my very special thanks for bringing me together with members of FUNDAFACI. Without his skillful support, I might not have been able to return to the Yanomamö in 1990 to resume my studies.

Two longtime friends and colleagues, William Irons and Raymond Hames, read portions of the manuscript and offered valuable suggestions. I thank them both for their prompt readings and their useful corrections.

Another person I must thank is Peter Matthiessen, whose sensitive writings on various native American peoples are literary landmarks. He read and offered valuable suggestions on portions of this book.

Gregory Gomez, my Apache brother, deserves my gratitude as well. He accompanied me to the Yanomamö in 1992, a dream we had shared for many years. We both hope that the experience will lead to a greater understanding among all Native Americans of the similarities and differences in the way they have been treated by invading cultures, so that past tragedies can be avoided for threatened groups like the Yanomamö.

I am especially grateful to Venezuelan President Carlos Andres Pérez for his support of efforts—by me and many others—to ensure the Venezuelan Yanomamö and their neighbors a more hopeful future. The legislation he signed in 1991, making a very large portion of the Amazonas tropical forest a special biosphere reserve closed to exploitation, is a historically important act.

As will be apparent throughout the book, I owe a profound debt to individual Yanomamö, like Kaobawä and Rerebawä, for the many favors they have extended to me all during my research, right up to the present.

I thank Mary Ann Harrell of the National Geographic Society for her insightful suggestions and comments on various drafts of this material.

I am grateful to Dirk Brandts for his help with the graphs and diagrams, and to Swig Miller for help in producing some of the maps by computer.

I am also deeply indebted to Dante LeLuccia for many years of superb computer programming and help with some of the data analyses presented in this book—and for coming into the Yanomamö lands with me in 1988 to help develop a system for assigning official names to the Yanomamö. I also thank Gary Crown, an electrical engineer, who made sure that my solar panels were wired correctly and would not easily corrode; his efforts have kept my computers and GPS instruments running efficiently during the past three years. I thank Melodie Knutson for her critical readings of portions of the manuscript and for her helpful editorial suggestions, and Leslie Winders for her help in locating illustrations for the book in my chaotic photo archives.

Over the many years I conducted my field research a number of Venezuelans in the scientific community there generously provided support and encouragement. I am indebted in particular to Dr. Miguel Layrisse and Dr. Marcel Roche for their support early in my field research and to Beatriz Fair, managing editor of *Interciencia*, the superb Venezuelan science journal founded by Dr. Roche.

I am deeply grateful for the professional and personal encouragement that my colleague Issam Madi tendered at a time when most Venezuelan social scientists endorsed astonishing theories and rumors about both the Yanomamö and my research among them—and for courageously helping to correct the public record via sensitive and powerful articles in Venezuelan newspapers.

I am also grateful for the practical and logistical help that Juan Carlos Ramírez and Javier Mesa provided to me and Charles Brewer-Carías during our several recent field trips.

Several individuals and groups have generously provided legal assistance and other services on behalf of the Yanomamö and my attempts to aid them via the nonprofit organization I founded, the Yanomamö Survival Fund. Kathy

Pratt and the San Francisco law firm she works for, Heller, Ehrman, White & McAuliffe, have contributed their efforts on a *pro bono publico* basis. David Peri, a prominent Santa Barbara CPA, has also tendered his valuable and enthusiastic help on a gratis basis. Robert Papkin, of the Washington law firm Squire, Sanders and Dempsey and a member of the board of directors of AFVI, has unflinchingly supported my efforts to develop programs and contacts to help the Yanomamö, whether or not his efforts were specifically tied to our AFVI activities.

Members of the board of directors of the Yanomamö Survival Fund deserve my gratitude as well: Paul Bohannan, Garrett Hardin, Wendy Luers, Mary Dell Pritzlaff, and Edward O. Wilson. Our work is about to begin in earnest.

This book appears at a time when there is exciting and rapidly growing activity in Washington regarding native rights and conservation. Many individuals in and out of government are becoming interested in the issues discussed in the final chapter and have been generous with their time and recommendations. I want to thank Katy Moran of the Smithsonian Institution and Kathryn Cameron Porter of Conservation International for their encouragement and for making it possible for me to meet with prominent U.S. legislators and others to discuss some of the issues affecting the cultural survival of native peoples.

I am very much honored to have Edward O. Wilson, a longtime friend and colleague, contribute the foreword. He is a scholar who has admirably put his enormous prestige and wisdom behind the cause of conservation, the preservation of the world's alarmingly threatened biodiversity, and the cultural survival of threatened native peoples.

Finally, I owe the greatest debt to my wife, Carlene, who has patiently and selflessly encouraged me in this lifelong work, which has taken me away from her and our two children, and into unmapped and unexplored regions, for months on end. Few can appreciate how difficult this is for the family of a fieldworker, or the worries and concerns it causes. Our children, who visited the Yanomamö when they were infants, have grown up to be neat people, and their admirable qualities are in large measure due to my wife's indefatigable extra efforts to be a double parent. Our children used to think that everyone's father, when out of town, was living somewhere with "the Indians." Now that they are adults, they can appreciate what it was that compelled me to be away from them so often and so long, and I am grateful for their understanding. I also want to thank Carlene for her insightful suggestions as I wrote and rewrote some of the more sensitive portions of this book.

I want also to thank my son, Darius, who spent three months with me in 1991, among very remote Yanomamö groups, as my companion, friend, and coworker, but especially as my son. This was the most enjoyable field experience I have ever had—despite our malaria and our diarrhea, and despite our frustrating wait in a very remote place for our helicopter to pick us up, nearly a month later than it was supposed to.

N. A. C.

Suggested Additional Readings

There have been many books wholly or in part about the Yanomamö. Of the following three books I would recommend for the general reader, two concern the Yanomamö while the third is about Australian aborigines at a time before they were contacted.

Ettore Biocca, *Yanoáma: The Narrative of a White Girl Kidnapped by Amazonian Indians* (New York: E. P. Dutton & Co., 1970)

In 1935 a young Brazilian girl, Helena Valero, was captured by the Yanomamö in a very remote area of Brazil, near the Venezuelan border. She lived for nearly thirty years among the very same groups of Yanomamö discussed in my book and was married to several different men, including the renowned Husiwä, headman of the group from which Kaobawä's village fissioned. Kaobawä lived with her for many years.

Valero was repatriated in about 1955 by Padre Luis Cocco, who had just established his mission at the mouth of the Ocamo in Yanomamö territory, and she eventually returned to Brazil with her several Yanomamö children to search for her family. An Italian researcher, Ettore Biocca, interviewed Valero and documented her extraordinary experiences as a captive among the Yanomamö in this book. In addition to giving very perceptive, extremely accurate insights into many aspects of Yanomamö culture, her narrative also expresses intimate views of that culture from the vantage of a woman.

Jacques Lizot, *Tales of the Yanomami: Daily Life in the Venezuelan Forest* (Cambridge: Cambridge University Press, 1985)

This is a highly readable book of ordinary events and concerns in the daily lives of the Daiyari-teri, whose village is located within a few hours' walk of

Bisaasi-teri. It is an introspective, almost poetic view of Yanomamö culture, told through the words of Yanomamö individuals familiar to the author. Lizot, a French anthropologist, began his long-term studies of the Yanomamö several years after I started my work and generally concentrated his efforts in smaller, less bellicose villages. His academic and theoretical inspirations are very different from mine. He portrays the Yanomamö culture from a French structuralist, Marxist, and more Rousseauistic stance and often goes to considerable lengths to refute both my hard scientific approach and my empirical findings on violence and warfare, downplaying the significance of violence as a major determinant in the dynamics of Yanomamö society. His book, however, contains many explicit discussions of violence and lethal competition.

John Morgan, *The Life and Adventures of William Buckley* (Sussex, England: Caliban Press, 1979)

William Buckley, an English convict, was transported in 1803 to the penal colony of Australia. He escaped soon after reaching Australia and spent thirty-two years living among various groups of aborigines—then almost completely unknown and uncontacted. In 1835 he was repatriated and eventually related the accounts of his life, which make up the substance of this book. The similarity of his eyewitness accounts to Helena Valero's is striking and instructive, particularly his frequent discussions of conflicts over women and of the violence this provoked between neighboring tribes.

Index

Food:
  diet, *see* Diet
  feasting, *see* Feasts
  gardening, *see* Gardening
  gathering techniques, 77–79
  hunting, *see* Hunting
  sharing of, 17, 18–19, 157–58
  theft of, 200, 219–20
  trade and, 187–88
Foot people, 5–6, 53
"Four-Year Mortality Rates in
    Seventeen Yanomamö
    Villages," 266
FUNAI, 252
Fundacíon para las Familias
    Campesinas e Indígenas
    (FUNDAFACI), 253
Future of the Yanomamö, 289–94

Games, 155–57
Gardening, 79–90
  cotton, 85–87
  headman's garden, 89
  macro movements of gardens,
    94–100
  magical plants, 87
  micro movements of gardens,
    90–94
  new garden, making a, 80, 224
  protection by allies when driven
    from your, 183, 193, 225
  root crops, 82–83
  sites for, 79–80
  slash-and-burn farming, 87–89
  snakebites and, 58–59, 91
  steel tools for, 80–81, 82
  theft of food, 200, 219–20
  theory of soil depletion as
    reason for movement of,
    90–92
  time spent daily on, 100,
    154–55, 157
  tobacco, 83–85
Gathering techniques, 77–79
Genealogies, 23–33
  best informants for compiling,
    26–29, 31–33
  invention of false names, 24–25
  older informants and, 25–26

taboo against mentioning certain
    names, 23, 25
Geography:
  alliances and, 188
  settlement patterns and, 56,
    105–6, 107–11
  warfare and, 106, 107–11
Gift, The (Mauss), 189
Gold rush of 1987, effect on
    Yanomamö of Brazilian,
    248–52, 254–55, 259, 275,
    277, 281, 291
Gomez, Greg, xvi–xvii
Gore, Albert, 251
GPS (global positioning system),
    102
Great Plains Indians, 81
Grubs, collecting, 77–78
Guides:
  recruitment of, 40
  to remote villages, 41–54

Hairstyles, 64
Hallucinogenic drugs, 12, 64–68,
    140–41, 234
  in daily routine, 157
  at feasts, 200
  shamans and, 140–41
  violence and, 141
Hames, Ray, 114, 258
Hammocks, 86–87
Harkin, Tom, 251
Harmless People, The (Thomas), xvi
Harris, Marvin, 113, 114
Head lice, 64
Headman, 34–36, 160–64
  gardens of, 89
  incest and, 180–81
  violence controlled by, 162–63,
    211
Health. *See* Sickness
Hekura (spirits), 3, 139–40, 141,
    152, 213
Honey, 18–19, 77
House construction, 68–74, 153
  acculturation and, 261
  communal, 68–74
  huts, 74
  palisades, 74

Hunting, 60, 75, 79, 154, 157
  for feasts, 197, 198, 199
Hygiene, 15, 157

"Ideal Model of the Yanomamö
    Social Structure," 168–70
Inbreeding, 174
Incest, 122
  headman and, 180–81
  incestuous marriage, 175, 180
  kinship and, 167–68, 180
Infanticide, 36, 113, 114
Infant mortality, 3, 270
Insects, 69
Intergroup violence over women,
    112–15, 183, 215, 220
  abduction, *see* Abduction of
      women
  at feasts, 192
International interest in the future
    of the Yanomamö, 251,
    276–77, 292–94
Irons, William, 240

Jaguars, 230
  myths about, 123–31
Jungles, 56

Kaobawä, 33–36, 256, 257
Kayapo Indians, 277–78
Kennedy, Edward, 251
Kinship, 6, 36, 164–67
  breaking the rules of whom one
      can marry, 175–76, 178–81
  as dynamic, 180
  genealogies, *see* Genealogies
  incest and, 167–68, 180
  outsiders included in scheme of,
      166–67
  rules governing whom one can
      marry and, 164–66, 168–70,
      175–76
  solidarity and, 174
  violence and role of, 215
Koshland, Daniel, 239
Kuikuru of Brazil, 91

Women, 144–50
  abduction of, *see* Abduction of
    women
  decoration for feasts, 200
  exchange of, between villages to
    aid alliances, 183,
    184–85, 188
  fleeing to escape abusive
    husband, 149
  foods eaten by, as indication of
    status, 158
  intergroup violence over, *see*
    Intergroup violence over
    women
  intragroup violence over, 37–38,
    112–15, 147–49, 215, 216,
    221
  killing of, 29, 147, 225

  male-female relations in myth,
    121–23
  marriage, *see* Marriage(s)
  menstruation, 151–52, 233
  older, status of, 150
  origin myths for, 122
  physical abuse of, 34, 36,
    147–49, 162
  protection of, against raids,
    195–96, 226, 231
  work of, 69, 89–90, 145–47,
    148, 151, 155, 157
Work:
  acculturation and, 261
  in daily routine, 100, 154–55, 157
  evening meal, 157–58
  of women, 69, 89–90, 145–47,
    148, 151, 155, 157

World Wildlife Fund, 277

*Yanoáma: The Narrative of a White Girl
  Kidnapped by Amazonian Indians*
  (Biocca), 110
Yanomama: A Multidisciplinary Study,
  279
Yanomami, Marcelo, 276
"Yanomamö Cosmos, The" 117
Yanomamö, Davi, Kobenawä,
  275–76
Yanomamö Survival Fund, 287,
  292
Ye'kwana Indians, 5–6, 10, 81,
  114
  garden products of the, 82–83
  missionaries and, 256